But ... dent

Please r...

Kiki Archer

Title: But She Is My Student
ID: 12912953
ISBN: 978-1-4717-1897-7

K.A Books *Publishers*

www.kikiarcher.com

@kikiarcherbooks

Published by K.A Books 2012

Copyright © 2012 Kiki Archer

Kiki Archer asserts the moral rights

to be identified as the author of this work.

All rights reserved.

ISBN: 978-1-4717-1897-7

For Nikki x

'You honestly are the best person I have ever met and I promise to love you forever.'

CHAPTER ONE

<u>*Mon 6th September 8.35am*</u>

The day started with the obligatory *'stand up and introduce yourself,'* and after three school placements Kat realised that this was simply for the other members of staff to appraise you silently and decide upon your fate; most of the time they got it right. The Head Teacher signalled the chubby lady with thin brown hair, green felt suit and yellow sandals. The lady stood up awkwardly from her woven fabric chair and uttered in the tinniest, wobbliest voice, 'Hello, my name's Hannah Fag, spelt P.H.A.G and I'm the new IT teacher,' and everyone immediately knew that *Faggy* wouldn't last a term. It did not help Faggy's confidence when the two girls from the English Department failed to stifle their giggles. Kat managed to catch the new teacher's eye and give a reassuring smile, something that meant the absolute world to a very nervous Miss Phag. When it was Kat's turn to be introduced she breathed in, smiled, announced her own name with authority and warmth and noted a number of kind returning smiles from the other seated staff members. What she also noted were the whispers of the same English teachers. The one with the bright red lipstick, bleach blonde hair, and highly inappropriate red halter neck, raised her eyebrows and slowly looked her up and down. The other one, who looked like an airhostess from a low budget airline, frowned with her large nostrils flaring, and looked falsely perplexed, as if not understanding who Kat was or what she might possibly be doing here. Every workplace was the same realised Kat, always a couple of women who thrived on being complete bitches.

<u>*3 Days Earlier: Friday 3rd September 9.30pm*</u>

'Cheers! Here's to you, Kat,' shouted a slightly tipsy Jess as her auburn curls danced around her shoulders. She was toasting her best friend for the third time so far this evening as *Build Me Up Buttercup* rang loudly in their ears. 'You've been bloody boring this past year, so make sure you have a good time tonight. You deserve it. Let's get twiddled, do our dance and then you *must* have some fun!' Jess chinked her glass ferociously against Kat's, causing the dainty sparkling bracelet on her slightly plump wrist to quiver at the force. She winked and nodded her head far too obviously, throwing her auburn curls to the right, 'Look at her, Kat. She's gorgeous. Go on, let your hair down!'

Jess was right, she *had* been boring but it had paid off with a much coveted first class teaching degree, and tonight she was celebrating her last ever weekend as a student with relief, anticipation and hope. Miss Katherine Spicer was starting at Coldfield Comprehensive on Monday, she felt ecstatic. The school was great - categorised as *Performing*, ten minutes walk from the modern spacious apartment she shared with best friends Jess and Lucy; she was happy. Teaching was her lifetime vocation. Kat had a real passion for bringing out the best in her students, always managing to do it in such an endearing manner; never condescending or righteous, just patient and thoughtful. She enthused about everything to do with history and somehow managed to spark an interest and desire to learn in the most unmotivated and lacklustre of students. She was a natural teacher and her inner confidence had grown from school placement to school placement. She sipped her sparkling drink with a sense of pride and achievement. Miss Katherine Spicer was ready for the real thing and could not wait for the start of term on Monday. *Saddo* she thought.

Lucy stood at the busy bar, looking across the glowing dance floor at her best friends. Both were gorgeous but in completely different ways. Jess was short and curvy with masses of red curly hair jumping around as she laughed and toasted Kat, probably for the tenth time now. Jess embraced her voluptuous figure with confidence, confidence that was sometimes misplaced with a love of Lycra once again on display, but she was confident and happy and smiling and laughing. The type of friend everyone needed, always cheerful, always positive. Probably why she was the only one of them to have a partner, assessed Lucy, still waiting for the drinks. Gary and Jess, Jess and Gary, they came as a package and were destined to spend forever together. Always in the apartment but never a bother, a perfect guy that Lucy only wished she had unearthed first. The club was lively tonight as she hovered rather impatiently for her three white wine spritzers. They had decided to ditch the cheeky vimtos of yester year, declaring their new drink of choice as sophisticated and appropriate for their new found status - adult. *Worrying* she thought.

Monday 6th September 9.00am

Kat was not going to let anything taint her excitement and enthusiasm for the day ahead, especially not the judgements of two cheap looking English teachers. So she approached the morning with gusto, spending the majority of time in her cosy form room greeting with sincerity her first ever Year Seven tutor group as they each filed past her and found their desks. Kat could indeed remember her first day of Secondary School as if it were yesterday, having earlier ignored the jibe from a letchy looking male teacher whose name she did not yet know; but now in the calm of her own warm classroom she reminisced at the excitement of having a blazer with inside pockets for your pens. The silly buzz when buying new shoes, especially if you were allowed the shiny patent ones. The new tie that you proudly learnt to tie in a long _kipper_ until you realised that _kipper's_ meant geek and _skinny's_ meant cool. The thrill of anticipation when you got your new pencil case out and displayed, for the first time, all of your new pens and luminous highlighters. The utter joy of getting a locker then realising you didn't actually have anything to put in it. Kat spent a wonderful morning getting to know her new charges, issuing them with rough books, homework diaries, school maps - that made no sense whatsoever - and lesson timetables. She tried her absolute hardest to impart a sense of reassurance and confidence for their days ahead and wished them all good luck for the afternoon lessons. As the bell rang noisily for lunch she watched them get swallowed up by a swarm of Year Nine's charging down the inexcusably narrow corridor; she realised that it was sink or swim for her and her tiny pupils today.

Friday 3rd September 10.00pm

The three women spent most of their time in the heaving _'Cheese Room'_ where Chesney Hawkes's _I am the one and only_ yowled out at least three times a night. The dance floor was large and sparkling, encased by two never-ending bars that were overflowing with glowing liquids. There were two wall to wall luxurious deep seat lime green sofas and someone short like Jess could almost lie flat on a single cushion. The decor was bright and modern; the atmosphere always fantastic. All of these gorgeous well groomed guys thought Lucy, but none of them in the slightest bit interested in me or my fantastic boobs. At least someone was getting some attention tonight, she mused. Lucy watched as another woman gazed at Kat; she could be mesmerising. Her warm, deep blue eyes that always held your own, natural shoulder length blonde hair and fantastic elegant figure commanded attention. Her height also made her hard to miss. At 5ft10 Kat was a stunner, real natural beauty, she had it all; the looks, the brain, the personality, the type of woman most girls look at and say *bitch*! Lucy watched as Kat threw her head back and laughed; her smile was glowing and enchanting all who observed. Naturally charismatic was the term. Lucy had never seen a hint of arrogance in Kat, an absolute delight to be around and a lovely person to live with, never picking faults, never judging, always doing the right thing - *perfect bitch* she laughed to herself with the drinks finally in hand. Kat was always teaching her something that she did not know, but to be fair that was not hard as she was not the brightest button in the book, or was it box? pondered Lucy, striding towards her laughing friends. Anyway Kat knew an awful lot more than she knew or ever really wanted to know, and as an aerobics instructor Lucy always said, *'once you know your grapevines and shimmies then you know your grapevines and shimmies,'* and she certainly knew her grapevines and shimmies, hoping that one day Mr Right would step into her class and whisk her off her feet. Her ex boyfriend had claimed, much to the abhorrence and reassurance of her housemates, that she was the perfect woman - nicely toned with muscles in all of the right places, as long as she kept the brown paper bag firmly over her head. She wasn't bad looking, with her black bobbed hair, sharp fringe and strong nose, but she wasn't a patch on Kat, which was why she failed to understand why Kat never met the right person. Too nice, assessed Lucy, always making sure everyone else was okay before thinking about herself. One of those selfless people who end up hurt by some idiot who does not deserve them in the first place. Kat had excused her singledom and lack of love life on studying in her final year, or something like that - Lucy had not really been paying full attention. We will soon see, she thought, finally crossing the busy dance floor with their posh drinks in oversized wine glasses; it's time to get it started again Miss Spicer!

Mon 6th September 1.20pm

Kat spent most of lunchtime preparing her room for the first proper lesson of the day - A2 history with Year Thirteen. Janet Louza, her nice but slightly monotonous Head of Department, had been thoroughly sycophantic throughout her interview, praising her abilities and almost begging her - in a droning manner - to accept the job. The school wanted Miss Katherine Spicer. She had an outstanding CV, fantastic references and was incredibly likeable. She was perfectly qualified to teach A-Level and that was needed now Miss Pendleton had finally given up the ghost. Kat loved the school and jumped at the inevitable job offer, and now, as the final bell rang announcing the end of lunch, she made her way - after several wrong turns - into the noisy dining hall. She had been given her duty position and knew she had to shepherd stray children out of the littered hall and into their afternoon lessons. She inhaled and the smell of sponge and white custard brought back more nostalgia. She was so happy to have finally made it, to be here, a teacher in her own right. She had been assured by Janet Louza that Year Thirteen classes were fully aware of duty teachers being five minutes late to afternoon lessons so she checked her watch and walked a lost tearful Year Seven pupil to the sports hall, trying to reassure him that a detention for the wrong colour PE socks on the first day of school was highly unlikely. She then headed back towards her classroom, full of nervous anticipation.

Friday 3rd September 10.15pm
'Cheers girls,' hollered Lucy, as freshly filled glasses chinked together, only one bat wing in sight.

Just as they were about to take large gulps, the unmistakeable beat of Beyonce's *All the Single Ladies* washed across the dance floor. Kat, Lucy and Jess swished their glasses onto the closest table with enough effect to look dramatic, but not enough to cause precious spillage, and with shrieks of excitement arranged themselves into position. Many tipsy evenings in the apartment had been spent perfecting the dance and now it was time to show it off.

****

Freya was sitting on the huge lime green sofa with her cousin, watching the three laughing ladies try and body pop to the beat of Beyonce's *All the Single Ladies*. Jodi had been saying something but Freya had zoned out, fixated by the flawless tall woman with the striking face. Her unique body popping was as fascinating as her smile that seemed to glow on the dance floor, and the dark blue skinny jeans and white ruffled top were accentuating a body that most women only dreamed of.

Kat took pride in her appearance and always managed to get *'the look'* right; smart without being boring, sexy without being on show and tonight she was attractive without having to try.

'Surely she isn't?' asked a perplexed Freya, still staring at Kat.

'You should find out,' stated her cousin matter of factly, as if it was as easy as that; it probably was for her.

Jodi was twenty, short cropped bleach blonde hair, boyishly pretty, out since she was eight, or so she said, and the only gay woman Freya knew. Freya was confused. It was all well and good that being a lesbian was the height of fashion, but in the real world, her world, she dared not breathe a word of her inner curiosity to anyone other than her loud, but very loyal cousin.

Jodi had arrived at the *Elton's Annual August Bank Holiday Barbeque* with another attractive woman on her arm. It had reminded Freya of when a pageboy posed for pictures with the bride; cute in the photo, but odd when exposed as a couple. After the obligatory plate of meat and jug of summer punch, Freya, Jodi and *'Little Minx'* - as Jodi liked to call her - started to gossip. Freya had always been popular with the boys, her long wavy chestnut hair, pretty face and sparkly green eyes drawing attention, but she had never been in love, she knew that for sure. If she really searched deep enough she ended up panicking and scrambling back to the surface as fast as she could. Freya hadn't figured out who she truly was or what she truly wanted, but then at her age who had, she wondered? So when Jodi and *Little Minx* had posed the question, 'What do you feel like when you see two women kissing?' having exposed her and the rest of the barbequing Elton clan to an afternoon of opportunities to form their opinions, she had answered honestly - 'Well when it's you two I guess it feels like anyone else, I just think get a room,' she was being nonchalant, but then for some reason unbeknown to her she paused and answered openly, 'but then I guess when I think about it generally I'm just intrigued ... it seems exciting.'

Jodi had smiled and announced that it was *Gail's Gay Bar* on Friday for the curious one. And here they were, sitting quietly, on the biggest lime green sofas that Freya had ever seen, watching. Jodi had been great, giving her time to adjust to the scene, not pushing her to dance, just letting her relax and see if she felt comfortable. Freya didn't know what she felt, only that she could see the tall blonde dazzling lady approaching. Maybe she was going to tell her off for staring. Oh wow, look at those blue eyes she thought, almost out loud.

Monday 6th September 1.30pm

Kat checked that her white fitted shirt was tucked neatly into her slim fit black trousers, pushed her fingers through her loose hair, jiggled her oversized red beaded necklace and entered the room. Look good, feel good, she thought. There was shuffling, then staring, then silence. She scanned the classroom and smiled warmly. 'Welcome to Year Thirteen history. My name is Miss Spicer and I will be your new teacher for this final year.'

There were a few mumbled 'Hi Miss's' and then the blue door slowly creaked opened and a very tall, great looking lad, with impeccably styled brown hair and the longest natural eyelashes Kat had ever seen, tiptoed to the desk at the front in a manner that can only be described as overly dramatic.

'So sorry Miss,' he whispered, then looking up stood straight as a dart, threw his hand to his hip and squealed. 'Oh my! History has suddenly become enchanting,' and without stopping for breath and talking as fast as was humanly possible he continued, 'I'm Harley, you look divine, oh sorry Miss, I didn't mean that, well I did, but you know what I mean. I was just not expecting a fabulous history teacher what with old Miss Pendleton last year, she taught my mum you know and my gran says she knows her from bingo and anyway, what a nice surprise. You are qualified aren't you Miss, only I need a B to get into uni and there is so much stress going around and I only hope-'

'Nice to meet you Harley. I'm Miss Spicer.'

'Oh this gets better, what a perfect name. We will be best friends by the end of the year Miss, I am telling you now!'

Kat read the slogan blazoned across his bright green t-shirt - *Yes I am*. The class had started to mutter and she needed to take back control. 'Well I'm not sure about that Harley,' she spoke in a firm but kind manner and addressed the rest of the class, 'but what I can tell you all with certainty is that you will get out of these lessons what you put in and the grade you receive next summer will be exactly what you deserve.' She tried to connect with everyone in the room. 'I will work my absolute hardest to ensure you all fulfil your potential,' a couple of the girls seemed to relax and nod in appreciation, 'but it is you who must want to strive to reach that potential,' a couple of the lads groaned.

Friday 3rd September 10.25pm

Lucy and Jess had seen the pretty woman with brown wavy hair sitting on the lime green sofas and noticed that she was mesmerised by Kat, so when the hilarious dance finished Lucy announced that it was now or never, get back in that saddle and ride the horse out of town, was that right she thought? Oh never mind it sounded good. Kat was always nervous when it came to her love life. Jess and Lucy were constantly frustrated with her inability to realise what a fantastic catch she would be and just how beautiful she had become. Kat knew she had been a plain child, never encouraged to do her hair or wear nice clothes or take an interest in her appearance, and her self-doubt had remained even after the blossoming of the late teenage years. But now, early twenties and full of body popping confidence, she thought *why not,* and made her way across the dance floor to the lime green chilling area.

'May I join you?' she asked, directing her attention towards Freya.

'Go for it girlfriend,' jumped in Jodi. She stood up, not very far, she was only 5ft2, and pulled up her loose fit jeans, only a third of her branded pants now on show. 'I was just nipping to the ladies. There is always a queue here, so I may be a while.' Jodi scurried off making funny eye movements to Freya as the reflector strips on her tight t-shirt beamed light in all directions.

Freya sat motionless with the stunningly attractive woman about an inch away. A younger looking *Elle McPherson* with something unique, Jodi had declared when earlier assessing her beauty. Freya hadn't commented, all she knew was that she had never seen anyone quite as beautiful as her before; and now she was sitting here, next to her, looking at her with perfect blue eyes.

'Hi, I'm Kat,' she spoke in a warm and soft voice.

'Freya,' said Freya, trying her best to stop her heart from jumping out of her slightly revealing black top.

Kat bit her bottom lip and looked in the direction that Jodi had just taken.

'She's my cousin.'

'I thought maybe -'

'No, no...' she paused in an attempt to gain composure, 'no she is just showing me the sights.'

'And do you like what you see?' The quick comment caused a deep wave of embarrassment to course across her cheeks. *What on earth am I doing?* She cursed herself, feeling devastatingly out of practice.

Freya propped herself up and urged her confidence to grow. 'I think you know the answer to that.'

Kat's heart started to pound, Freya was making her nervous. There was something about her green eyes that was drawing her in and controlling her gaze. The chemistry was incredible. She had been out of it for a while but this was unmistakable, a buzz of something new, something fresh, something real.

Freya met her warm blue eyes and whispered, 'You're stunning.'

Kat could feel her heart growing and smiling inside; just go for it she told herself. She realised that she had never been a typical student and that her behaviour had been far from outrageous, so as she sat on her final weekend as a *'student,'* she plucked up the courage and spoke softly. 'I would really love to kiss you right now.' Jess and Lucy would be proud.

Freya had never felt so much romance in such a direct way. She managed to nod her head slightly and Kat moved closer. It felt like slow motion. When the gentle lips touched her own Freya felt a sensation run all through her body, pure emotion, pure power, and pure lust.

Kat kissed her slowly, softly parting her lips and feeling the warm mouth against her own. The feeling was so tender, so caring and yet so arousing. Kat kissed deeper and Freya responded, kissing her back with as much meaning and passion as she had felt in a long time.

Freya never wanted it to end. It was without doubt the best kiss she had ever had. It had so much energy without being hard, so much emotion without being soft and so much meaning. So much meaning for her because she knew in that one kiss that it was this she wanted, this was what she was, this was her, meaning brought to her life by this kiss.

Kat met Freya's eyes as she opened them after what seemed like an eternity. 'I think I did this the wrong way round, but can I buy you a drink?' She smiled a warm and genuine smile, completely embarrassed by her uncharacteristic forwardness.

'Yes please,' was all Freya could manage.

Kat made her way to the bar and noticed the winks from the other side of the dance floor where Lucy and Jess were now trying to do the Gaga.

Freya's haze was rudely shattered by a sharp grab on the arm and a swift yank off the sofa. Jodi hauled her up, pulled her across the bustling dance floor, and literally pushed her out of the open fire doors.

'Go, go, go!' she shouted. 'Oh shit, if she catches me I'm in the absolute shitter.' Jodi was screeching as she rushed them onto the street and hailed a taxi, throwing Freya inside.

'What on earth are you doing?' she cried, finally catching her breath. Their black taxi pulled out of Lord Street and onto the expressway.

Jodi glanced over each shoulder, making sure the neon lights from the club were disappearing safely into the distance. She caught her breath. 'My ex, Trina, was in the queue and tried to corner me, I had to run. I can't be dealing with all that shit again. She was literally chasing me. She's a psycho.' Jodi relaxed as the bright lights of the expressway started to stream past her window. 'Phew. Sorry babe. Are you okay?'

Freya didn't know what to feel, what had just happened? All she knew was that she had just experienced the best moment of her life to date.

Monday 6th September 1.40pm

'Right,' said Kat, 'we have a fantastic class size, just ten of us, so first of all I want to find out a bit more about all of you.' She leaned back slightly and perched gently on the edge of her wooden teacher's desk. 'What you got in your history AS last year. What you hope to get this year and then maybe something interesting about yourself.' Kat realised that she would be making quite accurate assessments of each of them in the next twenty minutes or so, as would they of her. She reached for her black register, 'Okay, Harley Adams, you're first.'

Harley seemed to prune his hair every time he embarked on a sentence as if getting ready for the masses of dialogue to come. 'Well, Miss Pendleton didn't like me-'

'Not interested in that,' she cut in.

'Sorry Miss, crikey you're firm but I love it! Anyway I got a C in AS, but then I'd also just split up with my boyfriend, he's twenty three Miss, and there was stress, but anyway I need a B this year-'

'Thank you Harley,' she announced, firmly signalling the end of his time slot. Kat noticed the two lads sitting at the middle desks, there could have been ten years between them, but both were looking incredibly shy. Tom Wood had a full, slightly ginger, goatee beard and Kat judged him to be at least 6ft1, completely taking over his chair and table. The other lad, Jason Sparrow, looked about twelve; fresh faced, keen, glasses, smart shirt and trousers, and very red cheeks. She hadn't noticed their quiet exchange as Harley continued his monologue, both admitting to one another that their soldiers were saluting the new fit history teacher and they prayed they would not have to stand up and speak.

'Okay, Beatrice Belshaw please.'

'Hi Miss, it's Bea.'

Kat looked across the room and saw a beautifully exotic, naturally tanned girl, with her hand raised. She noticed the clothes and bag, they did not flaunt their brand but she could tell they were highly expensive. Pairing this with the model looks and pout, Kat began to make a judgement. Then Bea spoke again.

'Okay, I'm Bea, I got a B last year. I love history. I want to get an A and I'm willing to work really hard, and something interesting about me is that I love poetry,' she enthused.

'Yeah she won the young poet of the year competition last year,' declared Harley, the fountain of all knowledge.

She smiled a soft shy smile that contradicted her dark passionate looks and Kat realised she had been wrong, Bea was actually thoughtful, sensible and nicely modest.

Friday 3<u>rd</u> September 10.45pm

'Typical,' laughed Kat, 'a gorgeous girl, a perfect kisser and what happens ... she can't get away from me fast enough.' She scanned the busy room. 'Did you see where she went?' already realising that her two best friends had been far too busy throwing shapes on the dance floor to notice.

'Nope, sorry hun. Plenty more dogs in the pound,' shouted Lucy.

'What?' frowned Jess.

'Oh you know what I mean, but I didn't mean dog, she was stunning. Well done. Back in the saddle.'

Kat smiled, 'That's the last time I take your advice!' She shook her head and gently bit the inside of her lip. 'She was lovely though.

She had the most gorgeous green eyes.' She snapped out of it. 'Hey ho, nothing is spoiling my night, let's dance ladies.'

Jess watched Kat's blue eyes, they always told the real story, disclosed her true feelings and Jess could see now that she was trying to hide her disappointment and embarrassment. But as the night went on and the drinks continued to flow Kat concluded that the evening had been everything she had hoped for - fun, flirting and friends; she had everything and more. She was filled with pride and emotion, she had done it; she had made it.

'The next chapter of my life starts in two days,' she toasted, somewhat nervously.

Monday 6ᵗʰ September 1.45pm

'Right, next up,' clapped Kat, really relaxing into the lesson, 'Freya Elton'.

Silence.

'Is Freya here?'

A timid hand appeared in the far corner. Someone had shuffled so far down into their seat that Kat had failed to notice them before. As Freya sat up, raised her hand and met her teacher's eyes, Kat's heart pounded. _Oh Shit._

CHAPTER TWO

'What the friggidy frig am I going to do?' hollered Kat, as she swung open the weighted apartment door.

Jess and Lucy were stood at the large black ash table looking really pleased with themselves, presenting a buffet and wine. 'Ta dah! Happy first day Miss Spicer.'

The modern apartment was impeccable as always, lots of floor space, two large black leather sofas decorated with masses of red cushions, and a lovely high tech black kitchen - diner with splashes of red accessories complimenting the theme that ran throughout the open plan living area. They had three large double bedrooms all with roman blinds that opened to reveal stunning views of Coldfield Park.

'Don't girls, don't!' wailed Kat, as she fell backwards onto the cold leather sofa, popping her head back up to say, 'but thank you.'

'What's happened hun, did they pick on you?' exclaimed Jess in her most sympathetic, yet told you so tone of voice. Her red hair was bouncing around as curly as ever. 'Obnoxious little nerds the lot of them!' Jess worked with children and had since decided that she didn't ever want any, the only area of dispute between her and Gary. She had quickly come to realise that her job as Primary School Secretary was much more than just typing and filing, constantly bombarded with children with body pains and playground grazes, all of which seemed remarkably healed with a slightly damp, green paper towel. There were children who wanted her to pull out their loose teeth, squabblers who were told to cool off right next to her hatch; they were everywhere. The paperwork side of the job was great, but the interaction with those clingy, little people - who clearly loved her to pieces - she could do without.

'No it's bloody worse than that, I can't believe it. I just can't believe it. I'm fired. They will fire me.' Kat covered her face with a large red bobbly cushion. 'I might as well just resign tomorrow!'

Jess signalled to Lucy that this must be serious. Rarely did their flatmate swear and rarely did she over dramatisize events. 'What's happened hun?' she asked, genuinely concerned.

'Freya, the girl I kissed on Friday ... she is in my BLOODY CLASS!'

Jess took the party sausage back out of her mouth. 'Which class?'

'My school class today, my A-Level! She was sitting in my BLOODY A-LEVEL CLASS!' Kat wailed, still in shock.

'OH MY GOD!' shouted Lucy, leaving the buffet behind and racing to the black leather sofa. 'This is hilarious!'

'No it BLOODY isn't.'

'Oh shit, sorry mate,' said Lucy shaking her blunt black fringe, trying desperately to compose herself.

'Yes, oh shit.' She breathed deeply, relieved to have finally been able to let off steam. It had been hard work to maintain her poise in the staffroom at the end of school when asked by Janet Louza how her first day had been.

'Does anyone else know?' asked Jess concerned, but still standing in close enough proximity to the buffet.

'I don't know, I don't think so.' She sat up and regained her composure. 'I'm so sorry about the swearing, that just isn't me. I just don't know what to do, I can't believe it. I am in absolute despair.'

Lucy clicked her fingers and grinned, 'Okay, so let us get this straight,' she liked to summarise and clarify everything, 'the gorgeous brown haired lady ... who looked about twenty five ... that you snogged the face off on Friday night ... is actually a seventeen year old girl in your A-Level history class?!' Lucy had to keep pausing in an attempt to stifle her giggles. 'Well that's put a fly in the dung.' She loved using the little sayings that she had recently discovered in her Auntie's pristine toilet. She thought they made her sound wise and endearing, and was intent on practising them so she sounded thoughtful and clever when Mr Right finally showed up.

'Yes, what on earth am I going to do?' whined Kat, all hope lost. Three years training and she had lasted a day, *fantastic*.

'Well what did you do?' asked a pragmatic Jess, offering around a large packet of ever so moreish *Hob Nobs*.

Kat declined. 'I just carried on. She introduced herself, said she was called Freya - like I didn't know - said she got an A last year, which someone else told me was the only one in the class.' She paused remembering Freya's intense presence. 'She seems really bright you know … and her eyes, they were so sharp, as if-' she focused back on Jess, '…anyway, sorry, then she said she plays tennis for Coldfield Tennis Club-'

'Kat you love tennis!'

'Yes I know thanks Lucy. Anyway she just said she would work hard and try her best.'

'Ah that's sweet.' Lucy reached for the depleted packet of biscuits.

'So I just said hello back and carried on. I introduced the class to the 1834 New Poor Law, you know, the one which was passed by the government of Lord Melbourne and which largely implemented the findings of the Royal Commission…'

Lucy could see it in Kat's eyes, she was off, enthusing about something no one else had ever heard of, something about old peasants or something like that. 'What did she look like? Was she in uniform? *Hit me baby one more time,'* she sung, laughing at her own giggly excitement. 'Sorry, sorry, I just think it's quite funny. You weren't to know.'

'I know I wasn't.' She sighed with despair. 'She's in Year Thirteen and they wear what they want.'

Jess had so far made three return trips to the buffet table for just one more mouth sized sausage, and now decided to make her way to the foot of the black leather sofa with the tray. 'What was she wearing?' She was just as nosy as Lucy but tried to sound objective.

'Um,' Kat didn't have to remember. The vision of Freya was etched into her mind. 'Just a pink shirt and pale blue skinny jeans. To be fair she looked great.'

'Is she out?'

It had not even crossed her mind. 'I don't know.'

Jess knew Kat would be in turmoil. 'What did you feel when you saw her?'

She took a deep breath and looked up at the white ceiling. 'Honestly it was shock, then just embarrassment, more for her than for me. Then I don't know, regret I guess.' Kat looked back down. 'I just felt awkward, poor girl.'

'So no thoughts of snogging her again in your dimly lit store cupboard?' probed Lucy, trying her hardest not to be titillating or shallow.

'No!' she exclaimed. 'No, no, no, no, no.' She was chopping her palm with her hand. 'No way. It's gone, it's forgotten, I'm her teacher and that's how it has to stay.' Kat didn't mention the way Freya's pretty green eyes seemed to ache as they met hers at the end of the lesson, and she was not ready to admit to herself, let alone her housemates, the way that had made her feel.

****

Jodi was sitting in absolute stunned silence as she heard the full unedited story from Freya. 'You lucky bitch! That is my number one absolute fantasy.' Jodi preened her bleach blonde quiff and shuddered with desire. 'I once bumped into my French teacher in the swimming pool and spent the whole time, goggles on, under the water.' Jodi closed her eyes dreamily. 'I still remember now how her massive breasts bobbed up and down, and up and down-'

'This is serious.'

'Sorry babe. Okay what do you want me to say?' asked a calmer, more thoughtful, but very jealous Jodi.

Freya looked around the single room flat. It was cosy and warm, always reminding her of a little den. Jodi's prized music posters were hanging from the walls and the main feature piece of the room was the purpose brought super king size bed with red satin sheets. It was the perfect retreat for when Freya wanted to chill, or gossip, or just hang out. Jodi was good like that.

'I want you to tell me everything will be okay. That she won't think I misled her into kissing me. That she won't think of me as some stupid schoolgirl,' Freya went quiet and felt her heart quicken, 'that she will like me.' She pushed herself up against the red suede headboard. 'She was just so vibrant today, so motivating, and so intelligent. Even Big Tom thought he was capable of getting an A by the end of the lesson.' She paused remembering the connection, '...and the kiss. I mean I have literally not stopped thinking about it.' She closed her eyes and her whole body tingled as she re-lived Kat's delicate smooth mouth pressed against hers, her touch, her perfume. It was a rich smell of flowers and amber and other things that she could not distinguish, even today as she inhaled the same scent passing her on the way to the door.

Freya had actually thought she was going to faint when she saw Kat through the glass topped door adjusting her shirt and sorting her hair, neither of which needed altering; she had looked perfect. Freya literally stopped breathing and sank to the bottom of her seat in the corner of the classroom as Kat sashayed in with the same elegance and confidence that she had had when approaching her on Friday night. Freya didn't know what she had hoped Kat would do when she finally realized she was there, in her class, in her school class. Did she want her to say, '*Phew, I thought I would never see you again?*' Or '*Never mind that I'm your teacher, lets go out on Friday because there was an unmistakable chemistry between us?*' Freya was not stupid and could tell by the way Kat handled the class that she was the absolute professional. Firm but fair was the class's initial assessment when debriefing their new teacher in the Sixth Form common room, oh and 'bloody gorgeous as well,' Big Tom had added, promising not to miss a single class this year.

'Do you think she's married?' He had asked.

'Someone like that,' the tiny bespectacled Jason had announced with authority, 'is bound to have plenty of fellows chasing her.' Freya remembered how he'd put his right hand into his yellow corduroy trouser pocket and started to pace, saying, 'She probably has some rich fiancée who owns a yacht or the like.'

Big Tom had winked, 'Well I'm not being funny but she definitely checked me out.'

Harley had hooted, 'As if! You've got more chance with me than her, big boy!'

Bea had joined in, 'I think she's incredible, so smart and so confident-'

'Yeah yeah teachers pet,' Tom had joked, admiring Bea's ever so tight black *Armani* jeans.

Freya had remained quiet; her assessment of the new history teacher was completely inappropriate.

'You know when you kiss a guy,' pondered Freya, hands behind her head staring into space, completely at home spread across the red satin sheets.

Jodi grimaced, 'That's one misfortune I've never had the pleasure to experience.' She was not fussy with her women, she liked them Lipstick, Butch, Sport Dyke, Blue Jeans Femme, Pillow Queen, and her favourite was Gold Star Lesbian like herself, never slept with a man and have no intention of ever sleeping with a man.

'Get out!' shrieked Freya. 'What, you've never kissed a guy?'

'As if?! Why would I? I'm a lesbian? I love women. The thought of kissing a man seems so unthinkable to me, so wrong, so unnatural, so cringe worthy. I would just never do it.' Her small body shook with revulsion.

'Well you know what?' declared Freya, '…don't! I mean their mouths are so big and stubbly and they have these huge tongues like slabs of meat pushing in and out and-' she shuddered at the thought; a thought that last week would not have warranted such a negative reaction. Now however, she was aware of what it was like to kiss a woman, and it was incomparable, something so different, so meaningful, so complementing. Freya realised that women's mouths fit together in a way that men and women's don't. She got the electric pulses.

'Roll on Thursday Period One,' giggled an excitable Jodi, wishing the drama was her own.

CHAPTER THREE

Kat was sitting in the old fashioned staffroom on a free period where she had not, for once, been stung for cover. She was sure that *Kathy from Cover* deliberately targeted her, but then again every other member of staff seemed to have the same gripe. Today however she could relax. She looked around at the clusters of brown woven, foam filled chairs. All had owners and she had learnt early on to stand until you were officially allocated a chair. The same with the mugs piled high in the sink waiting for *Carole the Cleaner* to scrub them in a hopeless attempt to remove the permanent brown circles etched around the inside. Kat always washed her own cup. She had again learnt in her first ever school placement that if you dared to use someone else's cup or sit in someone else's seat you were subject to absolute and utter contempt, the misdemeanor remembered for your entire placement, confirmed with tuts every time you entered the room and met the eyes of their original owner. The cluster of chairs worn more than any others, she decided, were the ones strewn around the English Department desk. Stray exercise books sitting amongst a cluttered table full of trashy gossip magazines and what looked like a pair of makeup bags. The whole department could always be found huddled together at break and lunch - ideal for any students needing to find their teacher with a question or late homework - but Kat could not recall a single knock on the door and request for either of the English Department girls. She smiled to herself, feeling that silly buzz she used to get when permitted to enter her old school staffroom, being asked to carry textbooks or pick up a folder from a pigeonhole. Staff had to be very cautious about letting students into their domain, mostly because of notice boards like the one she was reading now. Strewn in big red letters it said, 'Calvin McGee isolated - told Miss Phag (with the original F crossed out) to, "Go screw herself sideways."'!

Kat was sitting, cradling her warm coffee, and reflecting. Lessons were planned, books were marked, two months in and she was thriving. Her Year Seven's had won the first two attendance reports, her Key Stage Three classes were going swimmingly and her A-level history class had been adorable. All ten students had handed in a fantastic first essay on the 1834 Poor Law. There had been a wide range of grades but Kat could tell that everyone had tried their absolute hardest. Big Tom's was a bit short and little Jason's was slightly pontificating, but all had tried. What had really surprised her was Freya. She had been mature, smart, funny and normal. Nothing had been mentioned, she had not hung around at the end of the lessons, and there were no longing gazes, no screwed up love notes. Kat snapped out of it, what was she thinking? Of course there would be none of that. Freya was clearly highly embarrassed about mistaking a dancing girl in a club with a boring history teacher. She had undoubtedly decided to bury it as a never to be repeated, cringe worthy memory, and that suited Kat just fine; especially when she found herself warming to Freya's kind personality and marvelling at her fierce intelligence, telling herself that she was just growing fond of her like she was growing fond of Harley's private anecdotes at the start of most lessons, and little Jason's authority on all things *woman* - even though he had zero experience. And Bea, she could not forget Bea, she seemed to get more beautiful every lesson, passion filling each perfectly articulated thought, her desire to understand glowing from her deep brown eyes. Yes it was fine, Kat decided, what had she been worrying about?

****

Freya spent another lesson stealing glances of Kat whenever she turned to face the interactive white board. It was common school knowledge that Miss Spicer had knocked Miss Pity from English off the *best backside* top spot and as Freya looked at her today, wearing another pair of perfectly fitted grey *Whistles* trousers, she ached. Freya was an intelligent girl and knew she had to act normally, show Kat how mature, clever and funny she was. There was no way she was going to mention the kiss and act like an infatuated school girl or crazy stalker. What she deduced was that Kat had to be attracted to her. She liked her looks enough to kiss her without even knowing her, so now if she could show her the whole package, the personality, the charm, the maturity then Kat would acknowledge her in the way she hoped for every single moment of every single day; and it seemed to be working.

Bea tapped Freya with her pen. 'What do you keep looking at?'

'Nothing,' she replied sharply, returning her eyes to her weighty textbook.

'It's okay; I think she's gorgeous too.'

'What are you talking about you weirdo?' laughed Freya nervously.

Bea let it drop.

****

As Kat enjoyed her second coffee in the quiet staff room, Ben Puller, the handsome but rather scruffy business studies teacher, sauntered in. 'Bloody little buggers those Year Eights. Someone's got one of those watches that turn the TV on and off and apart from strip search them, could I find out who it was? Could I buggery!'

Kat was really fond of Ben. He was blonde haired, rugged, and slightly dishevelled, but reports from her tutor group hailed him as a great teacher. He had befriended her in the first few weeks and laughed off the catty comments coming from Diane Pity and Fiona Mews the English Department cows - one of whom was clipping her way to the staffroom as they spoke.

Ben had drunkenly snogged Diane at last year's *Summer Bash* and she had been trying to get her perfectly manicured claws into him ever since.

Diane Pity walked quietly into the staffroom, the noise from her ridiculous heels absorbed by the blue tiled carpet squares. She settled into her sunken seat and reached for a trashy magazine. Diane didn't like Kat and made no qualms about who knew. She had heard Ben ask her out on numerous occasions only to be rebuffed by the, *I'm too perfect for you Kat Spicer*, and now again looking over at the pair flirting on the other side of the staffroom, she felt jealous; jealous that the kids loved Miss Spicer, jealous that she was already being earmarked for an Assistant Head of Year role, *I mean who gets that after two months?!* She opened the clasp on her see-through lunchbox and bit nastily into a large leaf of lettuce, studying the backs of their heads; how dare *my* Ben have a new woman on the scene?

Kat had asked Lucy and Jess's advice one evening when it became apparent that Ben had developed a bit of a crush on her.

'Well done Kat, you don't usually notice things like that,' chuckled Lucy over a bottle of cheap white wine. She looked slightly odd, slumped on their voluptuous sofa with her black *Nike* leotard on.

Lucy had just finished a body building class and was back for the night. Kat stared at her perfectly toned muscles. It was true, Kat was terrible at knowing when someone fancied her, always assuming they were just being pleasant or kind. But this time with four actual dates proposed she got the message and needed some friendly advice. But as Lucy and Jess were heatedly debating her plan of action she was staring at the bulging thigh muscles pressed against her legs and questioning why she was not attracted to her perfectly sculpted housemate. She decided that it was for the same reason she was not attracted to Jess; they were friends before she started having feelings for women. For that reason they were more like sisters to her. There was never any awkwardness or tension, each valued and respected the other for who they were; and they had a blast all of the time, making the most of their weekends and fast growing pay packets. Kat loved her life and was ready to act on the advice of her two best friends.

'Do you want to tell him?' asked Jess, lifting the double layered chocolate box above her head to read the mouth watering descriptions underneath.

'Yes of course, but I don't know how he'll take it.'

'What does that matter?' scoffed Lucy.

'I don't know, it just does. He's a great guy and I want us to be friends and I don't want him to think I'm just some man hating butch lesbian.'

'Look at yourself, as if!' wailed Jess and Lucy in despair.

'I don't know. It's just hard knowing when to tell people. I'm not ashamed.' Kat clarified for Lucy, but also for herself. 'I'm proud of my sexuality, but I think I just struggle to announce it. It's just not important like that.'

'So why didn't you just say it when he first asked you out?' Lucy asked, nothing ever complex or complicated for her.

Kat thought back to the busy staffroom full of teachers. 'Well I wasn't sure he was and I didn't want to sound presumptuous and then he asked again and I knew Leery old Lester, the dirty old teacher I was telling you about, and the English girls were listening, and I don't know; I guess I just don't want my private life discussed by the whole staffroom.'

Jess offered the box hoping no one would pick the Turkish Delight. 'I get it hun, but you know people will find out don't you?' She popped it in quickly.

'Of course, but I just want it to come out naturally and in its own time.' Kat was the consummate professional in school and always tried to get the balance right with her classes. All of the Sixth Formers seemed to know the ins and outs of Diane Pity's love life which Kat believed was highly inappropriate and slightly embarrassing for Mr Puller. In contrast was the other extreme, Janet Louza, whom the students seemed to think slept in the dusty store cupboard, clearly having absolutely no life or interest whatsoever outside of school. Kat was consistent, firm and fair, but still interested, approachable and warm.

'Just tell him,' they had said.

So sitting in the staffroom with yet another proposition for dinner she just said it, 'I'm sorry Ben but I am gay.'

Ben raised his eyebrows. 'Oh okay, I didn't realize. No worries mate, at least I can stop thinking that I've lost my touch!' And with that it was done, all great, all fine. A perfect reaction thought Kat. What she failed to spot was Diane Pity almost choking on her salad sandwich and scurrying gleefully out of the staffroom door.

Diane Pity was about to explode. 'Run, run, run,' she squealed to herself as she tottered along the long corridor in a fashion that her ridiculously high patent heels and impossibly tight yellow satin skirt were unaccustomed to. Her surgically enhanced breasts were spilling out of her tight pink body top as she urged her trotting feet to take bigger steps; her current attire making it a physical impossibility. She sounded like a drum roll getting faster and louder as she tottered past classroom after classroom down the never ending pale blue corridor of B Block. Diane felt ever so disappointed when passing Miss Phag's classroom. The noise had not been as deafening as she had hoped and snatching a glance through the glass as it rushed by it appeared that some pupils were actually facing the front. Every teacher knew that you could judge a colleague by the type of noise coming from their classroom and as Diane finally approached Fiona Mews's room there was absolute silence. Diane did not bother to straighten herself up, she just threw open the door and exclaimed in a loud breathy fashion, 'I need a word please Miss Mews.'

Fiona Mews closed the lid of her laptop, hiding her facebook homepage. She stood up, flared her abnormally large nostrils and screeched in her high pitched shrill voice, 'If anyone even coughs they'll be in detention.'

Her class of tiny Year Sevens did not dare to look up. Miss Mews was rumoured to have perforated a boy's eardrum when he had, for the third time, pleaded that he did not understand. Her lessons were always the same, a very brief introduction, tasks on the board and forty five minutes of working in absolute silence. Fiona used the time wisely to keep an eye on her eBay bids and stay up to date with her 243 friends on facebook, some of whom she could not quite place.

The heavy classroom door thumped closed and the noise echoed down the long corridor. 'She's gay!' blurted Diane.

'Who?'

'Miss fucking universe. She's gay. I mean gay. Properly gay.'

Fiona was thrilled that her best fake friend had some incredible piece of gossip, but looking at Diane almost shaking with glee she could not figure it out. 'Who's gay?'

'Miss sodding Spicer, golden girl. SHE'S GAY'. Diane almost spat out the words. She had not felt excitement like this in months.

'Never?!' hooted Fiona, experiencing Diane's feeling of utter joy. Her face quickly straightened and Diane fully understood why the pupils called her horse-face. She flared, 'Is this just a rumour?'

'No!' giggled Diane, her thin pencil eyebrows raised higher than normal. 'I just heard her tell Ben in the staffroom. She said, "I am gay". She is a lesbian. A dirty little clitty-licker!'

They held each other's thin arms and did a little jump, a jump of pure exhilaration.

'We will bring her down with this,' shrilled Fiona, as her garish orange and yellow neck scarf danced in delight. The intense jealousy they had felt at the arrival of *Super - Teacher Spicer* was instantly washed away with those three little words.

Kat and Ben made their way out of the staffroom towards the dinner hall, aiming to avoid the surge that left tiny Year Sevens smeared against the narrow corridor walls. Ten minutes till the lunch bell, they had time.

'We are going out on Friday to *Gail's* in town if you fancy joining us?' It was a genuine offer and Kat hoped that Ben would say yes. It would be lovely for him to meet her housemates and nice to have a colleague that she could socialise with. Kat explained how they rotated venues each Friday. *Reflex* with the revolving dance floor for Lucy. *The Mailbox* with its gorgeous wine bars for Jess, and *Gail's* gay bar with its electric atmosphere for her. The girls had a great time wherever they went and this Friday, Gary, had agreed to join them. He usually insisted that Jess had a night with just the girls at least once a week, but this week they seemed even more in love than usual and he had asked to tag along. Ben jumped at the offer which buoyed her confidence further. As they approached the large hall there was a buzz of flustered looking staff. The busybodies from Reprographics were handing out a letter in bold red print. Of the twelve or so teachers milling around the hall, all seemed to read it, take in a gasp of air, shake their heads in absolute despair and look utterly horrified. Ofsted had just given their two days notice. Ben and Kat huddled over a discarded flyer. They were due in at nine am on Monday morning for a two day school inspection. As Ben mumbled expletive after expletive Kat decided not to panic. She would view it in the same way that she had viewed exams - a chance to prove what you could do. She had indeed been the annoying child waiting outside the exam hall with a feeling of actual excitement, she knew she knew the stuff and now she would show the examiner she knew the stuff - and she did - A's and A*'s across the board. This was the same she reasoned, yes there would be nerves, but hers would be nerves of anticipation, not nerves of desperation. As long as she planned well then everything should be fine. Kat went to touch the wooden table then stopped herself - Jess was such a bad influence. Ben looked pale; he needed their planned night out now more than ever.

CHAPTER FOUR

Kat rushed over to a slightly nervous, but still ruggedly handsome, Ben. They were half an hour late. 'I am so sorry, we got stuck on the expressway, have you been here long?'

The club was buzzing and Ben had spent his time perched at the neon bar clutching his pint of bitter, something that was not often ordered in the funky gay bar. He had been marvelling at this whole new world. 'A while, but don't worry about it, it's been an eye opener!'

Lucy chimed in, 'Hi, I'm Lucy and as they say, the early bird catches the worm!'

He stood up, smiled cheekily and kissed her cheek. 'Ben, hi, nice to meet you,' he paused eyeing her excited eyes, 'I love that saying.'

Lucy's smile stretched from ear to ear as she puffed up with pride.

Ben had spotted the group of friends entering and was intrigued by the powerful looking girl with black bobbed hair who reminded him of Catherine Zeta Jones when she played Velma Kelly in *Chicago*. She looked giggly and flirty and incredibly toned, with fantastic boobs; his type. He had no idea what he had been thinking last summer when he drunkenly snogged Diane Pity, the egging on from his mates and the numerous *Aftershocks* were his only justification; or possibly the absolute eyeful of tit she kept forcing on him. Ben thought that Diane and sidekick Fiona were nasty, no other word for it, just nasty. Neither enjoyed teaching, and they certainly didn't care about the kids welfare or educational and emotional development like he did; just such a shame that the Head of English was Leery Old Lester who they kept happy with their highly inappropriate and really rather dirty flirting. Kat's arrival at the start of the year had been a breath of fresh air in the often down-beat staffroom. He looked over at her now and still could not believe it. She was the most strikingly beautiful women he had ever seen and what had endeared him further was the fact she had absolutely no idea just how sensational she actually was. Gutted, he thought, as he saw Kat's eyes glance shyly towards a tall brunette stood waiting at the bar. He sighed defeated and turned his attention to Lucy.

The group chatted easily and laughed frequently as the giggly club night quickly became a roaring success. Lucy and Ben hit it off like an absolute house on fire and were now embarking on their second mammoth snogging session to the smooth sound of *New York* by Alisha Keys. Jess and Gary were laughing and smooching on the lime green sofas and Kat was enjoying the attentions of Emma - good looking, smart - from what she could glean from their brief first encounter - and very complimentary. She had discretely found out Emma's age and breathed a sigh of relief; hurdle one passed. Kat, who was so astute and on the ball in all other areas of her life, really struggled with relationships, and Jess and Lucy had given her strict instructions on what to notice: 'Is she always glancing over your shoulder? Does she look at you when you are talking? Does she listen, really listen, to what you are saying? Is she kind to you?' The list had gone on, but now with the new addition: 'Check she is not a school girl.'

Emma pulled Kat closer and they moved together in time with the music. To onlookers they looked incredibly sexy and erotic, but for Kat it was all about the atmosphere, the music, the dancing, and the warming feeling of another woman's body held against her own. Emma started to kiss her soft bare shoulder, quickly progressing to her long neck and then finding her mouth. The kiss was nice, soft, tender and warm, but not the same explosion of energy she had felt when kissing Freya. Her mind started to wander.

'Oh ... My ... Good ... God ... Miss!' The wail was unmistakably camp. 'You get on my bus! How superb! I would never have guessed, but then Damien, my latest squeeze, always says my Gaydar is broken, and I tell him it's not, but now I need to text him and tell him he was right, because I had no idea Miss, not a clue. This is fab, I love you so much Miss, do you know that? You were my idol before, but now you're my ... what's better than an idol? My enigma, is that right? I'm sure you know; you know everything. Oh wow, congratulations Miss, I swear I won't tell anyone, I swear. I am just so pleased, so thrilled.'

Emma quietly disappeared to the bar as the perfectly tweaked, great looking lad, continued his spiel.

Kat and Ben were sitting in a brown leather booth in the quiet area, soulful music creating the perfect atmosphere for the numerous amorous couples scattered around the room, splashes of luminous colours glowing on the black walls. Harley had soon disappeared with a new '*soul mate*' after many over emphasised reassurances that he would be forever loyal to his favourite all time teacher.

'He's a good lad.' Ben tried to sound heartening and gave Kat all of the information he knew.

Harley had come out at the start of Year Ten. He spent the first three years of secondary school as a shy quiet boy who hid under his mop of brown hair, never drawing attention, never excelling, but never underperforming. One of those students who just floated under the radar, the one whose photo reference you had to check when it came to parents evening. Then suddenly on the first day of term in Year Ten, the girls in his tutor group thought they had been blessed with a new foreign exchange student, probably from Italy but maybe from one of the romantic Spanish Islands. A perfectly pruned Harley - four inches of holiday growth taller and broader, with hair fashionably styled off his face - displaying for the first time his enormous natural eyelashes and beautiful features. He had waited for the questions to silence and then began, 'Harley Adams, been in your class for three years, barely been spoken to by any of you, but now I'm going to be heard. I'm gay and proud of it.'

Gay Harley quickly became popular with the girls. His harem expanded week by week, his affectations were developed and perfected month on month and his witty banter and quick comments endeared him to most of the girls and boys in his year. Yes there were always some over confident smart arse Year Eight lads who thought it was funny to shout '*Poofter*' as he sauntered down the corridors visualizing the runway of a Prada fashion show; but then it was the same kid who thought his mates would laugh if he shouted '*Hairy Marys*' at the Indian girls or '*Oi Ginger Pubes*' at the painfully shy chubby red head sitting eating lunch alone. Harley was well like and justifiably so. Much of it was an act, but he would inevitably tone that down when he realised, maybe in his twenties, that people liked him for him - Harley, who just happened to be gay.

Whether it was the growing realisation that she could not reverse the events of the evening, or the numerous spritzers that had been consumed following the whirlwind that had been Harley, Kat lay quietly in bed and decided to shrug it off. She thought he probably could be trusted, but in the same respect realised that he had not asked to know her secret. Secret, she thought, that made it sound so sordid. It was not a secret, but it was also not common school knowledge. Kat wondered, once again, how best to handle it. Do you stand up in the staffroom on day one and say, '*Hi, I'm Miss Spicer the new history teacher. I like tennis, my favourite colour is red and I'm gay?*' All the straight members of staff would not declare their straightness so why should she announce her lesbianism. Or do you answer honestly when the nosy Year Nine girl says, '*You got a boyfriend Miss?*' Or do you ignore the questions and genuine interest of students and completely avoid any discussion of your personal life; which Kat thought would leave her appearing cold and unapproachable. She looked up at her sparkling bedroom ceiling, glowing with tiny stars; they would shine for about half an hour before slowly fading into the darkness that surrounded them. She closed her eyes, pushed her head deeper into her plush feather pillow and tried to focus. She believed that speculation was worse than truth, and had to devise a plan of action for when the inevitable questions arose; but with the loud noise from Lucy's room she was struggling to formulate one.

Ben skilfully manoeuvred Lucy into the reverse cowgirl and they started riding each other once again. Another position, another fantastic chance to feel Ben's enormous manhood reaching places Lucy never knew she had. She could not believe it, she was in complete heaven. Kat had failed to describe Ben's generous good looks, the way his bushy blonde hair stuck out slightly at the sides, the way his full lips and strong chin drew your eye, how his biceps pushed against the fabric of his black short sleeved shirt. At 5ft 9 and muscly, Lucy struggled to find a man who would dominate her, overpower her and take control. Well now, as Ben lifted her across to the top of her wooden chest of drawers, she realised she had. She could see his firm arse in the mirror moving in and out, perfectly timed to accentuate her every pulse. She screamed, he had done it again, it was her third orgasm of the night.

Lucy had ushered Ben into the back of their taxi and told him that she was not about to get rid of the goose that laid the golden eggs; he seemed to be the only one who understood what she had meant and laughed a warm genuine laugh that made her hold his strong hand even tighter. Kat had winked as Lucy manhandled him into their apartment and she could hear them now. The rhythmic rocking followed by the dull thumping, climaxing in the hard pounding. Lucy had tried to stifle her screams but the walls between the bedrooms were paper thin and Kat could not help but picture her own sexual experiences with men, each and every one a complete and utter disaster. She lost her virginity at eighteen to her older and much more experienced boyfriend. Brett had assured her that it was the next natural step, even though nothing about their heavy petting or subsequent sexual encounters felt natural. She had pictured music, candles, petals on the bed, an experience so perfect it would make her forget her doubts and worries and realise that yes this was fantastic and exactly what she wanted. Unfortunately he had hands the size of baseball mitts, stubble that rubbed painfully against every area he was hopelessly trying to arouse and big hairy balls that Kat could barely look at, let alone cup in her mouth as he had so masterfully instructed. Brett had done the obligatory nipple tweaks, rummage around in her downstairs area and was sure she would now be ready for the real deal. He pushed his way in and after about four strokes turned her over into the doggy position to finish himself off.

'Wasn't that perfect babe,' he had whispered in her ear as he cuddled her from behind.

Kat managed to say, 'Yes,' as she lay lifeless on her side, a slow tear running down her cheek and onto the cold pillow.

A year later it was Craig who she really believed she loved. She assumed the sex would be better, but played dead as he pumped and pumped and pumped, grinning down at her and complimenting her puppies as he stared perversely at her full breasts jiggling up and down. She had tried to switch off and grin and bear it, but when a bead of sweat dropped from his nose into her eye she had had enough. She told him to stop, simply saying, 'Sorry it's just not happening for me.'

Craig had asked if they could cuddle instead, but Kat decided it was best if he just left and in that one instance she had morphed from thinking she loved him, to never wanting to see him ever again, she was so completely and utterly put off.

She had ignored the glaringly obvious and gave it one last shot with Paul; perfect Paul. They had been dating for about two months when he suggested a night away in a posh hotel. She had never let it go any further than kissing and he assumed she was playing hard to get. He was smart, attractive, well paid, kind and honest and Kat knew if it did not work now, it never would. Everything was exact, a gorgeous room in the grounds of a leafy country hotel, expensive truffle chocolates on the pillow, champagne and strawberries ordered in advance. They started kissing on the romantic four poster bed and took things really slowly. Kat helped direct his hand, as she always had to with male partners, having learnt with Brett that not doing so resulted in many faked orgasms to bring an end to the sanding down of her delicate areas. Paul tried really hard bless him, but literally nothing was happening and when he asked for a hand to try and revive his wilting soldier she decided enough was enough.

Inevitably, she started to acknowledge her inner sexual attraction to women, and when a female flatmate at uni got into her bed one drunken night and kissed her in a way that words can still not describe Kat knew; and what followed made everything make complete sense. Sex was amazing. Sex was incredible. Sex was the most intense pleasure that all of her teenage magazines had described; only this time it wasn't a party sausage and two hairy dumplings that she had to contend with, but gorgeous curves and soft skin and warm moist openings that called for her delicate fingers. It was an experience that was repeated with a number of women over her three years of study, never cheap or meaningless, there was always that emotional connection. Kat reminisced and as silence fell from next door she slid her right hand into her pyjama bottoms; she was aroused. She closed her eyes and Freya was there, kissing her with passion, holding back her hair, finding more of her mouth.

'Stop it.' Kat spoke out loud to herself as she opened her eyes. She felt dirty, the student teacher boundary had always been so clear, a position of trust, a position of responsibility and consequentially, a position of power. She thought of Freya and the way she presented herself in lessons, she was the powerful one, so commanding and confident; so full of life. She tried to close her eyes again and give herself what every inch of her body needed right this second; but she couldn't. Freya's face, with sparkling green eyes and long chestnut brown hair kept appearing. She rolled onto her stomach, shoved her hands under her pillow and told herself to, 'Get a grip.'

CHAPTER FIVE

Kat had spent the entire rainy weekend perfecting her lesson plans. Year Eight Period One, Free Period Two, Year Seven Period Three and A-Level Period Four and Five. She had also exchanged a couple of flirty texts with Emma, arranging to meet on Thursday evening. She seemed nice enough and Kat knew she needed to get her love life back on track; an evening in a nice wine bar, chatting and laughing and getting to know someone new was exactly what was called for. She realised the more she tried to shake Freya's kiss from her mind, the more it kept appearing; she was involuntarily re-living the experience at least once in each lesson as she glanced over at Freya who was always head down working away. A couple of times her stare had been caught and met with the mischievous green eyes holding her own for that split second too long.

Kat walked confidently down the B Block corridor, secretly hoping that she would be observed. She had experienced Ofsted on her final school placement and realised the inspectors movements were known by no one until you spotted them sitting at the back of your classroom. Kat wondered if she had lipstick on her teeth when her regular smile was met with giggles from two Year Nine girls as she passed them in the hall.

There was absolute silence in the stuffy staffroom as Head Teacher, Kirsty Spaulding, introduced the five Ofsted inspectors who tried their hardest to smile and look reassuring; they failed. The only staff member who seemed at ease during the falsely optimistic staff briefing was Diane Pity who shot Kat a look that she struggled to place. She was being competitive judged Kat, even though not directly named in the report it was easy to determine which teachers got which grades and Miss Pity clearly wanted to come out on top.

'Good luck,' spat Diane, as she pushed her way out of the staffroom door at the end of the morning briefing.

Kat realised that it was the first time Diane had ever spoken to her directly; *what a privilege* she thought unfazed, tucking her detailed plans for the day under her arm, ready to embrace the challenge ahead. The inspectors had left five minutes previously and were already sitting patiently in their unsuspecting victim's rooms.

Diane trotted down the corridor, a feat made slightly more easy than usual due to her smart, properly fitted, but rarely worn, navy blue trouser suit. She had Year Thirteen A-Level English for a double period and had a choice of lesson plans depending on the inspector's whereabouts. As she marched past Miss Phag's room she could see the chubby balding inspector take his seat. 'R.I.P Faggy,' she hissed under her breath.

As Diane stood at her desk, triple checking for extras in her classroom, she smiled and reached for lesson plan B.

Freya and Bea had never seen Miss Pity so enthused. She had given them the English curriculum at the start of the year and from then on it had been *'Independent Learning'* as she liked to sell it. They were managing to cope because they were conscientious, naturally intelligent and very hard working, but poor Big Tom would be lucky to scrape an N.

'Right,' announced Miss Pity. 'I thought that given the circumstances I would meander away from the poets today and focus on a more relevant topic.' She was relishing every word.

Freya and Bea nudged each other under the table, they had never seen anything quite like it.

'Question....' pause for effect, 'what have Oscar Wilde, Truman Capote and Patricia Cornwell got in common?' She was pontificating and highly excited.

'Authors,' said Bea.

Miss Pity's room was not adorned with the usual colourful posters and displays that you would expect to see on the walls of an English teachers classroom, and there were certainly no signs of students work proudly displayed for all to see. Instead she had a wall dedicated to Peter Andre and a collage of photos from her tacky nights out with Miss Mews.

'Think outside the box Bea, clarify, clarify.' Miss Pity was doing her best teaching act. It had always been an act with her, never having that natural ability to guide and empower, to impart knowledge and create a thirst for learning; to be honest she could not really be bothered. The internet had so many great lesson plans now which included printable resources.

Freya whispered, 'What is she doing?' Bea was staring in disbelief, so Freya continued, '...do you think she's practicing her teaching in case she gets watched by an inspector this afternoon?'

'I don't know, but I know what she's getting at.' She spoke up, 'They are all gay Miss.' Her tone was sharp.

Freya wondered how Bea knew this. There was so much of Bea that still remained a mystery. She had transferred to their Sixth Form from John Taylor's last year to study philosophy as well as English and history, a combination that her previous school could not offer. Their first meeting was one they laughed about whenever patrolling the corridors together at break on their weekly *Sixth Form Community Service.* Freya always thought it sounded like a punishment as opposed to a responsibility which they had been encouraged to sign up for in an effort to ensure their CV's looked appealing on their upcoming UCAS Forms.

Freya had been the first to sign up to *Community Service* at the start of Year Twelve, loving everything about the Sixth Form. The fact she could finally wear her own clothes; often simple items accessorised with scarves and jewellery. The *'Gap Girl'* had been her label at the end of week one - a much nicer tag than poor Poppy Jones who was now known as *'Charity Shop Pop.'* Freya empathised with Poppy. It had been the same throughout the school on *Non Uniform Days.* Children from very poor or unloving families stood out a mile and whilst the day was anticipated by most with such excitement and minute outfit preparation, the odd few chose to stay at home or wear their uniform, pretending they had forgotten, simply to avoid the truth being known - their family had no money and the few clothes they did have were old hand me downs that didn't fit.

Freya had been patrolling the corridor on the second week in Year Twelve. It wasn't the power or authority that she enjoyed, but the feeling of responsibility, and with university choices next year she had started to think seriously about going into teaching. Her thoughts about where to go were interrupted by the sight of Chianne Granger, Year Ten, bitch, pushing a tiny innocent boy to the ground.

'See these feet?' she barked, 'worship them.' The fat bulging out of Chianne's shoe made her feet look exactly like trotters which matched the rest of her piggy appearance.

Freya knelt quickly at the crying boy's side. 'Hi, I'm Freya, lower sixth, are you okay?'

'Yes,' whimpered the tiny boy whose new blazer absolutely swamped him.

'Is it your first week?'

'Yes.'

'Well don't worry about Chianne,' she raised her voice, 'the whole school knows she had to get a license for being that ugly.' Freya stared up at Chianne as she helped the shy boy stand.

'What did you just say?' The growl was fierce and her mob of mates started to jeer.

Freya was only a year and a half older than Chianne but would never stand by and watch anyone suffer at the hands of a bully, no matter their age, size, or sometimes even the danger of the situation. By this time the boy had disappeared having been handed one of those lifetime memories from an unforgettable Chianne Granger.

'Hi there, I'm a human being, what about you Chianne?' She held out her hand.

A crowd had started to gather in the corridor. 'Go fuck yourself Freya.'

'Don't you dare swear at me you nasty bitch. What's your problem? He's Year Seven. What did he ever do to you?' Her temper flared.

'He asked me how to get to the library. I mean come on get a grip geek!' Chianne was addressing her audience with relish. Mobile phones had come out and she needed to look her best for the YouTube upload. She knew Freya already warranted a smack but if she was to beat her record and get over 5000 hits she needed to build it up.

Freya turned to leave. She had learnt how to control her fiery temper better over the last year or so and knew it was time to breathe deeply and walk away, report it to the Head of Year Ten and forget about it. Nothing would happen she realised. All the kids knew there was no punishment that school could give them that actually meant anything. Exclusions rarely happened because of the effect they had on the league tables, and expulsions were never heard of - *'Managed Moves'* was the new term where two schools would swap their offending youths.

'Go finger fuck yourself again Freya like you used to at primary school.' There were howls and more recording mobiles.

Freya spun back around, 'Shut your fat face, Chianne.'

A small bottle of blue *Impulse* body spray blasted like a stun gun into Freya's eyes.

Chianne blew a kiss to the cameras and thumped off.

'Are you okay?' asked Bea now at Freya's side, having been unable to penetrate the tight circle around the show. Bea guided a blind and flowery smelling Freya to reception and as Freya listened, with eyes closed, to Bea chatting away, she realised that she had judged the new comer completely wrong; hourglass appearances and pouty features meant nothing she realised.

Now sitting here a year on, she reflected on everything she knew about Bea. They were friends, yes definitely, good friends, but different to friendships she had formed lower down the school; more real, more rewarding, more grown up. Freya admired her for her intelligence and work ethic, the way Bea could hold her own in a debate without exhuming the frustration and irritation that she sometimes did. She loved her creativity and originality, her deepness, her passion. They proof read each other's essays and often studied together at Freya's house; never at Bea's. She had not once invited her over and Freya had never met her parents, both supposedly successful artists. Bea was certainly modest about herself, her smouldering looks, her model figure, her clearly wealthy background, never splashing herself with labels, but definitely buying from gorgeous shops. Freya assumed it must be the same with her parents, not wanting to show them or their house off.

'Spot on!' exclaimed Miss Pity with a clap of her hands. 'I am here today to reassure you...' pause for effect '...to put to rest the doubts floating around in your little heads.' Miss Pity felt like a wave hurtling towards the shore, building and building getting ready to crash with one final explosion of power.

'Miss are you okay?' asked a genuinely concerned Tom Wood who had never seen Miss Pity so full of emotion.

'Yes, but are you Tom?

'Yes thanks Miss?'

'Look, these authors are gay but they have still achieved success. Just because someone is gay it does not mean they are any less capable.'

'We know that Miss,' said a spotty girl whose name Miss Pity had misplaced.

'Obviously,' retorted Freya.

Not quite the response Miss Pity had been hoping for, but she carried on unabashed. 'I know that some of you in here do history as well and I just want to go all *"cross curricular,"* said with a large quoting finger gesture, one of those initiatives Diane actually knew little about.

'Miss can you get on with it please as we really need to finish *The Ancient Mariner.*' The spotty girl was tapping the syllabus timeframe she had planned out on her own.

'Oh cut to the chase class, I know you have all been worrying about it. I've heard nothing but concern and anxiety in the corridors this morning.' She lied. 'Being homosexual is not a taboo. She is just as good a teacher as anyone else.'

'Who?' smiled a quickly excited Tom.

'Miss Spicer of course.' Diane stood waiting for the smart remarks, looks of disgust and howls of laughter, but they did not come. They are in shock she thought. 'Yes, Miss Spicer has decided to finally step out of the closet. Miss Spicer is gay.' She almost shook inside with pure exhilaration at having broken the news. 'She is a lesbian, a dyke, call it what you will.'

The class were sitting open mouthed and there was no stopping her now. 'All sorts of names, let's get them out there, no need to feel ashamed. Rug Muncher, Vagitarian, Queer, Peanut Flicker...'

Bea stood up and walked out.

A very shrill Miss Mews had been teaching the same lesson to her Year Nine's and their excitement at the gossip thrilled Fiona, even though it seemed to be more of an interest and intrigue, than the disgust and abhorrence she was expecting; the class had Miss Spicer twice a week for history.

'I wonder if she's got a girlfriend?' one girl had asked.

'Yeah probably, she's so pretty, and clever,' said another from the other side of the classroom. The lively discussion continued with numerous - normally silent - pupils voicing their opinions.

'She might be married.'

'It's called a Civil Partnership actually. My auntie is in one,' piped another.

'So is my step dad. Well he was my second step dad then he left my mum for Chris from over the road.'

'Well *More* magazine said that everyone has got it in them.'

'What?'

'A bit of gayness and it says you should experiment if you want to.'

'Well I heard that Chianne Granger snogged Chantelle Mann up the field last Saturday.'

'Yeah I heard that too.'

'Yeah but then she gave Davey Jakes a BJ while Chantelle filmed it on her mobile.'

'I bet she fancies you Miss,' screeched a lad just pleased that they were actually allowed to talk and say whatever they wanted for once.

'I hope not,' scowled Miss Mews, adjusting her garish neck scarf.

'Why not Miss? She is so fit, you should be honoured!'

'Right let's calm it down,' hushed Miss Mews, but it was too late. She had allowed the atmosphere to develop and it would be hard to regain control.

She shrieked, 'Silence.' Or maybe not.

Kat was sitting in the staffroom pleased to have escaped *Kathy from Cover*. A great first lesson she thought, shame it wasn't watched. I wonder how poor Hannah Phag got on? Kat had passed Miss Phag's classroom and seen the look of worry on her face as she stood at her desk flustering with the controls for the impossibly complicated interactive white board.

'Can I have a word?' Hannah Phag's very red face appeared next to Kat's as she cosied into Janet Louza's seat, her green felt skirt brushed itchily against Kat's bare knees.

'Of course,' she smiled, 'how did it go?'

'I got a satisfactory!' Hannah exclaimed with absolute pride, rubbing two eczema covered hands together, causing dry crusty skin to fall and stick to her green felt skirt.

'Oh well done Hannah, I'm so pleased for you,' and she was. Kat liked Hannah Phag, even though she was one of those teachers who walked down the corridors looking straight at the ground, avoiding the shirts hanging out, the running, the eating in between lessons, the swearing; knowing that any involvement would end in disaster. But when Hannah was in her classroom she tried, she tried really hard and the endless hours spent preparing lessons and marking books were starting to pay off. Students could tell quite quickly which teachers cared about them and their education and which didn't. Miss

Phag did and even though she flapped and fumbled and looked as embarrassed at the front of the class as she would have done had she been stood there naked, she managed to show the pupils that she knew her stuff and wanted them to do well. Behaviour was starting to improve.

'Hey and don't you worry,' said Hannah, putting an itchy hand on Kat's smooth knee, 'no one will care.'

'Thanks,' was all Kat could manage, slightly taken aback by the contact from Hannah and the suggestion that she may underperform with Ofsted.

Kat spent break time in her room making sure everything was just so. Books were laid out, the white board was on, spare pens were handy for the girls whose pencil cases no longer featured in their small handbags - rucksacks were only acceptable for '*square*' girls.

The door flew open and crashed noisily against the dented grey filing cabinet, 'Miss!'

'Harley hi, are you okay?'

'Miss it wasn't me I swear.' His enormously long eyelashes were fluttering in double time.

Her stomach filled with alarm. 'What?'

'Everybody knows. The whole school is talking about it. I swear it wasn't me. I only told my best friend Mimi, and she swears she only told Crystal, and Crystal is best mates with Alisha who is in Chianne's gang, but she swears she didn't tell her, but Chianne knows and so do a group of Year Nine's I just passed, I could hear them talking about it.' Harley stopped to catch his breath. He knelt down next to Kat's chair and took hold of her soft, warm hands. 'I am so sorry Miss.'

Kat was embarrassed; she had had all weekend to prepare herself for the undoubted fact that her sexuality would eventually become hot gossip at school, she just did not expect it to happen so soon. 'Get up Harley, it's fine, no big deal. I always knew it would come out at some point. Don't worry.'

'Are you sure Miss?'

'Absolutely, I'm great, don't worry.' She tried her best to reassure. 'I'm sorry you had to see what you saw on Friday.' Her cheeks blushed.

'Ooooh I'm not, you two looked hot!' He flicked his wrist and winked his eye.

He was fine decided Kat.

Her Year Seven's filed in more quietly than normal, took their seats and looked up with eager smiles. They all loved Miss Spicer, she was kind and helpful and encouraging. They sat in silence.

'Okay,' said Kat. 'Egypt. Who found out how they managed to build the pyramids?'

A flurry of hands shot up. The ones who had heard the news wanted Miss Spicer to be okay, to keep teaching them, to want to teach them, to want to stay at their school; they had to show her that she was still their favourite teacher. The lesson went well, much to Kat's surprise and she questioned whether Harley had once again exaggerated the drama. The only indication that her sexuality was the latest bit of school gossip was the usually timid David Haverley who whispered, 'You're not going to leave us are you Miss?' as he stood in the doorway, last child out.

Kat chose to stay and eat her lunch in her room with the door locked. From its position no one could see her desk; no one could see her sitting on her own in silence. She needed some time alone to think. There were several loud knocks throughout the course of the hour and the door handle wiggled each time she failed to reply. What did she feel? She could not decide. Was it fear, or dread, or maybe worry? One thing she did not feel was ashamed. She was a lesbian. She had come to completely accept it and value it; it was a huge part of who she was, but it did not define her, it did not characterise her, it just classified her sexual preference. She thought of her father, *always tell the truth and you will never have to remember your words*.

Kat unlocked her door and waited for the arrival of her Year Thirteen class. Mr Bridges, the lead Ofsted Inspector, took an exaggerated, apologetic step into her room.

'Katherine Spicer.' She put out her hand and shook his sweaty palm firmly.

'Mr Bridges. You won't notice that I'm here.'

Her Year Thirteen's wandered in, all observing the chubby balding man sitting at the back. Emergency Year Assemblies had been called on Friday to prep the students for the incredibly important Ofsted visit. 'We show them how we walk in the corridors. We show them how we enter our classrooms quietly. We show them our respect for our teachers and for each other.' Head Teacher Kirsty Spalding had tried hard to ensure her statements did not sound too pleading; they did. The kids knew all about Ofsted. They knew teachers would suddenly come to life, allowing them to do experiments and activities, adding some zing to their mostly boring lessons. Mrs Spalding had sent Chianne Granger and Chantelle Mann to Reprographics first thing in the morning, telling them it was their obligatory work experience day, even though its real purpose was to keep them hidden; something that Hannah Phag and her *Satisfactory* were eternally grateful for.

Freya saw the inspector as she entered the room. *Oh shit* she thought as she took her seat and looked at Kat. She wanted to get to the front, surround her with a warm hug and tell her she was great, perfect, the best teacher in the world who had absolutely nothing to worry about; no one cared about the rumours spread by the witches of English. But she couldn't, so she sat quietly with the rest of her classmates, no one daring to speak.

Kat started off as normal. 'Hi everyone, good day so far?' Her smile was warm as usual.

There were a couple of small, reticent nods. Not the expected response.

Kat stood with gusto, 'Right lets debate! What really started the First World War? You've read the literature, you've seen how history books reported it throughout the decades and we have studied several eye witness accounts. Let's have some views.'

No one spoke.

Kat fiddled with the blue Y shaped Indian necklace she had chosen to compliment her outfit; the small pale teardrop stones twirled under her fingers. 'Remember when we looked at the marking criteria it clearly shows how all sides of the argument need to be explored and addressed before you reach your conclusion, so who wants to start?'

Silence. No one knew what to say. Not because they didn't have their views on Archduke Franz Ferdinand or their own theories about *The Family Affair*, but because they didn't know how to handle the situation. Everyone was talking about it, even the teachers and unlike her Year Seven class, these seventeen and eighteen year olds did not feel that over enthusiastic answers would give Miss Spicer the reassurance they wanted to give; not to mention the fact that an Ofsted Inspector was sitting at the back of their class already writing away.

Kat widened her eyes and nodded at them whilst Mr Bridges continued to scribble noisily.

'The shooting started it,' said Bea, deciding to get things moving. She looked smart and sophisticated as usual, with the addition of some oversized black fashion spectacles whose only job was to add to her glamour.

No one spoke.

'Come on guys, what's up with you today?'

Big Tom was the only person who failed to spot the inspector on his way in and had been sitting quietly trying to decide how best to broach the subject. It had to be mentioned he thought. They all had such a great relationship with Miss Spicer and it was so odd how everyone was sitting here now, not saying a word. He was sure that Harley was going to race in, smothering his favourite teacher with congratulations and shrieks, but he hadn't. Harley had clocked the inspector and walked in quietly without saying a word.

Kat sighed; there was nothing more damning than an unresponsive class. This had *Unsatisfactory Lesson* written all over it.

Tom laughed nervously, 'Is no one going to say it?'

Freya coughed and little Jason went to grab Tom's knee under the table, but grabbed his fellow saluting soldier by mistake and quickly realised with disappointment that it was much bigger than his own. The thought of Miss Spicer with another woman was such a turn on that they both knew there would be a mexican wave going on under the table with one popping up, then one going down, then back up and then back down each time the thought of Miss Spicer caressing another woman's big tits entered their minds; Miss Spicer kneeling at another woman's love slot; Miss Spicer naked, tits everywhere ... Tom snapped out of it. 'Miss, are you gay?'

The silence was deafening.

'Because no one cares here either way, but everyone is talking about it and I thought I would just ask.'

The only noise was the sound of Mr Bridges putting his pen and paper firmly on the floor. Kat clasped her hands together tightly and leaned against her reassuringly strong wooden desk. 'Yes I'm gay.' She looked at them all individually. 'Anything anyone else wants to get off their chest while we're here?'

People started to shuffle. Jason put his hand up and looked at the inspector, who gave a nod of encouragement. 'Well, do you think you were born that way? Because what I know about lesbian women is that some could never image being with a guy, some don't mind being with a guy and some think they are guys in girls bodies.'

Freya felt a surge of panic, *poor Kat,* she looked so fragile and vulnerable stood at the front suddenly faced with this onslaught; but as Kat continued, Freya started to relax.

'Thank you for that insight Jason,' she paused running her fingers through her loose blonde hair, she would just have to go for it. 'I simply developed a preference for women, just like I developed a preference for sports and music.' Sod it, she thought. I know I'm a good teacher, my classes know I'm a good teacher so what is the priority for me right now? She realised that it was to deal with their genuine questions and issues, so she sat on the wooden desk and smiled. 'Come on, let's debate it.'

'Are you sure Miss?' asked Bea, lifting up her black fashion spectacles and nudging her head towards the inspector.

'Absolutely,' said Kat with true meaning.

The class debated thoughtfully and logically. She was proud of them. Everyone got involved, critiqued their own opinions and developed their arguments further. Ten minutes left until the bell, where on earth had the time gone she thought, completely engrossed in the unique once in a lifetime lesson? 'Right, let's summarise. Bea, some quick questions; Coke or Pepsi?'

'What, you want me to say what I prefer?' Bea adjusted her posture and sat tall in her chair, loving the engagement.

'Yes.' Kat knew this game inside out.

'Coke.'

'Ant or Dec.'

'Ant.'

'Take That or Westlife.'

'Westlife.'

'Eastenders or Corrie?'

'Corrie.' Bea raised her eyebrows as if that was obvious.

'Summer or winter.'

'Summer.'

Kat was firing off the questions. They were tame compared to the ones asked by a slightly tipsy Lucy on Saturday night during their pizza, film and wine evening.

'A face full of warts or permanently bad breath,' Lucy had giggled.

'Warts,' said Kat. 'I would get them removed.'

'You can't they're permanent.'

'Okay bad breath then.'

Lucy sucked in a large breath of air and grinned. 'Give a tramp a blow job or drink a teaspoon of your own period blood?'

Kat and Jess screamed.

'I'm going to be sick.' Jess was telling the truth, she thought her lingering stomach bug had gone; it hadn't.

'The tramp has got lots of knob cheese.' Lucy was in her element.

Their stomachs had started to ache from laughing too much.

'My period blood,' said Kat retching at the thought.

'Let a man wee all over your face or let him poo on your tits?'

Kat was in absolute hysterics now. 'Poo on my tits.'

'McDonalds or Burger King?' asked Kat, her mind back in the classroom, focusing on Bea.

'McDonalds.'

'Red or blue?'

'Red.'

'Men or women?'

'Women.'

'Okay do you see what I'm getting at,' said Kat, not registering her final answer. 'It should make absolutely no difference to anyone other than yourself whether you like guys or girls. Who cares? It's your preference and you should treat it in the same way as all of your other preferences, just something that lets people know a little bit more about who you are and what you like.' She raised her hands and looked at the class in summary. 'Bea likes Coke, McDonalds and...' Kat suddenly realised, '....Corrie.'

The bell rang and Mr Bridges was the only one to get up and leave the room, shutting the blue dented door behind him. Freya was staring at Bea.

'What Freya?'

'Wow!' She put her arms out and squeezed her friend tightly.

Tom and Jason did not want to stand up, both now had images of Miss Spicer spanking Bea's pert naked bottom.

Harley squealed, 'That was the best lesson of my life!' He meant it. 'Miss...' dramatic pause, 'Bea...' dramatic pause, 'We are taking over the world!'

As they all finally left her classroom, Kat sighed. What was her alternative she thought? Desperately trying to convince herself that she had done the right thing.

CHAPTER SIX

'Will you come to mine for a bit?' asked Bea as she walked alongside Freya heading out through the busy main entrance, both oblivious to everything outside of their little bubble; a bubble full of the days adrenaline and intrigue.

'Oh I would love that. I have always wondered what your home was like.' She linked Bea's arm, then groaned. 'Ah sorry I walked in today, Mum needed the car.'

Freya only lived ten minutes from the school but would always drive in when possible and would have loved to have driven Bea on their first outing to her house. Freya's father's car sharing idea seemed to be working well and the family's new pale blue *Clio* was starting to be referred to as *Freya's Car*. As an only child her parents were wary of spoiling her, but in the same respect they were so proud of her for passing her test first time that they devised the car sharing scheme. Freya would have access to a nice, new, safe car but with the additional responsibility of knowing she always had to ask when she wanted to use it; another method for the *Elton Parents* to keep tabs on their very pretty, very grown up, only daughter. She was their pride and joy, excelling at school, performing well on the tennis court, always being referred to as a *lovely young lady*. Yes she had caused some huge family arguments in her early teens with her outrageous temper, but they were pleased to have seen it subside over the past few years. *Furious Freya* had disappeared; *Fiery Freya* was still known to appear every now and then, but predominantly the person remaining after the turbulent time called *Puberty* was *Pretty Freya*, the girl with the glint in her sparkling green eyes.

'It's fine, I always get the bus,' said Bea.

Freya still found it hard to imagine her getting on a bus and likened it to Jennifer Lopez shopping in Aldi - something that just doesn't look right.

'Little Maston isn't it?' She knew the area, but had no idea where Bea's house actually was. She had driven through there with her driving instructor who always made the same comment, *"How the other half live,"* much to her annoyance. But then to be fair Freya had made her own conclusions when she heard that the new smouldering girl in their A-Level history and English classes, with the lovely clothes and bags, lived in one of those posh houses in Little Maston; *not my sort of person* she had thought at the time.

'Yes, I get the number nine.'

They stood at the public bus stop on the main road opposite the school. There were far too many pupils crammed on the chewing gum covered pavement, all shoving and barging around trying to decide whereabouts the bus would stop. It was imperative that you got a good seat. It classified power and popularity for some and simple desire to stay alive for others. Chianne Granger was pretending to push Chantelle Mann into the furious oncoming traffic, much to the amusement of her mobile phone holding fans. Bea did not care where she sat, but she always tried to read her latest book, never actually managing to absorb the chapter or so which she then had to re-read later at home. She would often pick out the most vulnerable looking child and guide them into the window seat next to her for the journey. The chosen child was safe and forever grateful to the gorgeous, tanned Sixth Former, who they regarded as their guardian angel. Today however, the vulnerable would have to go it alone and swim in the dangerous Chianne infested sea.

'Joy, it's here!' she groaned as the red double decker approached the curb in a highly inappropriate manner given the number of children diving around on the pavement. The overweight and under shaved driver didn't care; he hated most of his route which stopped opposite Coldfield Comp. His usual passengers chose to stay at the bus stops and wait an extra twenty minutes for the number twelve. In particular he hated the big thumping girl who looked just like Miss Piggy with jet black hair and a gravity defying quiff. She had once offered to give him a blow job instead of her £1.20 which she wanted to spend on cider at the corner shop.

'Coming through,' boomed Chianne. 'Oi move out of my way you dirty little scrote.' Chianne claimed her back seat as usual and plonked down hard making the tear in the worn red fabric even bigger.

'This is horrible.' Freya could hardly believe her eyes. Coldfield Comp students had taken over the bus, pushing, shoving, hurling bags and shouting abuse.

'You get used to it.' Bea had yet to pass her driving test and make use of the brand new red sports car sitting on her parent's huge gravel driveway. She was an over analyser in all areas of her life and this included driving. Forty three lessons and four tests in and she had resigned herself to the fact that it may take some time. She had questioned whether the examiner had taken an immediate dislike to her, or was it because the day was overcast, or was it her inability to just turn left when asked instead of debating whether it would be better to take the second left instead? She acknowledged that her braking could do with some work; *should she brake yet, no not yet, not close enough yet, is that close enough, no, wait, hang on, BRAKE,* and her timing on the clutch was not great either; *change gear, crunch, oh hang on, clutch down, clutch up, change gear, crunch, BRAKE.* So she took the bus to and from school every day, feeling sorry for the people at the stops who stood up when they saw the number nine approaching and straight back down when they saw its contents. Often passengers who had timed their journey poorly and got on before the pickup opposite Coldfield Comp enjoyed a long refreshing breath of fresh air on their way home, having jumped off at the very first available stop, counting their blessings that they did not have children, or that their son had never brought home anything as abhorrent as that Miss Piggy lookalike, or that they had opted to send their children to John Taylor's down the road instead.

The bus was pulling away and picking up speed, tilting deliberately at corners and braking sharply whenever possible, the hacked off driver giving the shouting, standing, and sometimes moonying kids exactly what they deserved. Chianne had taken up her residence on the middle back seat. She sat opened legged - standing was far too much effort for her - and anyway, anyone who was anyone was close enough to hear her latest crude anecdote or see her latest footage on her state of the art phone, recently nicked from a girl in Year Eight.

'Oi Pissy Pants.' Chianne was hollering at a small, immaculately uniformed Year Eight girl.

The girl froze.

'Oi Pissy, you with the frizzy hair.'

The girl with the frizzy hair looked straight ahead, shaking inside.

'What's in the box?' Chianne had instructed one of her henchmen to grab it.

The girl panicked. *Where was that nice Sixth Former?* The girl turned to see a skinny blonde Chantelle Mann reaching for her case. 'Please don't, it's my new flute.'

'My new flute,' scoffed Chianne in the poshest voice she could manage through her badly bucked teeth. 'My new flute. You rascal give it back, scoff scoff.'

'Please I only got it today.'

The girl's parents had been saving up for lessons and she had been thrilled when called, with a variety of other students, to pick up their instruments on loan from the LEA. She had been delighted with it, excited by the hard black mottled plastic box. Her best friend had picked up a violin and her other best friend had picked up a trombone and all three had walked around the school paths at lunchtime with their new, interestingly shaped, black boxes on display; they felt incredible.

'Please, you don't open it like that.' A tear started to roll down her cheek. 'Please, it has got a clasp.'

'Give it here,' barked Chianne, quickly impatient with a fumbling Chantelle. The case cracked open, three pieces of flute hit the ground, two rolling quickly down towards the front of the bus.

Chianne picked up the remaining piece. 'Only one use for this now,' she wailed, spreading her legs akimbo pretending to work the flute. 'Ooo, look at me, I'm Miss Spicer, I don't like cock.' She jerked the flute and fluttered her mascara clogged eyelashes. 'I let my bitches use a flute on me instead,' she gasped.

'Here, Miss Spicer, let me suck your tits,' screeched Chantelle, adding to the chaos of the show. 'I'll let you suck mine.'

'Piss off Chantelle,' bellowed Chianne, chucking the piece of flute on the filthy floor.

Chantelle was always getting it wrong. Whenever she tried to impress Chianne it failed, even if she was doing exactly the same thing as her. She knew they were mates though; Chianne didn't let just anybody carry her bags or spray her black quiff ... or take the rap for her.

'What the tall history one? She likes tits?' yelled a *Chianne Fan* as they were known to their leader. A heavily dolled up Chianne could be found chanting out, in Lily Allen style, on her YouTube homepage; '*My names Chianne, do you wanna be my fan? Well get off your ass and come and join my gang.'*

'Yeah, lesbo,' bellowed Chianne, with an authority that no one dared question.

'Dirty bitch,' jeered Chantelle.

'She's always staring at my tits,' lied Chianne - one because she was not in any of Miss Spicer's classes and had only seen her on a handful of occasions, and two because Chianne didn't have any tits. 44 double a; bras only available online.

'Yeah mine too,' nodded Chantelle looking for approval.

Bea and Freya had been sitting at the front of the bus and were not aware of the sex show going on at the back due to the deafening noise coming from absolutely everywhere. Freya looked out of the dirty window and Bea opened her weighty English novel, only to shut it again two minutes later. Slowly the bus emptied, the big crowd from the back got off at the Peachells Estate with most heading straight for the greasy chippy; the centre of their concrete domain. Freya started to relax and watched as the roads got gradually wider and quieter and the scenery got much prettier. The driver sighed and rolled his shoulders, the lunatics had got off and the nicest part of his route was coming up. Houses started to separate from one another and step back from the road. Wrought iron gates appeared and hanging baskets became flamboyant and large, with pristine gardens clearly in competition. The bus was moving calmly now as it finally drove down a picturesque road with rows of tall old oak trees standing magnificently on either side.

'This is my stop,' said Bea, flicking her masses of dark shiny hair with a sigh of relief.

They thanked the driver and got off the bus, their hearing still slightly impaired. The wind picked up as they walked quickly down a long wide pebbled footpath, neither wanting to start the incredible conversation they knew was ahead until they were well and truly warm and settled. Freya knew the footpath with its evergreen hedges and wild flowers would be utterly idyllic on a warm summer's day and hoped this would be the first of many visits. They turned a corner and she saw it. It was beautiful. A charming black and white timber thatched cottage extended and improved in its own original style. It was massive. It was quaint. It was just like Bea she thought; mysterious yet charming.

Bea didn't mention the red convertible sitting on the drive with number plate BEA 17. She was already eighteen and would probably be in her late twenties before she could drive it properly. Freya stared at it in disbelief as Bea fumbled in her Prada bag for her house keys.

The huge oak door swung open. 'Darling. Hi.' A handsome, slightly short, balding man, whose mild ethnic origin Freya could not quite place, stood open armed, kitted out with a paint splattered apron, corduroy shorts and fabric mules. He hugged Bea with meaning. 'The first time you bring a friend home and you got on that ghastly bus, you should have called me.'

'It's fine, Dad.'

He looked at Freya, 'I'm always telling Bea that I'll pick her up but she has none of it, she doesn't like the Bentley.' He spoke in a perfectly matter of fact, but friendly, manner.

Bea's tanned cheeks turned noticeably red. 'Dad this is Freya, Freya Dad.'

'Hi.'

'Hi there, call me Cal.' He stepped back and made a rectangle with his index fingers and thumbs, framing Freya's face. 'Natural beauty, real natural beauty, you would be a brilliant portrait, and those sparkling eyes, oh sensational.'

'Okay, yeah Dad thanks, we will be in my room.' Bea rolled her eyes.

'No worries darling,' he winked. 'I'll not disturb. Lovely to have met you Freya.' He meant it.

Freya was clutching her knees on the end of Bea's large soft bed, the embroidered white quilted divan felt heavenly under her bare feet. She looked up at Bea who was sitting shoes off, flawlessly dressed as ever with her legs crossed at the plump white headboard. Freya thought it was a lovely room up in the eaves of the old house. The views of the surrounding fields were beautiful; a derelict barn in the distance, horses galloping to the fence. Freya spotted the gate from the garden into the field; *surely the field wasn't theirs as well?* The room was decorated with pretty, large print wallpaper, similar to something Freya had noticed in the window of *Laura Ashley*, pink and yellow flowers the dominant design. There was a large oak wardrobe, two chests of drawers and a bookcase full to overflowing with more novels stacked neatly on the plush, deep pile, brown carpet.

'Okay where do you want me to start? sighed Bea, fashion glasses safely back in their Gucci case.

Freya felt childish. Being in Bea's presence sometimes felt overwhelming. 'Don't be silly. Look I'm just so glad you have finally let me come back here, your room is so beautiful, you're so lucky.'

'I know; my brothers are at boarding school so it's just me and dad a lot of the time. Mum is forever travelling with her art and yes, I guess I am lucky.' She paused and looked at Freya perched uncomfortably on the edge of her bed. 'Are we okay?'

'Of course, why wouldn't we be?'

'Because I'm gay.'

Freya giggled nervously, 'I know, you announced it in front of an Ofsted inspector in history today! Seriously though, I'm really pleased for you. Does your dad know?' She had spotted the wink in the huge oak hallway.

Bea flicked her hair. 'Does he know? He is the one who opened the closet door and said peepo!'

She laughed, still aware of the slight awkwardness between them. 'What do you mean?'

'Him and Mum, they outed me to myself.'

'Like what?' It was all so intriguing.

'Well when I was about fourteen they would have these chats like... "Do you know that most gay women have a ring finger longer than their index finger?"'

Freya looked at her own hands and made a mental note to *Google* that later.

'So I would look and say, well my ring finger is longer than my index finger, and they would say, "Oh really what do you think that tells us? Does it tell us that you're gay? Or does it tell us that the statistics are incorrect? Or does it tell us something else. Let's analyse"'

Freya scrunched her eyebrows in disbelief, 'That's awful.'

'No not really, it was all done with a bit of fun and they have tried their hardest to be the typical liberal parents.' She reached across to her iPod and it lit up with the smooth sound of *Adele*. 'I think they just saw something in me and wanted me to avoid the turmoil of having to think I had to try things out with guys to prove something to myself or to others, or to avoid the saga of coming out to them or whatever.'

'What else did they say?' asked Freya, finally making herself more comfortable.

'Well they would tell me stories about when I was younger and I would sit with my brothers watching *Blind Date*. We would all tie scarves around our eyes and pretend to be the picker and I would only pick from the women saying that they were nicer than the men. I don't know just stupid things. A typical tomboy I guess.'

How things have changed, thought Freya, looking at Bea and her seductive feminine beauty. 'So what happened?'

'They just had open discussions about sexuality, they love to analyse everything. I think that's where I get it from.' She laughed and shook her head in remembrance. 'I was walking around a shopping centre with my dad, I think I was twelve and we were playing a game where we would squeeze each other's hand when we saw someone we thought was attractive, and obviously he was being stupid and squeezing when he saw someone with a massive cleavage or short skirt, but he said that I squeezed when I saw a beautiful woman. I can't really remember it to be fair, but I guess they were right because I started to develop feelings for a woman at the stables where we keep horses and I didn't have to hide it from them. I had someone to talk to and I really appreciated them for that. I think if they'd not been the way they were, then I would have denied my feelings, or panicked, or started to act like a weirdo. Instead they just told me to accept it as a normal crush. We *analysed it!*' Bea laughed and took reassurance that Freya was now snuggling at her end of the bed.

Freya felt jealous. How nice to know, to know what you want, to be sure of what you want and to have support. 'What happened with her?' She needed the details.

'The lady at the stables?' She knew exactly who Freya meant. 'I used to go every day to muck out the horses and do odd jobs. She was there all of the time. *Rachel, the lead trainer.*' She spoke like a crush. 'It was her dad's business and I don't know, I guess by the time I was sixteen I knew it wasn't actually a little crush. I knew that I loved her, and I thought that she loved me.'

'No way,' said Freya in astonishment.

'Yes, we were together for just under a year. It finished the summer before I started at Coldfield.'

'No way!' She was sitting upright grinning from ear to ear. 'Did your parents know?'

'Yes of course. They discussed it within an inch of its life, how to handle it, whether to approach her with my feelings, what to say, how to deal with her reaction. I guess they responded like any parent would to a daughter who develops a crush on a lad and doesn't know what to do.' She looked away and started to fiddle with the tassels on her white bed throw.

'You are so lucky.' Freya knew she could never approach her parents about anything to do with crushes or feelings; it just wasn't like that with them.

'I guess.'

She looked at Bea. She was beautiful, truly beautiful, inside and out. 'Are you okay to talk about it?'

'Yes. It's fine. I'm okay now. I guess our break up is not any more dramatic than that of any teenage break up. She was *twenty one* though.' She raised her perfectly arched eyebrows.

'No way,' said Freya, continuing to be shocked, conscious of her sudden limited vocabulary. That was a bigger age gap than her and Kat. Harley had badgered Kat into telling the class the date of her birthday; he said he didn't want to miss the party. Kat was such a great teacher, so conscientious, so thoughtful in the way she explained things and so helpful in her comments. You would always find an essay of suggestions and hints in her beautiful looped writing at the end of your own and often her carefully crafted essay was longer than your original piece of work. She was so clever and smart, but also so funny and so chatty; Freya's mind wandered as it so often did these days. The relationship between all teachers, (apart from Miss Louza and Miss Mews), and their Sixth Form classes was much more relaxed than lower down the school. That was one of the incentives to stay at Coldfield instead of going to the local Sixth Form College. You could have the great *'tutor-like'* relationship with your teachers that you got at the college, but here, they had said on Open Evening, here you *would* be chased for essays and you *would* have to turn up every single day, which *would* in turn give you the grades that you deserved. Most didn't buy it and went to the college instead, where they could call their tutors by their first names and be treated like the young adults that they truly were, instead of the silly, spotty Year Eight child that the teacher at school would always remember. Kat was getting it right though, thought Freya - friendly, but not over the top, interested but not gossipy, respectful, and fast earning respect. August 31st, Kat's birthday, a date Freya knew she would not forget. That made just three years and two months between them, it was her 18th next week.

Bea brought her back into the room. 'I had just turned sixteen. I told her how I felt. How I loved our chats, how I loved what she taught me with the horses, how I thought she was attractive and she said she felt the same way about me.' Bea turned her attention back to the white bed tassels. 'Then suddenly at the start of the summer on the day of my last GCSE she said it was over. I was devastated.'

'Have you heard from her since?'

'No, she works at a different place now.'

'What did your mum and dad say about it all?'

'Not much,' said Bea finally untying a knot from a white tassel, 'but when I said I didn't want to tell people at Coldfield about my sexuality they were not particularly overjoyed. They wanted me to be more open and proud and said it was the only way I would ever be properly happy. They believe that being true to yourself is the most important thing in life.'

Freya marvelled at her poise. 'So what changed? Why did you decide to say *women* today? It would have been so easy and so utterly expected for you to have said men.' She had now positioned herself on her front, supporting her chin with her hands, mesmerised by Bea's depth.

'I don't know,' she picked up and hugged a large yellow floral print cushion, 'I guess it was Miss Spicer; her guts. I mean come on, that Ofsted guy was there. He was assessing her. The fact she put that on the line for the truth, her truth, then I don't know. I guess it inspired me to do the same.'

Freya shuffled up the bed and carefully wrapped her arms around Bea. 'You are one amazing person, Beatrice Belshaw, do you know that?'

'Thank you. Your friendship means so much to me.'

Freya gently shook her head, stirring the long brown waves that had been nestling neatly around her shoulders. 'You're so lucky you know?'

Bea pouted. 'Stop saying that. Everyone says that. I know. I get it. I have everything that a girl could possibly want and need, don't I?'

'Well haven't you?'

'No, not the one true thing I wish for.'

'What's that?'

'You,' she whispered, reaching for Freya's soft cheek.

There was a faint tap on the oak door and a very quiet voice, 'Hello? Hello, can I come in?'

'Don't be stupid Dad of course you can come in,' shouted Bea quickly dropping her hand.

Cal looked at his exquisite daughter and the brown haired beauty sitting incredibly close to her, he was thrilled. 'Can I take you girls to dinner?'

****

'Is anything going right for you at that school Kat?' huffed Jess in a manner that took her by surprise. Jess was usually so caring and upbeat and helpful; you could always rely on her for a positive spin on things. This evening, however, she seemed impatient. Something else was clearly on her mind.

'Yes it is thanks Jess. Look, don't worry about it,' she sighed preparing to raise herself from the deep black sofa.

'Oh sorry hun, I've just got stuff on my mind.'

She sank back down. 'Can I help?'

'No let's get you sorted first, come on, what exactly happened?' Jess got herself comfy amongst their numerous large red cushions.

Lucy shouted from the kitchen, 'She outed herself in front of an Ofsted inspector in lover girl's class today.' She was busy making a vegetable stir fry, wine glass in hand, oil spitting onto their bright red backsplash.

'Yes thanks Lucy,' shouted Kat. Lucy had been watching *Deal or No Deal* when she had arrived home. It had only taken the time between two banker's offers for her to listen, summarise and concluded the situation in a rather rude, but light hearted manner. *If only things were as simple for me* she thought, suddenly envious of Lucy's frivolous approach to life and all of its contents. She was happy, realised Kat; Ben had not stopped texting her.

'How did you do?' quizzed Jess, holding a red bobbly cushion tightly against her stomach.

'Well that's just it. Usually they stay behind at the end of the lesson and give you an initial assessment grade, one to four, outstanding through to unsatisfactory and then the full review goes to the Head before the final report is published a couple of weeks later.' Kat knew the system.

'You're buggered then!' shouted Lucy as she tossed in extra mushrooms.

Kat didn't take it personally, she wasn't being mean. 'I know.' She held her head in her hands.

'So did it all kick off?' asked Jess concerned, but also thoroughly intrigued. Kat's life had never been so exciting, at least not since that dreadful saga with her ex a couple of years ago.

'No, no nothing like that. We just had a lesson discussing sexuality. I tried my best to link it into sexuality through the ages, how times have changed from when it was a hangable offence in the Eighteenth Century...'

She was off enthusing again. 'Yeah, yeah we don't need the history lesson thanks Miss Spicer,' shouted Lucy, her culinary masterpiece finally prepared.

'Okay sorry, so anyway we debated and discussed and came to our own conclusions; which unfortunately had absolutely nothing to do with World War One. Oh and then the excruciatingly beautiful Beatrice Belshaw, the one I told you about, *well she came out!*' Kat declared in a falsely matter of fact manner.

'So that's not going to look good then either, Miss Spicer converting the inmates!' Lucy laughed, sucking a bean sprout into her already full mouth.

'I'm buggered aren't I? Excuse the language.'

'What about Freya?'

'What about her?'

'Well is she out? Was she open about frequenting gay bars and snogging gorgeous, intelligent, smart, attractive women?' Jess cuddled Kat, she felt bad for being sharp.

'No, she stayed quite quiet actually. I don't know what her story is and it's not my place to ask.'

'So no extra lessons yet then?!' mumbled Lucy, her mouth full, chomping away ever so quickly. She was sitting on the red leather stool at the tall breakfast bar and her huge leg muscles were visible through her tight blue tracksuit. Kat and Jess had never known anyone who ate so fast.

She felt her cheeks redden. 'It's not like that.'

'But you must find her attractive Kat, that can't have changed.'

She carefully formulated her answer. 'She is clever and thoughtful and quick witted and conscientious, clearly going to get an A and yes, Freya is very, very pretty.' She paused but could not help it, it was so easy to talk about her and she found herself doing it more and more often, especially with Lucy's persistent probes. 'It's like she has some sort of captivating fire in her eyes, sometimes she will look at me and I feel like she is staring into my soul, reading everything I am trying to keep hidden.' She snapped out of it. 'But she is *my student,*' she bellowed towards the kitchen diner.

Jess could see the signs but knew her friend was not yet ready to talk openly so she stayed on the topic. 'What will you do tomorrow?'

She sighed, 'I'll just have to take it as it comes.' Her housemates had once again managed to cheer her up and calm her down. 'What about you anyway Jess? How's things?'

Jess closed her eyes. 'I'm pregnant.'

'Holy shit!' shouted Lucy.

CHAPTER SEVEN

Kat had to put the unfolding events of last night and Jess's dilemma to the back of her mind. She arrived at school early following a very brisk and nippy walk - the weather was starting to turn, and now she was stood at her pigeonhole, note in hand. Things looked like they were about to get a whole lot worse.

Kat, Meeting in my office 9am. Kathy from Cover has your tutor group and first lesson taken care of. Kirsty Spaulding .

A panicked shiver made its way down her spine.

'Ai, ai, Miss Spicer,' Leery Old Lester approached his overflowing pigeonhole which was full of notes and memo's that he had absolutely no intension of ever reading. He pinched her bottom with his whole hand and she span around shocked and slightly in pain.

Kat doubled checked the staffroom, it was empty. 'Get your dirty hands off me and don't you ever, ever do anything like that again.' She was fuming and staring directly into his blood shot eyes. There was a definite whiff of booze on his stale breath. Dave Lester was about fifty five, fat and very hairy; hairs in his ears, hairs hanging from his nose, hairs joining his eyebrows and hairs high up on his cheek bones. Kat looked at his bulbous nose with its black pores that were deep and round, and studied the red veins that seemed to join together to form large shiny patches over most of his face. His eyes were pale and small and she glared into them fiercely.

He turned around and walked towards his sunken seat, wearing the same off white shirt he sported yesterday and most of last week, the loose collar around his neck was looking decidedly grim. 'Dirty lesbian,' he mumbled.

'Excuse me?!'

He didn't reply.

Kat was very good at staying calm, but she could not be doing with this. She had always been the same, level headed and composed;

always doing the sensible thing, always putting her head first. *Breathe, breathe,* he means nothing to you Kat, let it drop. She won herself over.

Slowly the staffroom started to fill, with most people sitting and checking lesson plans, the nervous buzz still in the air, final day of Ofsted. Ben sat down next to her; he looked good. His naturally messy fair hair had been brushed and was fairly level and his face was clean shaven. He had a new black shirt that was completely tucked in for once. Nearly all of the staff had made an effort, an effort which was highly visible in some cases due to the usually low standards. Diane Pity, for example, actually looked really nice in her navy blue trouser suit and appropriately buttoned light yellow shirt; even if it was its second outing in two days. Fiona Mews, however, still had her garish orange and yellow neck scarf tied tightly around her throat and her jet black hair was scraped up into an Essex facelift.

Ben turned to Kat, 'Lucy told me what happened in your Ofsted lesson, don't worry about it mate, everything will be fine.'

She handed him the note and he groaned. 'Oh babe, keep smiling. You're a great teacher and that's all that matters.' He squeezed her knee and this time the male contact felt good.

'Thanks, and I'm really pleased about you and Lucy, she is such a lovely girl; slightly crazy, but lovely.'

'I know.' He meant it. The sex had been wild and he was hooked, hooked on her weird and wonderful sense of humour and her simple no nonsense approach to everything; not to mention the muscles, in particular the bulging ones in her thighs.

There was no sign of the inspectors, probably already on their way to their first lesson of choice. A seedy voice boomed over two rows of chairs. 'You know what you need Spicer?' Leery Old Lester tried to joke loudly, 'A real man to show you what you've been missing, ha ha ha!'

'Shut up Dave,' barked Ben.

Staff muttered and mumbled under their breath; *about him or me?* thought Kat, deeply embarrassed. She nervously made her way down the long pale blue corridor past the IT and English rooms. She walked slowly, appreciating the relative calm and quiet. Tutor time, her little Year Seven's were sitting two blocks away, troubled that their favourite Miss Spicer had been replaced by the bearded supply man so soon after all of those horrible rumours. She finally pushed open the heavy metal doors from B Block and was met with a gust of cold wind that had been gaining speed and losing temperature over the littered tennis courts.

David Haverley from Year Seven scurried towards her over the concrete, his register held tightly under his arm. 'Hello Miss, you look nice today.' He smiled kindly and rushed off, determined to be the best register monitor that Mr Puller had ever seen.

Here goes, thought Kat as she entered the very warm, very grand, A Block, home to the *Main Entrance* - used only by visitors and staff, *Main Hall* - with its expansive stage and seating structure, used only on very special occasions, and *Heads Office* - used when firing a member of staff she thought.

Kat was sitting outside Mrs Spalding's office listening to the soothing noise of the mini waterfall that ran the length of the plush waiting area. Very rarely did pupils enter A Block with its flowers, new carpets, soft background music and airy atmosphere, a million miles away from the clamour of the cramped paint chipped blue corridors of B Block. She felt like she was sitting in a private medical centre watching the multi coloured fish moving peacefully with their serene composure in the purpose built two metre long aquarium tank. There was not a hint of a child anywhere to be seen, or heard. Register monitors were allowed to enter to collect and return their registers but apart from that you only got the privilege of entering A Block on *Awards Evening*, or *Speeches Day*, something that the more common of pupil didn't seem to attend anyway; some didn't even know that A Block existed. It was no longer a case of being sent to the Head's Office when naughty; Kirsty had a Deputy Head in B Block for that.

The square light on the office door turned green. Kat was allowed to enter. She felt about twelve.

'Sit down Katherine.'

Kat sat on the very expensive high backed white leather chair which squeaked as she adjusted her skirt. She felt incredibly uneasy.

'Well you have done it Miss Spicer.' Kirsty Spaulding was serious and monotone.

'Look I had no other choice-' She had prepared her speech in the waiting area whilst watching a slow John Dory swim through a front door and out of a chimney.

'I'm joking with you,' roared Kirsty, beaming from ear to ear. 'Oh Kat, what a find, what a find! I knew you'd be sensational when I hired you. That is one of my talents; I can spot a cracker when I see one!' She was raving. 'Sorry about making you wait, that was just my little bit of fun. I could see you the whole time on the camera!' She tapped the screen sitting on top of her expensive walnut desk and giggled.

The Kirsty Spaulding behind closed doors was not at all like the Kirsty Spaulding wheeled out on special occasions such as Ofsted assemblies. Most of the pupils could hardly recognise her. She was rarely seen in the corridors of B Block, especially at rush hour and she had herself almost forgotten which subject she was actually qualified to teach; it had been ages since she was properly inside a classroom. She had a sixty strong teaching team who dealt with the learning side of things; she dealt with the targets. She was a manager and proud of it. The school was performing as it should, according to the recent *Fischer Family Trust Value Added Score*; what mattered more though she realised, was its Ofsted report.

'Can I get you a coffee? Or a tea? Or something stronger?' She signalled to the fully stocked spirit cabinet complete with cut glass crystal tumblers. It was nine am.

'A coffee please?' said Kat raising her eyebrows not sure what on earth was going on.

The Head got up and walked to the expensive coffee machine in the far corner of her lavish office. She was wearing a smart blue V necked jumper, navy blue woollen pencil skirt, tan coloured tights and lamb's wool slippers.

'Excuse the slippers, but they are just so comfy.'

Kat watched her smile as she carefully made the coffee. She felt like she was looking at her for the first time. Mid fifties, slightly plump with rosy soft cheeks, mousey brown hair pulled into a wispy bun and glasses permanently lost on the top of her head. She wasn't ordinary and plain as she had initially thought - her only real assessment having been from her staffroom chair during their morning briefings. The serious lady who spoke at the front when addressing her workforce was a million miles away from the lady that now stood in soft slippers waiting on her at the coffee machine. This lady had bright eyes that seemed to shine with a definite hint of mischief.

Kirsty handed her the coffee and sat on the desk. 'Where do I start?' she laughed, lifting her arms and closing her eyes. 'Well first of all welcome to Coldfield Comp, I don't think we have officially met.' She slid off the desk, walked back over to Kat and held out an eager hand.

Kat didn't quite know what to do, she was finding it all very bizarre and fumbled with her coffee cup, eventually placing it on the floor, making sure it was steady so it wouldn't fall and ruin a clearly expensive carpet. She managed to hold out her hand and offer a nervous 'Hello,' unsure of whether to stand or curtsy or what to do.

'Clearly I wasn't on your actual interview,' said Kirsty making her way back to her perch. 'But I inspected those CV's with a fine tooth comb and wink, wink, nudge, nudge,' she tapped the top of her monitor, 'I knew you would be incredible. I like James to do the face to face interviewing, he has so much more to do with the staff, it makes sense, but never doubt that I am the all seeing eye, I have the final say on everything that goes on in this school.' James Dapper was the second Deputy Head and Kirsty Spaulding was getting even more excitable with her tapping hand gestures.

'Okay,' was all she could manage, unsure of how to behave.

'Look I'll cut to the chase. Mr Bridges the lead inspector came to see me at the end of school yesterday to give me a day one round up. I believe he came to watch you *Miss Spicer.*' She spoke with one eyebrow raised.

'Yes my Year Thirteen yesterday afternoon.'

Kirsty jumped off the desk. 'You got an *Outstanding*! He has already given our school an *Outstanding* in ECM all because of your one lesson!' She was gushing. ECM was the Every Child Matters policy, another one that rang a faint bell with Diane Pity, but not enough for her to actually remember what it was all about. 'He thinks you would be a perfect candidate to head up the new PSHE team.' Personal, Social and Health Education; nope, Diane Pity would not be able to place it.

'Oh right,' was all Kat could manage.

Kirsty pushed a wisp of mousy brown hair back behind her ear and rushed forwards to grab her wrists. 'I mean, come on, he said you were sensational! He read your lesson plan so he knew what you were going to do, and he had looked at their work so he knew how they were performing, so he took the lesson as it came and he was blown away. His exact words were...' she released her grip and searched for her glasses, locating a second pair in the walnut drawer. She paused and transformed into the person Kat recognised, suddenly speaking loudly and seriously, '"*The lesson was outstanding in all areas. The teacher was able to adapt, to show initiative, illustrating a correct and measured response to the class' demands. The atmosphere generated was one of learning, of understanding and of respect.'"* She lifted her glasses and her pitch raised two octaves. 'I am thrilled Kat, because then further on it says-' the serious voice returned, *"'Coldfield Comprehensive School caters for the needs of all of its pupils on a personal and emotional level and is successfully meeting the Every Child Matters Criteria."* We have done it! You have done it! Not even John Taylor's managed to figure out the ECM policy!' Kirsty Spaulding was fit to burst.

Kat felt like she had been buffeted by a storm, now completely unsure of her whereabouts. 'Okay great, thank you.'

'Is that all you can manage? You should be thrilled! ECM policy! ECM policy! We did it! What a coup!' Kirsty did not seem to be enthusing her protégé so she calmed down and returned to her seat behind the lavish walnut desk. 'Look if you're worried about your lesbianism then don't be.'

Kat tried not to laugh but failed.

'Look I'm being serious. Ancient Maureen Taylor from cooking is a devilish old lesbo. Oh sorry I'm not meant to call it that anymore am I? I mean from food technology.'

Kat's smile widened as she finally started to relax, gently reaching for her coffee that stood untouched on the deep wool carpet.

'And pretty boy Jones in PE, he has been here three years and not yet owned up to living onsite with the caretaker. Poor Andy lives for that boy and can't stand it when he sees him pretending to flirt with the Sixth Form girls.' She signalled to the Oriental rug lying in front of her desk. 'Andy does my rugs and likes to chat, you know how they do.'

'Any advice?'

'Oh just do what you're doing love. You don't need tips from me.'

Kat kindly rejected Kirsty's suggestion to loiter around A Block and let the bearded supply guy finish off her lesson. Instead she made her way back up to her classroom brimming with confidence on a mission to reclaim her class. *Miss Spicer is here and she is here to stay* she whispered to herself as she waltzed out of A Block, knowing the chances of a child being around to hear were well below zero.

****

Kat and Ben leisurely walked the short distance to her apartment from school, both heavily relieved after action-packed days.

Ben had received a *Good* during lesson two and his usual rugged look had slowly returned. Now at four pm he had a loose tie and open top button, his black sleeves were pushed up to his bulging biceps and his fitted shirt was hanging out. He ruffled his messy hair and scratched his chin which was already starting to sprout short, stubbly blonde hairs.

'You're barking up the wrong tree there Mr Puller,' shouted a smiling Year Ten lad who zig zagged past on a small black BMX bike.

Kat recognised him as Davey Jakes, a lovable rogue who she taught in bottom set GCSE history. 'In his dreams Davey, in his dreams!' she shouted back.

'Nice one Miss! See you tomorrow!' and with that Davey Jakes sped off, cutting into the road and the oncoming traffic.

'Fair play!' said Ben looking impressed.

'Well that's not really me but I just feel great. I feel like a huge weight has been lifted off my shoulders and I feel confident.' She linked his strong arm. 'Thanks for your support.'

'Me? I haven't done anything.'

'Well I know Lucy will be thrilled to see you.'

His eyes twinkled excitedly. 'I was desperate to come over but you know how it is, this had to come first.'

'I'm glad it was only a two day inspection.'

'Me too, but trust bloody Pity and Mews to get away without being watched.'

'Well I'm not going to waste my time thinking about those two alley cats.'

'Touché Miss Spicer, touché!'

Lucy lay on the sofa with her back to the apartment door and shouted, 'What drama happened today Kat? Did your dress fall off in front of the class?'

'Boo,' whispered Ben in her ear, bending over the black lounge sofa.

Lucy leapt up, wrapping her tight legs around his stomach. He dropped his bag and staggered towards her room checking the route in between loud, hard kisses.

Kat sat down in Lucy's warm spot and heard the bedroom door slam shut, followed by a wail of giggles. At least someone in this flat is trouble free she thought, questioning why she still considered herself troubled. She could not quite put her finger on it.

'Hi Kat,' said Jess returning from the bathroom and slumping into the sofa with a heavy thud.

Kat looked up at her full face which was usually glowing, so full of life; vivacious was how she would normally describe her, but now she saw tears and red eyes, even her bouncy auburn hair looked flat. She was sobbing.

'Oh come here.' Kat enveloped her with soft, warm arms.

The safe cocoon hug felt lovely and Jess inhaled Kat's beautiful smell.

Kat could feel her weeping. 'What can I do?' she spoke quietly and lovingly stroked her curly auburn hair.

Jess reappeared, eyes red and cheeks burning. 'I just don't know what to do.'

The events had unfolded last night with the loud and clear message that Jess did not want this baby. 'Have you told Gary yet?'

'I can't. I know I said I would, but I can't. I don't want a baby.'

'What does Gary want?' Kat asked softly in a way that only she could manage, probing without causing offence.

'I don't know do I, but I know he wants me, I want him, we are so happy. Everything is perfect exactly the way it is right now. I am twenty two for God's sake. I can't handle a baby at twenty two. Can you imagine a baby here?' Jess looked pale and exasperated.

'Well it wouldn't be here would it? I would assume you would move into Gary's?'

'I don't know.' She thought about Gary's flat, it was nice enough but would there really be enough room for a baby amongst all of his computers and sound systems and boys toys? 'What am I even doing thinking about it? There is no need, it's just not happening.' She looked adamant.

'For me Jess will you think about just one thing? I promise I will support whatever decision you make-'

'I've made it.'

'I know, but please just think about telling Gary. You know why.'

'I can't.'

'Just think about it. You love him.'

She buried her head in her hands. 'I can't do this. I need to get it sorted. Will you help me?'

'Oh Jess come here.' Kat bundled her back into her arms.

Jess felt safe and warm but knew what was coming in Kat's ever so soft and delicate manner.

'Not unless he knows Jess.'

CHAPTER EIGHT

'I promise, Bea, I must have had some sort of food poisoning from those oysters your dad made me try.' Freya was whispering, trying to assure her that it honestly was a stomach upset that had kept her off school and not the topic of conversation from the previous evening. Freya really wasn't used to the rich and expensive cuisine that Cal and his refined family took as standard.

'Girls if you could remain in silence please.' Kat spoke firmly.

It was the end of term informal, but important, history test. Both Freya and Bea were finished, checked and content with their work and had fifteen minutes to spare. From their seats at the back of the warm and friendly classroom they could time their whispers perfectly as Kat slowly paced back down the aisle. Big Tom shuffled noisily in his tiny plastic seat and Harley, who was sitting right at the front, let out another exasperated puff, checking the clock and continuing his frantic scribble.

Bea quietly reached for the rough piece of paper folded in the middle of the desk. '*R U OK?*' she wrote.

Freya leaned in and disguised her pen with her left arm. '*Fine Y?*'

'*U no Y.*'

'*It's fine.*' She glanced up to check for movement.

'*Sure?*'

'*Yes don't worry.*' She wondered how many times she would have to reassure Bea.

'*Sorry if I freaked U out.*'

'*U didn't. It's cool*'.

'*Will things change?*' Bea passed the tatty note and let her little finger deliberately brush against Freya's.

'*No.*'

'*At all?*'

'*No.*' She gently put her biro down.

The note came back. *'Oh OK.'*

Freya really did not want to get caught playing pass the schoolgirl note, but had to reply. *'In what way?'* She suddenly realised what Bea had meant.

'Us.'

'Not sure what you mean.'

'I don't expect anything but what do U think?'

'?'

'Don't worry, ignore me.' Bea passed the final note with a definite sharpness.

Freya felt the whoosh of cold air as Kat swooped in for the piece of paper.

Kat shook her head, screwing it up with one hand and walking briskly to the front of the classroom. She threw the note into the large dented metal bin, turned to the class and announced that time was up. Freya tried to catch her serious stare but failed. Kat deliberately avoided eye contact and walked around, quickly collecting in the finished exam papers.

When the bell rang, signalling the end of the lesson, Freya approached the large wooden desk at the front of the classroom and finally managed to connect with Kat's striking blue eyes. Her excuse was poor. 'Sorry, we had both finished. Please don't think we were cheating.'

'I don't. Have a good half term holiday.' Kat spoke kindly and offered a smile.

The scraping noise of metal chair legs being shoved back under worn desks and the shuffle of people moving loudly out of the room and into the heaving pale blue corridor had no effect on Freya, she was in a muted bubble, 'You too,' lost in Kat's eyes.

Harley squealed, 'Ooo she will. She is out tonight. I heard her talking to Mr Puller. Some tall bird called Emma!' He quipped and winked, sashaying out of the door, relieved to finally talk again.

'Enjoy then,' said Freya, starting to blush.

'Thanks.' Kat felt awkward. The green questioning eyes were holding hers for far too long.

****

Kat relaxed on the heated balcony of the exclusive wine bar, *Lightbag,* and admired the wall hung lanterns that were illuminating the glimmering waters of the canal. Emma was late. It was meant to be their first date since their chance encounter at *Gail's* and Kat was not impressed, especially since it was not even her who had pursued the idea of 'get to know you' drinks. She had sent Emma a text message fifteen minutes after their agreed meeting time - '*Just arrived...*' she did not want to sound eager '*...sat outside what can I get you to drink? x*' She had actually been early and was now starting to get restless. '*Two ticks babe*' was all she received back.

Kat loved to people watch, always wondering at the vastness of life, every single person inside the bar had a story, a life full of issues and experiences and dilemmas and dramas just like her own, no one's predicament worth any more or any less than the other persons. She believed if someone came to you with a problem then the problem should be treated with absolute care and significance, no matter how irrelevant it could be deemed. It was their problem; a problem and an issue of upmost importance in their life and their world at that point in time. So when Lucy had asked advice about Ben and his desire to spank her - which went against Lucy's principles - Kat treated the issue with thought and care and Lucy realised she would never be as good a person or friend as Kat was to her. But now after forty five minutes of pondering the possible problems and solutions of the customers of the *Lightbag,* she had had enough.

'Not going anyway were you babe?' Emma leaned down to a shuffling Kat who had been working her way off the trendy but uncomfortable wrought iron picnic bench. She kissed her hard on the mouth.

Kat coughed, nervous by the gesture and slightly overwhelmed by the strong exotic smell of her very dominant perfume. 'No, no, just getting another drink,' she lied. They had nearly reached their conversation record. Kat always found the first date difficult, especially if the initial meeting had been somewhere loud and busy where confidence was easy to find.

'Mines a Becks then please babe.' Emma allowed her to struggle off the bench and quickly shuffled into the warm seat. 'Oh and some crisps or something, I'm starving.' She put her hands behind her head and cracked her shoulders, nodding Kat in the direction of the bar.

Kat could recall that Emma was a physiotherapist at a private health clinic. That she had been tall, with dark hair, attractive and fairly complimentary, but now on her way to the posh bar she questioned her initial hazy experience and positive judgement. The service was quick and friendly, but incredibly expensive and she returned to the balcony assuming the next round was on her date.

'Cheers babe, what a nightmare week.' Emma was whining as she put her hand on Kat's thigh under the table and squeezed her leg.

Kat felt uneasy. Kissing someone you hardly knew in a buzzing club after a number of drinks was a lot simpler than this. 'What happened?' she asked, slowly trying to edge away.

'Well I had Mr Peters with the groin strain, and I'm telling you now, no one wants Mr Peters with the groin strain.'

Emma was not giving much eye contact and Kat found it hard to connect.

'Then yesterday I had the swimming pool with the old ladies from the Friary - the old people's home?' She looked at Kat as if she should know exactly what the Friary was, where it was and what it involved. When Kat didn't reply she raised her eyebrows and tutted. 'And anyway you have to help change them and they are in the pool and it's just a nightmare with their wobbly legs...'

Kat was trying really hard to pay attention, but with her date staring around at whatever took her fancy she was finding it difficult to concentrate. 'Oh right.'

Emma gulped her beer and swallowed a little burp. 'Then we do rehab and the stories, I mean I don't want to know thanks all the same. There's enough heartache to deal with without someone else's sob story. So I just do the muscles and say I have to concentrate and then...'

Kat had used up her variety of interested two syllabled sentences - *'oh right, uh huh, really, I see,'* and was now, many anecdotes later, just sticking with 'right.' Emma was boring her and the buzz of other people's conversations from the nearby tables seemed so much more appealing.

'Give me a kiss babe.' Emma suddenly put her arm around her neck, catching her completely off guard and pulled her in tight for the embrace.

'Um...' Kat didn't have chance to rebuff as large lips pressed forcefully against her own, '...okay...' She kept trying to break it off, '...mmm...' but failed.

Emma wiped her mouth with the back of her hand and let out a small breathy burp. 'That was nice babe. Any chance of another drink?'

Kat looked down at her white wine spritzer, still half full, and recalled Emma's fast gulping between the tiresome self indulgent tales. 'I've got school tomorrow so it can't be a late one for me sorry. But yes of course, the same again?'

'Cheers babe.' Emma squeezed her leg once more under the table, moving her hand a couple of inches higher this time.

Kat stood at the bar shielded by a group of ogling businessmen with smart suits and loose ties. She discreetly sent Lucy the message. *'Give me the phone call in 5.'* Both knew what it meant. She slipped back onto the hard wrought iron bench with her purse nearly empty.

' ...and then I had the whiplash guy and I mean I have been seeing him for months and everyone knows it's insurance...'

Had she paused when I went to fetch the drinks wondered Kat?

Nokia ringtone. Kat wasn't very technical and was perfectly happy with a normal ringtone even after a Katy Perry - *I kissed a girl* - Bluetooth download from Lucy. She turned to Emma, 'Excuse me,' and reached for her phone. 'Hello?...Yes...Okay...No worries.' Kat was an awful liar, the only time when she struggled to keep eye contact.

There was another immediate tutting sound. 'That was not *the phone call* from *the flatmate* was it?' laughed Emma, looking directly at her for the first time.

Kat realised she was actually really attractive with strong, high cheekbones and full lips, dark wedged hair that reached her sharp jaw line and large deep brown eyes that were now looking sultry. Emma smiled and her whole face transformed into the person she recognised from *Gail's*. 'Sorry babe, I've just had a hectic week, let me make it up to you?'

'Um, it wasn't-' She couldn't lie.

Emma nodded, 'It was. Look, I remember you told me that you liked tennis.' She smiled as she noticed the look on Kat's face.

'Yes?'

'See I do listen. Anyway, I used to play for Coldfield Tennis Club and I'd love to book us a court for Saturday.' She continued to charm and looked up with big brown puppy dog eyes. 'Please. Let me make it up to you. I was a bit nervous I guess and I just rattled on.'

Kat wasn't sure whether she believed her, but was always willing to give people the benefit of the doubt; often to the annoyance of Lucy and Jess.

'Okay, what time?' she smiled defeated.

'Ten?'

'Alright then, see you there. I really do have to go you know.' She edged out of the uncomfortable seat. 'School tomorrow. It's the last day and I cannot wait for my first half term break.'

'Oh yeah how's that going?'

Emma was already looking around before Kat got time to answer, 'Okay than-'

'Good good, see you Saturday then babe.'

Kat had already got up and Emma didn't bother.

'See you Saturday.' Kat was not sure if she heard.

CHAPTER NINE

The first day of the October break was glorious, and the warm sun was comforting as Kat sat book in hand on the white paint chipped benches outside the old tennis pavilion. She snapped the hardback closed; half ten, historical novel finished and still no sign of Emma.

'Hi.' The voice was gentle.

Kat turned around and saw Freya stood nervously in a black fitted tracksuit with her long chestnut brown hair tied up into a high pony. She looked fresh faced and rosy cheeked.

'Hello.' Kat smiled and stood up unsure of how to greet her. She tried again. 'Hi, how are you? What are you doing here?' She looked at Freya's red tennis bag and white shock absorbing tennis shoes and felt stupid.

Freya didn't try to be funny, 'It's my birthday and my mum and dad have barred me from the house for a couple of hours. They are clearly planning some sort of embarrassing surprise and so I just thought I'd come and have a bit of a knock about.' She put down the heavy red bag and stood awkwardly, suddenly unsure of what to do with her hands. 'We are going out tonight so I thought a bit of exercise wouldn't go a miss.'

Kat didn't know whether it was Freya's rambling or slight embarrassment that made her so endearing, but she felt her heart glow and did the natural thing. 'Your eighteenth? Wow congratulations.' She hugged her and for a split second they both closed their eyes, involuntarily marvelling at the way their bodies seemed to fit perfectly together.

Freya's confidence grew as the smell of Kat's perfume and the feel of her beautiful hair now touching her face transported her back to their first kiss. Her birthday was already complete. She pulled back slightly with her hands still resting lightly on Kat's waist. 'Thank you. Look, I just wanted to tell-'

The crunching noise of a weighty bag being hurled into the sandy gravel made them both jump.

'Hi babe, come here sexy,' Emma growled, as she grabbed Kat and span her around into her arms and onto her mouth.

'Um...okay...mmm...Emma, stop it!' She wiped her mouth aghast at the rough contact, literally shaking herself free to create some distance from her. She looked up apologetically. 'Freya this is Emma, Emma, Freya.'

Emma glanced across momentarily. 'Hi, look nice to meet you, but my babe and I have got some serious sexual tension to burn off. Come on gorgeous get over here.' She grabbed Kat's wrist and was about to insist upon another slap dash kiss when the *Hot Chocolate* Ringtone stole her attention. 'Wait a minute.' She reached for the Blackberry in her oversized tracksuit bottoms. 'Yeah ... what ... yeah ... piss off ... okay ... right ... fine ... no ... fine ... bye.' She shoved the phone back in her pocket and huffed. 'Bitch!' She turned to Kat. 'Look that wasn't *the call from the flatmate,* but I have to go. Mr Wright with the knee, remember I told you?'

Kat couldn't.

'Well I'm needed. What can I say? The demands of a good physio! He better bloody tip me this time! Play with your mate or something. Look I'll text. Maybe you can come to mine later babe?' She darted off, throwing her heavy sports bag over her broad shoulder. 'See you sexy'

The sound of the crunching gravel faded and Emma disappeared into the distance. Kat turned back around slowly and shook her head in complete embarrassment. 'I'm so sorry about that.'

'No worries, it's fine. Is that your girlfriend?' Freya couldn't even look at her because she felt so utterly humiliated at the secret thoughts she had been harbouring.

Kat waited and found her green eyes. 'No. That is someone I am going to try my best to never see again.'

She looked away. 'Oh right okay, not that it's any of my business, I just thought -'

Kat gently took her hand and waited for her eyes to return. 'I can assure you she isn't.' She spoke softly not wanting to question her burning need to reassure.

Kat's hand finally let go and Freya scuffed her feet in the dusty gravel as she changed the subject. 'Look I'm so sorry about school.'

'School?'

'The note thing.' Freya had played it over and over in her mind, chastising herself for being so childish. 'Did you read it?'

'No, why would I?' Kat had been tempted and it had taken great restraint to stop herself from sifting through the pencil sharpenings and browning apple cores to leave the scrappy note where it sat discarded at the bottom of her metal classroom bin.

'Sorry, no reason, I'm just being silly. Look, I have a court booked. I was just going to use the ball machine but we could play if you fancy?' Freya looked away again, she could not read the situation - was Kat recognising the looks? Was she feeling the intensely charged atmosphere? 'Or I understand if you just want to get off.'

'I would love a game.' She meant it.

'Fantastic.' Freya's green eyes twinkled, 'I'm good you know.'

She spotted the glint. 'So am I,' she smiled.

Kat had started to sweat. Freya had been serious about her ability and on match point she realised her game was up. The pair pounded the yellow furry ball, both playing to impress the other. Kat noticed Freya's agility, speed and focused determination; the way she placed every shot with power and meaning, each ball with a perfectly thought out final destination - just inside the white line. Freya noticed Kat's body, the way she moved, the way she looked, and the way their arms had brushed together each time they passed at the slightly sagging green net.

Kat played with real emotion and feeling. 'Ah, damn it! Good shot Freya, well played. I believe that is game set and match to you!' She puffed defeated and jogged into the net.

'Well played. Good game I enjoyed that, you are really good.' Freya exaggerated.

'Oh thanks, but not quite up to your standards.' They shook hands.

Freya held Kat's grip, 'Yes you are.' Her leading voice and intense stare gave away her meaning.

The pair walked to the edge of the court and slumped against the green wire enclosure. Kat felt in her bag for the high sugar energy drink but found instead her recently finished historical novel. 'You might like this,' she said, lifting it out and handing it over.

'Is it good?' asked Freya, now patting her chest with her small black sports towel.

Kat had not been able to ignore her magnetising figure. The way Freya's incredible body had moved powerfully across the court, or the way her tennis whites fitted her beautiful body perfectly, or now the way a minute bead of sweat had dripped slowly down her glistening chest. 'Yes, hang on.' She rummaged for a pen and opened the inside cover. *Dear Freya, Happy 18th Kat Spicer x,* 'Happy birthday.' She smiled apologetically, 'I'm so sorry, I didn't realise it was today.'

'How were you supposed to know? But thank you, that's really nice of you.' She smiled and once again held Kat's stare. The atmosphere was electric.

Kat had given Harley a pair of luminous green leg warmers on his 18th, one of many lying around the apartment from a promotion Lucy was involved with. She had thrown them his way at the start of a history lesson and this was no different she reasoned. 'Oh it's fine, it's nothing really, I hope you enjoy it.'

'I will,' said Freya, still controlling the connection.

They stood up slowly and gathered their belongings, heading into the old fashioned changing rooms. It was quiet at the club this weekend as a trip to the NEC's *European Tennis Championships* had taken away most of the regular members. Freya would have gone had it not been her birthday weekend and strict instructions from parents to *keep it free*.

They entered the stuffy changing rooms. 'I have really enjoyed myself, thank you.' Kat spoke with a meaning that made Freya's heart hurt.

'Me too,' she added, aching inside. There was so much she wanted to say and so much she wanted to do but didn't know how. Surely she can feel it too she thought? Surely she can sense it, the chemistry, the atmosphere, each look with its crushing, aching effect on my chest, each touch with its electric resonance across my body?

They sat in the yellow tiled changing rooms, neither knowing what to do. There were no individual cubicles, just a row of pegs above the long wooden bench that was fixed to three of the walls. On the fourth wall there was a row of open showers. Both had their wash bags and change of clothes. Kat had assumed she would have a drink in the clubhouse with Emma, and Freya needed to look good for the surprise at home, which now had absolutely no chance of beating the fabulous events of the morning. Freya had to get washed and changed, she had no choice, but she felt uncomfortable - why was Kat just sitting there in silence, fumbling around with her white laces?

Kat felt uncomfortable, she could not just leave without a shower, that would be unhygienic - but why was Freya just standing there messing with her towel?

'I'm going to have to go in. I think my parents have invited the whole extended family to shout *Happy Birthday* and pounce out at me.'

They both laughed nervously.

'Yes no worries,' said Kat trying to sound relaxed, still messing with her laces that were already untied.

Freya turned to face the chipped yellow tile wall and lifted off her white tight fit t-shirt revealing a *Nike* sports bra and flawless smooth stomach. She breathed in and her heart fluttered; *had she read this wrong?* She would soon find out. Freya turned around.

Kat looked up and felt a rush of desire.

'Are you coming in?' Her green eyes were radiant and the atmosphere was intense, charged with emotion that neither had felt before.

Kat was screaming, her mind and senses in overload. She needed to look away but she couldn't; Freya looked magnificent, so perfect, so beautiful, so sexy. She had to stop it. 'I have to go Freya,' she paused, 'you know why.' She dropped her eyes and tried to sound normal, 'I'll see you next term and you make sure you have a fantastic birthday.'

Freya watched and waited for her to finish messing and stand up. She found the connection once again and paused, 'I will, thank you.' She spoke with confidence, holding Kat's intense blue eyes until she finally turned to leave.

CHAPTER TEN

The October half term break was passing far too quickly for Kat's liking. She decided to ignore the temptation that Freya had caused at the start of the week, filling each day with family and friends, desperately trying to forget the issues causing havoc in her head, hoping maybe they would just go away; maybe she would forget the way Freya's eyes had pulled her close and enticed her to stay. The sun had been shining through the large apartment windows, warming the black leather sofa in the lounge as she lay comfortably, once again slipping into her daydream, only to jump at the sudden buzz of the apartment bell. She pulled herself up and gently padded across the wooden floor to the heavy apartment door, opening it, conscious that her cheeks were flushed. 'Oh hi, Gary, how are you?'

He hadn't been around for over a week and looked tired. Kat had known him for years. He was in his late twenties, but today he looked about forty five with dark sunken eyes and pale fading skin. Gary leaned down and pecked her warm cheek. He was well over six feet tall, slim with a small but attractive face. Unfortunately his mousy brown hair had started to recede badly and his attempted growth of the good bits to form a modern comb over was simply not working.

'Not bad thanks,' he did not sound convincing as he huffed into the cosy apartment. 'Sorry I forgot my key.' He had come straight from work and Kat looked at the name tag still fastened to his bright orange t-shirt - *Gary Peters Customer Service.*

'Jess isn't in, do you want a drink?' she asked, walking towards the sparkling kitchen. Lucy could be slightly messy at times, but all three of them took pride in their apartment and always cleaned up carefully after themselves. 'I was just about to make myself a coffee,' she lied.

'Is it Boxercise or Zumba tonight?' Gary adjusted his fold of hair and looked like he was about to burst into tears.

Kat watched him in the reflection of the chrome cooker hood. *What if he asks me?* She took her time to fill the oversized red kettle. 'Lucy dragged her off to her new Zumba class for an honest opinion.' Trying to lighten the mood she added, '...she thinks it might be too provocative for the older members of her group.'

He stood awkwardly, neither drawn to the inviting black leather sofa whose red bobbly cushions still held the imprint of Kat's outstretched body, or the tall red leather breakfast stools. 'Oh,' he managed.

Kat turned round and clapped her hands. 'Tea of coffee?' This felt incredibly strange. Gary was behaving like a complete newcomer to the apartment that he pretty much lived in. Each member of the gang had their own special place to sit when snuggling in for the weekly DVD night. Lucy and Kat shared the black leather sofa, Kat always on the left, Lucy on the right. Jess tended to lounge gracefully on the matching single sofa seat, stretching her short legs onto the pouffe, leaving Gary with the red bean bag and wooden floor.

'Do you know?' He finally spoke and made his way down onto one of the red leather breakfast stools that Jess had to hoik herself up into; their height difference was incredible, but they looked great together, they always had done.

She turned the kettle off and gave up on the drinks. 'Know what?' She sat down beside him and swivelled round so that their knees were nearly touching.

Gary studied her. Everybody knew that she couldn't lie, that her eyes gave away the true story. 'What's going on with Jess?' He watched them flicker. 'She's been a different person these last few weeks and I'm just so worried that she's going to finish things.'

Jess and Gary had been childhood sweethearts and Kat could not recall a single serious row - yes Jess could be moody like all girlfriends - but Gary seemed to compensate and compliment with his relaxed and loving, laid back persona. She slid off the stool and stood next to him. 'Oh come here.' Wrapping her arms around him she felt a warm tear seep through her shirt sleeve. Gary was such a nice guy and so in touch with his emotions - maybe too much - always the first to cry at their often romantic films. She didn't know what to say.

He sniffed back a tear and messed with his thinning mousy hair, not quite knowing where to start. 'It's just that I love her so much and I could not bear to think of my life without her. We've been together five years now and I love her. I love her so much.' His comb-over flap was now truly ruffled.

She was unsure of her words. 'Do you think something's going on?' She paused. 'I mean is there something going on between you two?'

Gary pulled a thin brown hair between his fingers, one that had no doubt recently given up the ghost and fallen from his bowing head. 'I have no idea. I just know she's not talking to me, she doesn't want to be around me. She's touchy and snappy and I can't do anything right.' He looked up and pleaded, 'Tell me the truth Kat.'

She looked away.

'Is there someone else?'

She turned and stared directly at him. 'No, I can promise you that. She loves you.' Kat was a firm believer that proper communication solved all issues. 'Just talk to her.' She realised how hypocritical she sounded given that neither her or Freya were daring to mention the enormous elephant present in every single room they ever found themselves in. Their meeting in *Gail's* and subsequent skin tingling kiss had literally never been mentioned.

'So there is something then?' Gary pulled away sharply, quickly straightening on his stool.

'I'm not saying that. I just know that talking, and talking properly, always solves everything. Not that I'm an expert on relationships!' She tried once again to lighten the mood. It failed.

He took a deep breath defeated. He'd heard enough and smiled weakly, 'I'll have that coffee if it's still on offer?'

She knew exactly how he liked it, milky with three sugars. 'I'm doing it now.' She switched the warm kettle back on, relieved that he did not want to probe her further. 'What have you got planned for the weekend?' Jess would usually have him over every evening of a half term that was free from early starts, but so far this week this was his only visit.

'Nothing.'

'Well they should be back soon and we could all get a film or something? Ben is with them, poor thing. Lucy brought him some men's leggings and, again it's not something that I'm an expert on, but he need to be careful with his hip thrusts!'

'Lucy said he was a donkey!' He smiled and exhaled, relief brought by Kat's kind gesture. 'A film would be great.'

'Singin', do wah diddy diddy dumm diddy do,' thrust. 'Did you see it that time?!' wailed Lucy as they piled through the apartment door with Ben prancing around, thrusting his incredibly mobile third leg.

'Singin', do wah diddy diddy ... Oh hiya Gary,' muttered Jess, noticing him settled on his red beanbag.

Gary looked up. 'Nice to see you having fun.' He meant it.

'I needed a pick me up.' She walked over to the lounge, bent down and nuzzled into his chest, they looked good together. 'I'm sorry babe, I've been a nightmare. Forgive me?' Her bright red cheeks were still burning from the hardest Zumba workout of her life.

'I don't know what you're talking about. Come here.' They hugged lovingly and he rubbed her moist back. He loved every inch of her, especially her ample, cuddly love handles. 'Kat thought we could all watch a film tonight?'

'Sounds good to us,' shouted Lucy and Ben, half naked on the way to the shower. 'Give us five.'

'Ten if I have my way!' growled Ben, chasing her with his leggings and their pointy contents.

One hour later and they were all sitting in the dark lounge watching *The Notebook*. Kat observed the way Lucy and Jess became entwined in their men, comforted by their arms. She shivered and hugged her own knees, gently wiping the slow tear that was sliding down her cheek. A lovely film, she thought.

****

Bea linked Freya's arm. 'You still have the marks from the glasses.' She touched her nose gently as they walked away from the brightly lit cinema complex towards Coldfield Park.

'So do you,' said Freya, looking at Bea's dark brown eyes, now more of a mystery than ever.

Bea took a deep breath. 'I just want to say sorry for what I told you. I shouldn't have said what I did. I realise that I've put you in a really awkward position.' She had analysed and debated over and over in her head. Maybe she had misjudged Freya and the schoolgirl infatuation she thought she spotted with Miss Spicer. 'I just thought, or maybe hoped that you were the same.'

'What do you mean the same?' asked Freya as they slowly descended Coldfield Park hill towards the dark and poorly lit path back through to Five Oaks. On a warm summers day the park was beautiful.

There was a large lake with pedal boats for hire that gently rocked alongside families of moorhens, overfed ducks and elegantly graceful, yet viciously fierce, swans. The paths and trails, all of different, clearly coloured, magnitude, wandered through areas of birch, bracken and heather, taking the walker through areas of wide open space, followed by pockets of shrubbery filled enclosures. Freya had a favourite private place just off the blue nature trail. A perfect suntrap whose small grassy hollow was protected by heather. She called it her *sand dune* and had spent many an afternoon revising, sunbathing and relaxing, sheltered by its secret nesting.

Bea had noted the tone. 'Nothing, sorry. You know me, I spend so much time thinking about something that I end up convincing myself of something completely different.'

'What do you mean?'

'Well you know I like you,' Bea looked apologetic about it, 'and I don't know, I guess I just tried to look for signs that you might like me too.'

'Did you find any?' asked Freya, genuinely intrigued.

'I don't know. Not really I guess.'

She stood still, their arms were still linked and it forced Bea to do the same. 'You know you are my best friend, don't you? You know I think the world of you. I admire you. I envy you sometimes, and I value you so much. I value us. I just don't know what I'm thinking anymore.' She looked across the moonlit lake.

'I'm so sorry to have confused you.'

'You haven't.' Freya watched a small circle ripple on the water and thought of Kat.

'Look I'm here if you want to talk, or so is my dad!' They both laughed and resumed their slow walk, huddled closely together, protecting themselves from the winter weather that was fast approaching and giving each other some much needed reassurance with their gentle touch.

CHAPTER ELEVEN

Kat was sitting at the breakfast bar in her favourite warm pink and white checked pyjamas, sharing Lucy's thick buttered toast. Last night's heart warming film had been long and she was determined to make this final holiday weekend a relaxing one. 'I'm so pleased that Jess seems to have cheered up,'

'I know. I think it's just the relief.' Lucy spoke with her mouth full.

'What relief?'

'I thought she told you?'

'Told me what?'

Lucy took another huge bite. 'She asked me to help her.'

Kat was getting anxious and placed her toast back down. 'What's happened? Lucy? What have you helped her with?'

She swallowed her mouthful and spoke clearly for the first time that morning. 'She asked for my help. We booked into a clinic. You saw her last night, she was a different person.'

Lucy was right, why hadn't she noticed? 'What about Gary?' She paused and whispered, '... how could you?'

Lucy pushed away her crumb filled plate, suddenly taking in Kat's quiet anger. The sudden silence was broken by the click of her bedroom door and both paused as Ben wandered into the kitchen looking completely dishevelled in a pair of grey pyjama bottoms and pink slip on slippers. 'What's up ladies?'

Kat stared at her plate and said nothing.

Lucy felt sick. 'I think I've done the wrong thing. I have haven't I? I've got it wrong.'

Ben yawned and rustled his bird's nest hair, eager to salvage the left over toast from Kat's plate. He grabbed a piece and started to chew. 'Why? What's happened?'

She took a deep breath. 'I helped Jess.' Inhaling sharply she suddenly realised the enormity of her actions. 'I helped her; she was pregnant.'

'What?' Ben suddenly came to, dropping the toast back onto the plate.

'She asked me to help her sort out where to go. She's my friend. I'm not going to tell her what to do. I don't know what's best for her.'

'Does Gary know?'

Lucy shook her head.

'Well what about what's best for him?' spat Ben.

Kat was so cross that Jess had not come back to her. Why on earth had she gone running to Lucy?

'Gary doesn't know? You helped Jess abort his kid without him knowing?' He was incensed.

Lucy's bottom lip quivered and Kat was taken aback, she had never seen Ben angry, not even with the worst class of bottom set boys.

'I didn't think about that.'

'You never do,' he shouted, turning his naked back on the pair of them. 'You fucking women, you're all the same! It's always all about fucking you!' He shook his head violently in disbelief.

'I just did what she wanted me to.' Lucy was now crying, trying to call him back. 'She didn't want me to come so I didn't. She said it wouldn't take long and that she'd be back later.'

'It's today?' roared Ben, turning back around. 'When? Where?'

Lucy was in pieces.

He shook her arms roughly. 'Lucy! Where?'

'Down at the Trust League Unit in Mormley, at ten.'

Ben looked at the oversized clock and raced to the hall shoving on his old trainers and brown bomber jacket. 'For fuck's sake!' he shouted, as he grabbed his keys and slammed the heavy apartment door.

****

Gary stood motionless in between the laptops and the blank DVD's, it was a quiet morning and the plinky repetitive store music had sent him into a trance.

'Gary, mate!' Ben rushed through the electric doors looking absolutely ridiculous.

Gary didn't even notice his jumbled attire. 'Hiya, what are you in for?' He signalled with two hands to shelf after shelf of discounted electrical equipment.

'You have to come with me. I'll explain in the car.' Ben grabbed his arm, 'NOW!' and marched him out of the store, shouting a vague message about a family emergency that was not quite understood by the underwhelmed supervisor. He pushed him into his blue battered *Golf* that was sitting directly outside the store with its driver's door still open. He jumped back in and sped towards the car park exit, desperately trying to navigate his way out of the retail outlet maze. 'She's having an abortion,' he spluttered, trying to stay calm.

'Lucy?' Gary was hopelessly trying to plug in his seatbelt but the sharp turns and sudden screeches made it difficult.

'No, Jess.'

'What?!' His seatbelt pinged back up to his left ear.

'I'm sorry mate, I just found out. It's at ten. We might get there in time.' Ben was fuming with Lucy. 'I had to get you. These fucking women don't give two shits about anyone but themselves.'

He was dumbstruck. 'My Jess?'

'Yes your Jess, your kid. Come on. Where the fuck is the exit?'

Ben skidded into the *Trust League* car park as Gary jumped out of the car. Twenty past ten, too fucking late, he thought as he flattened his wild hair in the rear view mirror. He breathed a sign of despair, not just for Gary, but for Lucy. His Lucy, who he thought he knew. His Lucy, who he wanted to love. His Lucy, who had let him down.

Gary slowed to a halt as he approached the buildings huge white doors, and watched as Jess pushed through from the other side, out into the sharp biting air, out into the cold dull morning where he stood motionless. 'Jess?'

'Oh Gary!' The white doors slammed shut behind her and she raced into his outstretched arms as tear after tear streamed down her face.

He held her for an age before sinking to his knees. He clung to her waist and placed his ear against her stomach. 'How could you?' He looked up in total despair.

'Gary-'

'Our baby?'

'Gary-'

'I would have loved you both forever, you know I would. You know me Jess. How could you?'

'Gary, I-'

'How could you? How could you?' He was shaking.

Jess wriggled down beside him and held his head in her hands. 'Gary I couldn't.'

His eyes filled with tears. 'You haven't?

She shook her head.

He's here. Our baby's here?'

Jess nodded. 'He or she is here.' She held her stomach. 'I love you Gary. I'm so sorry. Forgive me?'

A cold burst of wind took Gary's breath and he paused, looking deep into her repentant eyes. 'Marry me, please. I love you Jess. Marry me? We can be a family.'

She smiled gently and in that instance Gary knew he could not be without the one thing he never even knew he had. He lifted Jess up and shielded her under his forgiving arm, turning their backs on the building and making their way back towards her car.

CHAPTER TWELVE

Freya was sitting on Jodi's red satin sheets, half term history paper in hand. 'She gave me this back today.'

Jodi swiped it from her grasp and read it out loud, softly, sexily, *'71/75. Grade band A. Freya this is a testament to your hard work, aspiration and intelligence. You should be incredibly proud of yourself. A performance like this in six months will give you the grade you strive for and deserve. Keep up the good work. Proud of you.'* Jodi threw it down on the bed, slammed herself against her red suede headboard and screamed. 'Oh my god, Freya, she wants you!'

'No she doesn't,' said Freya despondently, her attention drawn to Jodi's huge Jessie J poster blue tacked to the wall. 'I just feel so stupid.' So far this term Kat had hardly spoken to her and their encounter at the tennis club made Freya worry that she had spoilt everything. 'I stood in front of her in my sports bra and tennis skirt and asked her to take a shower.'

Jodi had requested exact minute by minute, second by second, details of the birthday encounter and had yet to tire of hearing it repeated.

'It is just so cringe worthy, what on earth was I thinking?' Freya shook her head, still not wanting to acknowledge her own stupidity. 'She just left, walked out and left me standing there feeling so childish.' She reached for a black cushion and buried her face, eventually surfacing for air. 'I was so sure I felt chemistry,' she paused and clutched the cushion against her aching heart, 'no, I know I felt chemistry and I was sure she had too.' She threw the cushion back down. 'I must have been wrong though. What an idiot.'

'What did she do that gave you the impression she felt it?' probed Jodi, loving every moment of the deliciously juicy, but heartbreakingly painful, scenario.

'We just get on so well.' Freya smiled in remembrance. 'We laughed all through the game - I know she was taking it seriously

87

though and I could tell she was really trying to win - but we laughed and we chatted and I don't know, we just had fun.'

Jodi's wiggling eyebrow ring signalled for her to continue.

'It was relaxed, enjoyable, entertaining, exciting and...' she paused trying to find the word, '...natural. There was no awkwardness. It was just a great game, and she was good, she played some good shots.'

'And then?' Jodi was lying on her stomach with her feet dancing in the air, twiddling the front of her new blonde Mohican. She had a good love life, but nothing as explosively dramatic as this.

'That's when she gave me the book.' She produced it for the third time of the evening.

'*Dear Freya, Happy 18th Kat Spicer x'* Jodi moaned with desire.

'Stop it, I really don't find this funny. I can't stop thinking about her, literally, I can't stop. But we've hardly spoken this term and it's crazy, but the less we speak, the more I hang on every little word, look or brief *work related* encounter.'

Jodi did not want the torrid love affair to fizzle out so got her straight back on track. 'So you got a kiss, but not a love, and you got her first name, but also her last name. It could go either way babe!' She glanced at the back cover and after a quick read of the blurb passed it back, something historical and boring did not appeal to her at all. 'Have you read it?'

Freya beamed, 'From cover to cover. I started after my party and didn't stop until I'd finished. I kept thinking what Kat would have been feeling and thinking at different parts, imagining why she had stopped when I saw a folded corner.' She hid once again under the soft black cushion. 'I'm a stalker aren't I? I'm a sad school girl with an infatuation for her teacher.' She peeped over the top of her hiding place. 'I even smelt it.'

'Smelt what?'

'The book. It smells like her. It smells of her gorgeous rich perfume, and I've decided there is definitely jasmine in it as well.'

'What are you now, a *perfumer* as well as a stalker?' Jodi teased, meaning no harm. She could see her cousin was in that familiar place of first time female love and sincerely hoped, for her sake, that it wasn't unrequited. 'Seriously babe how do you feel?'

'I feel like I look at her and get lost in her eyes.'

'Oh Freya, come here babe.' Jodi reached across and hugged her lovelorn cousin.

CHAPTER THIRTEEN

The term had been busy and Kat's conscious decision to keep her head down and avoid Ben had proved easy; but as she looked over at him now, sitting alone in the quiet staffroom, she realised this had been the wrong course of action. In the same respect her deliberate avoidance of eye contact with Freya had also failed to work. She had put it off for too long. Ben hadn't been to the apartment for over a month and looked scruffier than usual with his stylishly messy hair now disheveled and his designer stubble now beard like. Kat walked over to his area and crouched down next to his brown fabric seat. 'Hi how are you? Isn't this term the worst, always so busy in the run up to Christmas?'

Ben looked up and smiled warmly. 'I know, it's been hectic.'

She took the sunken seat next to him, relieved that their only company was Carol the Cleaner who was standing at the sink with a mound of stained coffee cups, not quite knowing where to start.

He smiled again, 'How are you? Not been avoiding me have you?'

She knew he was teasing because he had been doing exactly the same thing as her. She adjusted her position on the itchy brown chair, unable to get comfortable. 'No, Kathy from Cover keeps cornering me. I'm meant to be free next, but instead I have Year Nine hockey!'

'Oh unlucky, it is bloody freezing outside!' Ben offered her a biscuit from the precious business studies biscuit tin but instead of a luxury cream filled chocolate treat pictured on the lid she had a choice of digestive or digestive. It was the same in every department - wonderful tins restocked with bulk bought rich teas or malted milk.

The ice had been broken and now Ben just felt silly. He reached for her warm hand. 'I just didn't want to put you in an awkward position with Lucy and everything. I just think it all happened so fast with me and her. We didn't really know each other that well and-'

Kat squeezed his hand in return and cut in, 'You were great together, and you know that.'

'I know, but I can't forgive her for being so callous.'

'Thoughtless and silly sometimes yes, but callous no. She was trying to do the right thing for her friend and didn't look past that point. She is really upset, she misses you Ben.' Kat finally managed to push a piece of yellow foam, which had been scratching her bare legs, back into the brown woven fabric seat.

He shook his head. 'I just can't be with someone like that.'

Kat hushed her voice as the bearded supply guy entered the staffroom. 'Why is it such a big deal to you? Gary forgave Jess instantly, what's your involvement?'

He paused and ruffled his messy hair. 'Because Gary got to keep his baby, I didn't.'

'Oh Ben-'

'Look I don't want to talk about it. It was a long time ago, it's fine, it's forgotten and I want it to stay that way.'

Kat nodded compassionately.

'How is she anyway?'

She thought she would try, 'Lucy?'

'No Jess.'

'She is pretending to be a reluctant mother, moaning about the timing of her maternity leave, the baby is due just before the summer holidays, and complaining about her figure.'

Ben chuckled.

'Hey don't be rude'

'It's a good job she likes Lycra!'

'Anyway she is secretly excited. I keep catching her looking on the internet at baby clothes and prams and cots and she has every pregnancy book going, marking dates on her calendar and Gary takes a photo of her bump every Sunday night. They can't wait to tell people.'

Ben relaxed in his chair and reached for a slightly chewy digestive. 'How is he?'

'Thrilled. He is taking her away over Christmas and is going to propose properly. They want to have a small Easter wedding.'

'Really?! Oh wow, that's great, good for them.' He loved hearing all of the news, he had really missed the gang.

The bearded supply guy was hovering around the overcrowded notice board, intrigued by the latest list of students in isolation whose crimes ranged from smoking, to boob flashing. Kat turned closer to Ben's ear and placed her hand on his well defined leg. She whispered, 'She wasn't going for an abortion. It was only the first counselling appointment. Lucy was all flustered and didn't really understand the whole process of it.' She squeezed his knee. 'She wishes you would return her calls.'

'Really?' He paused absorbing the first bit of news. 'Well it's still the same principle, Gary should have known from the very beginning.' He sighed, he had been dying to know, 'What has she been up to anyway?'

'What, apart from killing herself at the gym? Just the usual really, classes and brushing up on her reading, she wants to win you back.'

'I guess I've been a bit of a melodramatic idiot.'

'Well do something about it then!' she urged, finally comfortable in her chair.

He needed some reassurance. 'It's past that now. I've left it too late.'

'No you haven't, just come round tonight, surprise her.'

'I miss her.'

'Well come home with me.' Kat was getting excited, Lucy had been utterly miserable for these last few weeks.

'Are you sure? Are you sure that's what she wants?'

'She would love that.' The loud bell rang and Kat jumped up. 'Wish me luck, Chiquita Granger and a hockey stick next! I am not looking forward to it.' Kat headed for the green staffroom door whose latest sign read, *Good teachers are costly, but bad teachers cost more.* Underneath someone had scribbled, 'Yeah Faggy!' so Kat ripped it off and screwed it into a ball. The only provocative thing that each *thought for the week* provoked was ridicule.

'Good luck, hey and Kat ... thanks.'

'No worries, meet you here at four.'

****

Kat pushed open the battered wooden door to the girls changing rooms and was instantly hit with the unmistakable PE changing room smell. She tried not to breathe as she shouted, 'Let's get changed quickly please girls.'

'Urrr Miss get out, you can't come in here.'

Kat edged her way through the mass of girls. 'Excuse me Chiquita but I think I can. Miss Titley is away and I will be taking you for hockey today.' Kat hated the PE changing rooms, always so dark and fusty smelling, stray socks and clumps of turf littering the cold tile floor and twenty five girls clamouring around one tiny mirror trying to correct the damage that an hour in the wind had inflicted on their hair.

Chiquita put two hands on her waist and wobbled her head, 'Well I ain't getting changed. My sister Chianne said you're a lezza and it's against the law for lezzas to come in the girls changing rooms.' Chiquita was thinner than Chianne but apart from that their features were almost identical.

'Shut up Chiquita,' shouted a couple of girls as they put their thick blue rugby tops on over their school shirts.

'No I won't shut up, it's wrong.'

'Just because she's a lezza don't mean she's gunna fancy you Chiquita,' roared a laughing girl who was pulling long blue socks over her school tights.

'Yeah it ain't like you got the bloke teachers falling all over you Chiquita!' The noise started to escalate.

'Miss Spicer is Premier League, Chiquita, and you ain't even made it on the pitch!'

'Whatever,' said Chiquita, giving in and pulling a damp PE kit out of a ripped plastic Tesco bag that had been festering in her locker all term.

Kat spoke loudly, 'Right now that we've all finished, can you make sure your jewellery is off before we go outside.' She knew what was coming.

'I ain't taking my sovereigns off Miss, Gemma Pickers is a thief.'

'No I ain't Chiquita.'

Kat stood and sighed as voice after voice rose up from the benches.

'Miss, I can't take my earrings out, they've only just been pierced and the holes will close up.'

'Yes you are, Picker the nicker. That bangle ain't yours, I put it in the valuables box last week and you nicked it out.'

'Can I put plasters over mine Miss?'

'Miss, if it rains we are coming in right? Cos I straightened my hair this morning and I've got Mr Puller this afternoon and I ain't going in looking like no frizz head.'

'I haven't got my PE shorts Miss and I've only got a thong, I'm not playing hockey like that, can I go in goal?'

'Yeah the helmet suits you.'

'Miss, I've got a music lesson at half past so should I bother to get changed?'

'Oh roll on lunch,' muttered Kat, marching the rabble out to the soggy pitches, no hope of the ball rolling more than a metre.

****

Kat and Ben pulled up their collars and decided to make a dash for it across the potholed school car park. Halfway across and a car pipped. A voice shouted through the lashing rain, 'Can I give you two a lift?'

'Cheers. Come on Kat.' Ben opened the door of the pale blue Clio and jumped in the back. Kat smiled through the open window at Freya whose face was already spotted with rain. She walked quickly round to the passenger side. The connection felt good. Kat had continued to be the best possible teacher that she could, but had consciously avoided looking over at Freya's back table as she worked, and tried her hardest to avoid any personal chats or involvement in her funny anecdotes. But as she stepped into the warm car and smiled once again at Freya, she realised just how much she had missed her knowing green eyes.

'Bloody nightmare this weather. Thanks Freya, just up past Coldfield Park.'

'Okay, no worries Sir.' She pulled out of the school car park and into the standstill traffic, too many Sixth Formers with cars was the complaint from local residents who wished the school had a side entrance.

Ben shook himself off and sprawled across the back seat. 'Did Freya tell you she was the only one in my class to get an A*, can you believe that was nearly two years ago? Uni for you soon hey?' Ben relaxed, searching in his well worn backpack for the remainder of his lunch, his recently depleted appetite had suddenly returned.

Freya was trying her best to look relaxed and confident whilst also remembering *mirror, signal, manoeuvre*. 'Well I've got to get the grades first Mr Puller.'

Kat realised that Freya had never addressed her, not once, as Miss. How does she manage to get my attention in class? she wondered, allowing herself to look across at her for the first time properly in about a month. Kat had deliberately tried to avoid too much eye contact, worried that the feeling would return; the feeling that seemed to take over her, the feeling she was struggling to control.

'So how is *Eager Elton* doing in your class then Miss Spicer?'

'Brilliant Mr Puller, but I think she needs to stop using that *print an essay* website.'

'Kat! You can't say that!' said Freya, hitting the leather steering wheel in mock outrage.

Kat coughed nervously.

'Oh Kat is it?! I didn't know you were one of those *just call me Kat* teachers,' laughed Ben.

'I'm not.' Kat was embarrassed and Freya was blushing profusely.

'I'm sorry, Harley is always talking about you and calling you Kat and it just rubs off. Sorry.'

'I bet she is a massive topic of conversation for that boy,' laughed Ben, oblivious to the tension.

Freyagate, as it was now termed in their apartment, was a topic of restricted conversation. Kat knew that Lucy had been loyal and kept it private, even though she had suggested that Ben could be the look out while she had her wicked way with Freya over her classroom desk.

Freya wanted to make amends. 'She's a great teacher Mr Puller. Everyone is expected to achieve way above Miss Pendleton's predicted grades from last year.'

'Thanks.' Kat smiled at her and Freya glanced up and returned the smile apologetically.

Ben drew a heart on the wet window. 'A love in! Look we are steaming up, what will people think? Hey pip the horn there's Pity and Mews.'

Freya sounded the horn. How was she to know that Mr Puller had been messing around? She only realised when he disappeared from her rear view mirror and she spotted him hiding flat on the back seat giggling. How old was he again she questioned?

'It's a disgrace. Look at that, getting a lift home with a Sixth Former, a female Sixth Former.' Diane Pity shook her head. Her black roots were even more obvious in the heavy rain.

Fiona Mews shook her spotty umbrella and flared her nostrils. 'I am keeping a note Diane. I am keeping a note, don't you worry. Spotless Spicer will hit the floor soon and she won't be running, we will see to that.' She flared again, curling her lip up to the right. 'Head of PSHE, I mean what does she know about ... what is it? Personal, Special? No Social...'

Diane was even more annoyed than Fiona. 'That's the promotion I wanted. PSHE is Professional and Social and Health, no Happiness, no...' she shook the rain from her head, 'oh fucked if I know.'

'Where were you off to anyway?' said Ben in between large mouthfuls of squashed ham sandwich; Lucy and him could eat for England.

'Home to do her essay on the slave trade I hope,' smiled Kat, noticing the way Freya's knuckles looked white as she clutched the steering wheel tightly.

'I was going to Bea's. She only does Friday mornings, lucky thing. We are going into town tonight.'

Ben was naturally nosy. 'Whereabouts are you headed?' It was another thing that made him and Lucy a good match.

She checked her mirrors. '*Gail's* probably.' Her face reddened again.

'Oh yeah, I heard about Bea's revelation. How's all that going with her?' he chuckled.

'All what?' She noticed Kat discretely looking around the car, hoping desperately that she'd miss the two well thumbed gossip magazines sitting in the foot well. Freya knew she should have chosen *History Monthly* instead.

'You know. Her *sexuality*?' He mouthed the word.

'I don't know Mr Puller, why don't you ask her! You are so nosy for a man!'

'Feisty Freya, that's the other thing I used to call you wasn't it. Miss Spicer you need to watch this one, they always say it's the quiet ones, the ones you least expect and then whoosh, she blows!'

She slowed the car cheekily. 'Do you want to walk the rest of the way Sir?'

'Ha, no you're okay thanks. Third Friday of the month, that's your choice of venue isn't it?' said Ben directing his question at Kat.

The thought of bumping into Freya on an evening where she would undoubtedly look incredible and be perfectly able to hold her own in their company, worried her. 'Jess has stopped coming out and I think Lucy may change her plans once she sees you.'

Ben was talking as if Freya wasn't driving the car. 'No, I'm only coming in for a bit. A lot to chat about you know, but I have Jones' stag do tonight.'

Freya paid attention. 'Mr Jones from the PE department?'

Ben shoved in the final piece of bruised banana. 'Yeah, never met his missus though, it's all a bit strange. You two might bump into each other. Make sure Bea doesn't make a pass at Miss Spicer won't you Freya?!'

Kat felt embarrassed. 'I'm not sure we are going Mr Puller.'

'You always go, that much can't have changed in the last month! What are you doing calling me Mr Puller anyway? It's only Freya!' Ben was getting excited about seeing Lucy, he'd been an idiot and realised it.

'That would be nice,' said Freya, catching Kat's nervous eye.

'They'll be there!' said Ben, raising his eyebrows at her in the mirror. 'Just don't challenge them to a dance off, you have no chance!'

Kat directed her into the apartment bays. 'Thanks for the lift.'

'Cheers Freya,' shouted Ben already out of the car and entering the code into the communal lobby.

'See you later?' she whispered hopefully, as Kat slid out of the car.

Kat turned around. 'Maybe.' Her heart was urging her to stay and talk openly. 'Probably.' She smiled softly and left Freya with two hands on the wheel, heart pounding like a drum. It was back, both could sense it.

'Oh look,' said Jess to Gary, both huddled over the small pink laptop screen with their backs against the black leather sofa. 'He's bigger than a strawberry. Oh wow, his fingers and toes have completely separated, and you won't believe this, oh wow, no way, he can swallow and stick out his tongue.' Jess was glowing.

Gary leaned in further, 'Get out?! At eleven weeks?' He tapped the screen, 'That's my boy, testicles starting to produce testosterone!'

Jess giggled. 'I think he, is a she. I think we are having a girl, don't ask me why, I just have that feeling.'

Gary kicked the red bean bag with his outstretched toes. 'Maud and Penelope, I don't think we will be passing on the family names!' He loved every detail on this latest fantastic pregnancy website.

'Hey, I like my mum's name,' squealed Jess, moving the pink laptop from her knees onto the small black ash coffee table. She turned to tickle Gary. 'I love you so much,' she whispered as she quickly found herself wrapped under his warm arm.

'I know.'

'And I promise you, I would not have done anything without you. I just-'

'Jess, stop it, I know. I believed you the first time. It's fine. We are fine, no we are more than fine, we are perfect. Let's get that twelfth week out of the way, get engaged properly the week after-'

'Are you still not going to tell me where we are going?' She looked up with pleading eyes.

Gary tapped her round freckled nose. 'No, it's a secret, and then let's invite the whole family, and I mean the whole family, over for New Year and tell them our news.'

Jess joked, 'Hi guys, surprise! We are getting married in three months and there will be a baby arriving three months after that!' She was actually nervous. Her parents liked Gary, they approved of the relationship, pleased with the way both kept their independence, not rushing to get a house, secretly hoping he would start to move up the promotion ladder at work; but seeing their daughter made happy was all that really mattered to them. 'Things will be fine,' said Jess hopefully.

'Hello,' shouted Kat as the heavy apartment door clunked back into place. She added her beige belted rain mac to the array of coats hanging bulkily next to the door; Lucy's enormous yellow puffer jacket, Jess's black suede parka with slightly manky faux fur hood and Gary's orange work cagoule. Ben kept his brown leather bomber jacket on, standing nervously behind her, unsure of the welcome awaiting him.

'Hi Ben, long time, nice to see you back mate,' said Gary standing to shake his hand.

Ben looked sheepish. 'Hi, listen guys. I'm sorry. I've been a knob.' He edged further towards the lounge.

Jess remained seated on the floor.

'As Lucy once told me, only the wisest and stupidest men never change.'

Jess still didn't smile.

Lucy emerged slowly from her room. 'Ben?'

'Hi Lucy.' He had an audience. 'I'm a knob; I've just said it to everyone.'

'No you're not mate, don't worry about it,' said Gary, loudly patting him on his bomber jacket, trying to reassure.

'Yes I am. Lucy I am so sorry. Can you forgive me?'

Kat felt touched. Ben could be incredibly immature for a man of twenty six, but he was stood now with responsibility and heart.

'Lucy?' She looked incredible and Ben could see the difference a month in the gym had made, already perfect muscles bulging with even more power.

'Come here big boy!' she yelled, running through the lounge and jumping up to clasp her thighs around his stomach.

'I really am sorry, I-'

'Oh forget it sexy, you know what they say, "The weak can never forgive. Forgiveness is the attribute of the strong" Mahatma Ghandi.' She really did want to win him back.

Kat laughed. 'Anyone for a cup of tea?'

'And don't you think I will be ditching you Kat,' she yelled, being piggybacked into her bedroom. 'It's *Gail's* tonight Ben, our lovely Katherine needs cheering up, has she told you about that weirdo Emma?'

Ben didn't answer, he was too busy unzipping her tracksuit top and kicking the white bedroom door closed.

CHAPTER FOURTEEN

It was dark inside the taxi as Bea edged further towards the steamed up window, nauseous from the potent air fresheners that were scattered around the cab; the feeling of Jodi's leg brushing against her own making the situation even worse. Freya was in the front, chatting away over warbling Asian music, seemingly unaffected by the fragrant stench, reciting the boringly obvious - *'Have you been on long? What time will you finish? Where are you going next? I bet you get some right nightmares in here don't you?'* The tired driver was unresponsive, but Freya still chose his company over Bea's. Bea was annoyed.

Freya hadn't encouraged Jodi's plan to take Bea off her hands, but she hadn't rejected it either. She didn't want to think of her in that way, she didn't want her to enter the equation. Her thoughts were still undoubtedly for Kat. Kat was the one she wanted. Kat was the one she dreamed of. Kat was the one she knew she could wait for if only she could get one single definitive sign of encouragement. Freya turned to look at her two friends sitting on the grubby back seat. Jodi was open legged, flicking the clasp on her large eagle shaped belt buckle and Bea was huddled against the cold window.

'So have you been with many women?' purred Jodi, trying to sexily undress Bea with her come to bed eyes.

Bea was not sure what to make of the overly confident, pretty but boyish - clearly out - cousin, who came complete with flashing green eyebrow piercing. 'I've had a girlfriend, why? Have you?'

Jodi winked, 'Let's just say I know my stuff.' The plan was for Bea to fall for her, leaving Freya with her mind on the end game, bringing quickly into fruition the highly fantasised and seemingly inevitable student-teacher affair - that was Jodi's take on it anyway.

'What's your type of woman then my beautiful Beatrice?' She tried to brush a layer of loose velvety dark hair back behind Bea's ear.

Bea flicked Jodi's hand away and hushed her voice. 'I'm not going to spend time debating to myself whether or not you are trying to come on to me, so I will just risk sounding pretentious and put it out there,' she took Jodi's small, slightly sweaty hand in her own, 'you're not my type, I'm really sorry, you seem lovely but not for me sorry.'

Jodi smirked naughtily, 'We will see. I'm a grower.' She started to stroke the kind hand which was quickly removed.

Freya now felt devastated for the pair of them, Jodi was singing *Bea my, Bea my baby*, and Bea was staring out of the steamed up window, hands tucked firmly under her armpits, pretending to be mesmerised by the passing bright lights of the expressway. Freya gave up trying to talk to the driver and turned to face Bea. '*Sorry*' she mouthed to her friend who really did look sensational tonight.

Kat and Lucy sat in one of the *Gail's* infamous brown leather booths in the club's *chill zone*. The area had originally been intended for occasions such as this – two friends wanting a quieter area to have a good relaxing chat in. However more often than not when someone asked you if you wanted to, *'go to the booths,'* chatting was the last thing that you would be doing. Kat felt slightly squeamish as she pictured the visions of lust she seemed to encounter when passing the booths at the end of most evenings. Lucy's clasped hands and authoritative voice suddenly focused her attention.

'My book said that grudges are a non cathartic negative emotion.' She could not help but smile each time she delivered a saying in the way that it was intended.

'Wow you really are trying to brush up.'

She grinned. 'I don't understand it, but I know I feel fantastic.' She waved her hand dismissively. 'Yes Ben was mean to me, but I deserved it and now things are fine again so as far as I'm concerned it is all forgotten.'

'Do you wonder why he reacted so badly?' Kat wasn't going to break a confidence.

'Oh no, just blokes isn't it. They can be as temperamental as women. It won't be mentioned again, onwards and forwards as they say!' Lucy swung her sharp black fringe in time with her marching quotation.

'Oh bless you.'

'What?'

'Nothing. How's work?' Kat reached for her drink and tried hard to avoid another quick scan of the room.

'Great thanks, they've asked me to put on an additional Zumba class because of its popularity, and I'm going into primary schools as part of some fitness for life programme. I can't wait; get some practice in as they say!' She winked.

'For you and Ben?!'

'Don't be daft, for little Jessie! I'm so pleased for them.' She took a large refreshing gulp. 'I guess we will need a new housemate, do you think I should bring it up with Ben?'

'Wow, I hadn't even thought of that, where has my mind been?' Kat paused and delicately tried to guide her in the right direction, 'Um no, probably best to leave it for now, let him find his feet again.'

'He found more than his feet this afternoon if you know what I mean! The size of that boy! Pheweee!'

Both started to giggle. 'Not for me thanks,' said Kat shivering at the thought.

For a moment there was a silence and Lucy studied Kat as she sipped her drink. She had been quite quiet of late and she wondered once again whether her very best friend would ever be able to completely open up. 'Oh Kat how are things? Seen any more of that witch Emma?'

'She is not a witch, but no, I have politely refused a number of invitations.' She laughed at the memory. 'She even offered to give me a full hour long sports body massage, she said I could have it for half price!'

'Ha! The bitch!'

'She's harmless enough.'

'No she isn't Kat. You need someone nice, you deserve someone nice, look at you, you're incredible. What is it that you want?' Lucy was showing genuine concern.

Kat looked across the booth and fixed her mesmerising blue eyes on Lucy's. 'I just want to be loved.'

Freya, Bea and Jodi made their way across the large sparkling dance floor towards the long bar full of neon bottles enticing them to try the latest crazily flavoured shot. Everything about the room was intense, the lights, the beats, the atmosphere, the perfect place to let loose and party. Freya linked arms with Bea and Jodi, 'What will it be ladies?'

Jodi shook her off and re-straightened her blonde quiff. 'Sorry got to go, there's *Little Minx,* be back in a bit.' She strutted off with her right hand pushed into the back pocket of her baggy white jeans and her left hand on her hip. Bea wondered if she had a bad knee, it was quite a limp.

Freya looked at her friend apologetically. 'I'm so sorry about the taxi.'

'Why didn't you sit in the back?' The response was sharp.

'I don't know.' She looked around the busy dance room knowing that Kat would choose the cheese room over this music any day. 'What do you want to drink?'

Bea waited for Freya to focus. 'You don't have to be afraid that I will bite you.'

Freya slowly returned her eyes and lied, 'I'm not.'

'Yes you are, I can tell.' The voice was raised over the repetitive pumping dance beat. 'You won't look me in the eye anymore, our conversations for this past month have revolved around school and work and nonsense about TV and irrelevant rubbish. We used to chat so deeply about everything.'

Freya glanced at Bea whose brown eyes were downcast with hurt. She was right; things weren't the same between them no matter how hard she tried to ignore the situation. 'I'm scared Bea. I'm scared that if I do look...' she focused on the intoxicating dark eyes penetrating her own, '...that I won't be able to stop.'

'Would that be such a bad thing?'

She thought of Kat. 'Probably not.'

'So let's just have a good time, you mean the absolute world to me just as we are.'

Freya watched Bea's lips move as she spoke and thought for the first time of what it would be like to kiss them.

Lucy watched Kat elegantly sipping from her wine glass, she looked incredible this evening. Kat's warm blue eyes were smiling, probably remembering some memory that Lucy wasn't privy to. Kat was such a great listener but struggled to share her inner most thoughts and feelings, assuming they were of no interest or concern to her genuinely interested and concerned best friends. 'How's Freya?' She hadn't asked in a while, her recent attempts had been brushed aside briskly, knocking her confidence as a much desired and valued confidant.

'Oh Lucy don't.'

She was going to do it again. 'Why not? Who am I going to tell?'

Kat put down her glass and nervously tore a strip from the colourful beer mat. 'Ben?'

'You know I'm loyal Katherine! That is my best good point!' She feigned offence.

'I know. I know you are, sorry. It's just there is nothing to say.'

'What about feeling. What do you feel?'

Kat closed her eyes and ran her fingers through her thick blonde hair. She sat back against the warm leather booth and sighed, 'I am trying desperately hard not to let myself feel. I have to listen to my head Lucy, you don't understand the position I'm in.'

'I do,' said Lucy exasperated, reaching for her hands over the table, 'the age gap between me and Ben and the age gap between Jess and Gary is much more than you and Freya.'

'But I'm her teacher and it's not happening. What am I even talking about this for?!' She shook herself free, breathed deeply and sighed, 'There is no me and Freya.'

'Hello Miss Spicer,' smiled Bea, standing motionless at the end of the brown booth.

Shit, how long had she been there, thought Kat?

Jodi waltzed her way back across the sparkling dance floor, pulling up, once again, at her blonde quiff, making sure all and sundry could see her sexy swagger. Freya was standing alone. 'Sorry about that, *Little Minx* needed a shot of *Juicy Jodi!*' She purred and licked her lips.

Freya's eyes searched the dance room. 'Have you seen Bea?' The crowd of boppers sprayed with smoke were making it hard to focus.

'No sorry. You know I don't think it's going to be a go-er between me and her, I hate to admit it, but for once I think she is out of my league. Freya you should be honoured that she fancies you.'

'I am.'

'So what's the problem then?' Jodi spoke louder, not wanting her next epiphany to get lost in the loud music. 'You could always use her to warm up for the big event.'

'Jodi that's awful. It's much deeper than that with Bea. I just don't want to spoil what we have.'

Jodi looked at Freya's green eyes, they were usually so alive with passion and mischief, but now they looked heavy and concerned.

'Look Cous, it pains me to say it, but the ultimate teacher fantasy may just be that, a fantasy. You've got an exquisitely beautiful girl there who fancies the pants off you and I think you should go for it, you would look great together.'

'Oh I don't know, maybe. She does look amazing tonight though doesn't she?'

'Sexy I think is the word.'

'Yes she is isn't she,' said Freya finally giving in and daring to entertain the notion of Bea.

'Look, you stay here and get us another drink, I'll have a look around.' Jodi had been looking for an excuse to prowl for prey as it was.

Lucy watched the colour drain from Kat's perfect face. She puzzled. Surely this womanly woman could not possibly be a pupil at Coldfield?

Kat spoke in her teacher voice that always made Lucy giggle nervously. 'Lucy this is Bea from my A-Level class. Bea, this is my housemate Lucy.'

'Oh *you're* Bea!' Lucy raised her eyebrows.

Kat kicked her under the table and widened her eyes.

'Sorry, I'm not being funny but I know I certainly didn't look like that when I was at school.' She gawped, trying to make light of the situation.

Kat corrected her, 'You left school at sixteen, Bea is eighteen.'

'Oh yes, so I did.'

Bea didn't smile. 'Miss I don't want to spoil your evening but can I have a word?'

She was looking more pouty than usual and Kat was struggling to read her.

'Miss. That sounds so funny,' giggled Lucy, fast becoming nervously delirious.

'If it's about the slave trade then no!' Kat tried to joke, but again, Bea stood stony faced.

'Definite no,' shrieked Lucy, one hand in the air, head tilted, tongue out, pretending to hang from a noose.

'Lucy what are you doing?' asked Kat embarrassed.

'Sorry I just feel all giggly, it must be the spritzers.' She downed half a glass. 'Oh look, empty, I need a refill, anyone else?'

Kat and Bea shook their heads as Lucy legged it from a situation she realised she was only making worse.

'Sorry, she won her boyfriend back today and has gone a bit loopy!' said Kat, watching Lucy totter her way to the bar with her calf muscles bulging; a side effect of the ridiculously high heels she had insisted on wearing. Kat moved her attention from Lucy, who was clumsily bumping into a couple of slow dancers, and looked up at Bea still stood at the edge of the brown booth.

Bea tested the water. 'Look tell me to go away and I will, I don't want to spoil your night.'

Kat tapped the plump brown leather seat. 'Don't be silly, are you okay?'

Bea edged her way in and sat intimidatingly close to Kat. 'I could do with some advice.'

Kat took a nervous sip of her fast depleting drink. 'Of course. I can't promise it will be the right advice, but I'll be honest.'

'I'm in love with Freya.'

Kat's stomach lurched, she felt winded. 'Freya Elton?'

'Yes, the same Freya.'

Kat had to concentrate, what did she mean *the same Freya*? She tried to focus. 'Does she know how you feel?'

Bea was looking at Kat's blue eyes, trying to gauge their reaction, but she couldn't catch them. 'Yes, well sort of.'

Kat tried to ignore the deep pain she felt in her wounded chest and concentrate on the issue at hand. 'Okay and what does she think?'

'I think she is scared, I think she is confused,' Bea pinned Kat's eyes with her own, 'I think she is infatuated with you.'

'Don't be silly,' laughed Kat, nervously trying to sip some more spritzer. It had all gone.

She paused, '...Okay, well I think she is definitely curious but is struggling to come to terms with it and I think you are the only person she would talk to, she idolises you.'

Kat felt incredibly uncomfortable. 'Look, it's not my place to get involved.'

Bea didn't reply.

Once again Kat felt the pull of her duty of care. 'How do you feel?'

'I feel like I have found my soul mate, like we were made for one another. She is just so funny and smart and caring and feisty and beautiful. Freya is beautiful.'

'I know.'

Bea shrugged her shoulders and bit her bottom lip. 'I just don't know what to do. I told her over a month ago that I liked her and things have just been a bit weird with us. Sometimes I think she feels it to.'

Kat's stomach lurched again.

'But other times I don't know what she is thinking. I don't want to spoil what we have got but I also want more, I want her.'

Kat felt decidedly queasy, what could she say? What other option did she have? 'Tell her how you feel. Tell her the things you love about her.'

Bea began to glow. 'I love everything. The way she strokes her earlobe when she is thinking. The way she chews her pen when she is writing. The way she laughs. The way she smiles. The way she is kind. The way she cares. The way she listens. Just everything. She is just incredible. I have never met anyone quite like her before.'

Kat was hurting, she had seen the same things, been drawn to the same things and wanted to cherish the same things privately to herself.

'Spritzers ladies!' sang Lucy.

'Oh thanks, but I better go. Thanks Miss, you have made things a lot clearer for me.'

Lucy guzzled one glass thirstily, waiting for the beauty queen to finally disappear into the pumping bass of the dance room. 'What the bloody hell is going on? Was she talking about your Freya? Is your Freya here?'

'Oh Lucy,' muttered Kat with her head in hands.

Freya watched as Bea walked across the dance floor, she was so incredibly sexy. She had passionate brown eyes that looked smoky with desire and her long layered hair swayed as her hourglass figure passed easily through the maze of dancers. Freya realised she was stunning and felt her eyes drawn to the rise and fall of her chest as she gently approached. She stopped at making a comparison to Kat - Kat was unique and Bea was – well, Bea was holding her waist and pulling her close and pressing her ear against her own. They swayed with the music, everyone else was moving in double time; Freya let herself go. She let Bea's fingers climb her open back, climb her neck and hold her head and she responded when Bea's tongue teased her own, her lips pressing harder and their bodies moving closer; chests pushed passionately together.

Kat stood immobile and watched with pain, a kiss of passion, a kiss of desire; a kiss that could never be hers.

Freya drew Bea close and opened her eyes, watching in sheer agony the torturous vision of Kat turning to walk out of the club.

CHAPTER FIFTEEN

Kat resolved that the kiss she witnessed was a blessing in disguise. Her heart was now back where it belonged and her head was fully resuming of duties. Yes it had hurt at the time, but it had also shocked her back to reality - what on earth had she been doing entertaining such ridiculous thoughts about a student? She viewed it as a narrow escape, a lack of judgement that potentially could have ruined her whole career. She was free, she was safe and Beyonce's *Best Thing I Never Had* was topping the most played list on her iPod. But when Freya had presented her with a Christmas gift on the penultimate week of term her heart revived to life and she ached once again. Kat had received a huge number of Christmas presents, many from her Year Seven tutor group who were yet to realise that the primary school tradition of mum's buying presents for teachers wasn't really replicated at the *big school*. Kat, however, had received gifts from students across all years and couldn't refuse when Freya knocked on her blue classroom door at the start of Friday's lunchtime and presented her with a pretty box, wrapped in deep purple delicate tissue paper, complete with black bow.

Freya had shut the door quietly and walked towards the large wooden teachers desk, smiling as she drew the gift from behind her back.

'Oh Freya you shouldn't have.'

'Are you going to open it?'

'Should I?' Kat leaned back from the desk she loved, the sight of Freya a wonderful reprieve from her monotonous marking.

Freya's green eyes sparkled with anticipation. 'Please'

She carefully pulled off the bow and gently drew open the deep purple tissue paper as she glanced up at the expectant eyes. 'You really shouldn't have.'

'Just open it,' she urged smiling.

Kat peeled back the wrapping to reveal the familiar white and gold box with large jagged purple writing. 'My perfume? Freya, I know how expensive this is!' Kat felt uncomfortable. 'I can't accept this. This is too much.'

'Well I can't start wearing it because then you really will think I'm a stalker!' she laughed, pulling up a chair.

Kat paused questioning her meaning. 'You have never given me the slightest impression that you're a stalker!' She studied the box, then tried to hand it back. 'I just think this is too much.' Freya was not accepting so she put the perfume down and picked up the pink doily. 'Look I got a hand knitted tea cosy from David Haverley's mum, three boxes of *After Eights*, two teddies, and an *I love you Miss* mug from Davey Jakes,' Kat was pointing at the gifts scattered across her desk, testament to her popularity. 'But this, Freya, nothing like this.'

'I was sprayed in Debenhams and I knew instantly that it was yours.' Not quite true. It had taken over two hours of toxic inhalation and every available area of free skin to finally find the scent; Kat's scent in it's beautiful purple bottle. 'It is yours isn't it?' She knew it was.

Kat smiled inside, 'Yes, it's my favourite. This means a lot, thank you.'

'Does it?' she paused, 'mean a lot, I mean?' Freya held Kat's eyes and the gaze was charged with emotional tension.

Kat looked away. 'Yes all of my gifts do. It touches me every time I receive something from a student. I don't like people spending their money on me, but it's the thought and the time the person has used going to the effort to arrange one that means the most. It staggers me really. But actually saying that a lot of the boys aren't quite sure what it is their mum has brought until I open it!'

Freya looked deep into her blue eyes, they were smiling with warmth. 'People really love you Kat.'

'Thank you.' She felt strange being addressed so openly but touched by Freya's sentiment she let it go. The conversation flowed and they chatted for most of lunch about the circus of *Activities Week* that was to take the whole school off timetable in the final four days before the Christmas break. It was meant to be an incentive to combat the horrific behaviour that seemed to occur in most lessons at the end of term. Year groups were taken on different day trips and a variety of activities were put on in school, with staff having little choice of their allocated whereabouts, cursing those ending up with Alton Towers and Drayton Manor, but laughing when they saw Pity and Mews stuck on Year Nine Arts and Crafts day. Kat had a mixed bag, a Sixth Form spa day at *Cross Hall* the highlight, a Year Seven puberty workshop the lowlight.

Freya was chatting enthusiastically, 'So you don't have to pay?'

'No it's great. I've heard it's lovely.' Kat leaned back in her wooden chair, she was not high enough on the teacher ladder to warrant a budget spend on a leather swivel. 'I really need some R and R.' She was enjoying the carefree chat, but debating where to take it. 'How much did it cost you?'

'Thirty pounds for the day spa, but it's worth every penny, I went last year.' Freya closed her eyes and sighed at the memory. 'It is just so luxurious.' She snapped back into the room as a thought occurred to her. 'Who else is going? I hope it's not Miss Pity, she came last year and got a colonic!'

'Freya!' She laughed. 'Well Harley is the only boy to have opted for it over Go-Karting so Mr Puller has been told he needs to come along, and I think Miss Pity and Miss Mews have it on their schedule as well.' A staff list had been clearly displayed in the staffroom with shrieks of injustice against poor Kathy from Cover who always failed to appease everyone. 'I'm really looking forward to it.' She looked up at Freya's beautiful face, marvelling at her natural charisma and confidence.

'Yes me too,' she smiled, absolutely thrilled at the thought of sharing such a girly day with Kat.

'Hey and Freya,' Kat spoke as Freya slowly made her way to the door, 'thanks for the chat, and the gift, how could I forget the gift! Seriously thank you, it means a lot.'

'No worries, I'm glad you like it.'

She paused and dropped her gaze to the wooden desk. 'I'm sorry we missed each other last Friday.'

Freya rushed back and pulled her plastic seat back closer to Kat's, 'We didn't though did we?' She leaned in with an earnest desire to actually have a conversation of meaning.

The blue door flew open and its metal handle crashed noisily against the gray battered filing cabinet, causing them to jump, lean back and look guilty.

'I thought I saw you,' flared Fiona Mews, her long black ponytail still swinging with the force of her entry. 'There are to be no teachers alone in the classroom with a single pupil when the door is closed. Standard procedure Miss Spicer,' she snapped, 'standard procedure!'

'Excuse me Miss Mews, but could you please leave my classroom, I am in the middle of something very important.' Kat spoke calmly and with confidence, who the hell did Fiona think she was?

'Yes it looks like it,' she flared, looking down her long nose, alluding to the expensive bottle of perfume and dainty purple wrapping paper laid out on the desk. 'I think *this* needs to be passed on.' She marched briskly from the room and the noise of her heels echoed down the empty lunchtime corridor.

Freya sat open mouthed. 'Is she for real?'

'It seems like it,' sighed Kat, 'look don't worry about it, ridiculous rules that don't help anybody. Did you realise that PE teachers are not allowed to put plasters on children anymore? The crying girl who has fallen over and grazed her knee on the netball court is not permitted a hug or a hand up and certainly not a plaster on her knee. It's just ridiculous.' She was getting flustered. 'It's not as if any harm is done with the door closed. I mean what on earth does she think might be going on?'

Freya watched Kat messing with her blue biro, tapping the nib, flicking it round, tapping the end, flicking it round, she wasn't looking at her. 'You have nothing to worry about because nothing is going on ... is it?'

'No exactly,' said Kat quickly affirming her position.

'Okay, so no worries then.' Freya spoke quietly, got up slowly and turned to leave.

Kat looked up and watched her beautiful wavy chestnut hair swaying as she walked silently from the room, pausing for a second as if to return and say the unsaid, relief and disappointment conflicting for Kat as the stride continued through the door.

CHAPTER SIXTEEN

Kat inhaled deeply as she walked out of the safety of the private *Cross Hall* changing rooms and through the grand entrance to the main vitality pool. She composed herself and thought of Lucy. Kat had been hit by sheer panic the previous evening when Ben produced, with pride, his new pair of long orange surf shorts.

'This ought to do it!' he had grinned at Lucy, 'Don't want those randy Sixth Form girls seeing Mr Long!'

Lucy had made some ridiculous comment as Kat dashed to her wardrobe. It hadn't even crossed her mind. She was going to pack her bag in the morning, throw in her swimsuit and towel and enjoy a much needed spa day. She would be able to relax completely as she realised - as had the other lucky staff members - that there would be absolutely no need to supervise the twenty sensible young adults; gold star for Kathy from Cover.

Kat had walked barefoot across the polished lounge floor. 'Honest opinion.'

'Bloody hell Spicer! Where have you been hiding that?!'

'What?' Kat had started to shiver.

'The body Spicer, the body! Check it out!'

Lucy had bashed Ben across the chest. 'Don't touch what you can't afford matey!'

'I'm not touching her?!'

'You know what I mean.' She eyed Kat who stood in her gorgeous black bikini, its last outing being their fantastic girls' holiday to Crete. 'Kat you look fab! What's the problem?'

Kat continued to explain that she had simply assumed she had a swimsuit, but when it came to actually thinking about locating it, she realised she had not been the owner of a swimsuit for over five years.

So now as Kat passed under the large cream pillars and entered the luxurious spa room, complete with its heated stone loungers, salt water vitality pool and soothing mood music, she stood tall and thought of the alternatives - Jess's off black, slightly bobbly swimsuit, which was ridiculously baggy around the middle but chaffing in length, or Lucy's all in one swim outfit that covered ankle to wrist, with swimming cap optional. Ben and Lucy had both agreed it was Kat's perfectly reasonable, but slightly revealing, black beach bikini that won the hilarious, somewhat embarrassing, fashion show.

'F-wit, F-woo!' Harley sat up from his lounger, lifted his sunglasses and winked at her; the room was indoors and enclosed. 'Looking good Miss!'

She had deliberately taken her time changing, hoping the Sixth Formers would have scattered to the saunas, steam rooms, jacuzzis or treatment rooms, but most were lying around the pool on curved stone sun loungers with their iPod's beating, trying to catch an impossible tan.

She felt the force of Ben's body racing towards her, lifting her from the bottom and charging her into the vitality pool. They splashed into the warm water, shrieking with childish giggles, much to the annoyance of Diane Pity and Fiona Mews who were on the receiving end of their explosive splash.

Ben wiped his face and bobbed in the soothing water. 'Thought I'd give you a helping hand, you looked a bit lost!'

'Well it saved me having to decide whether to take the steps or attempt a dive!' She smiled and flicked her wet hair. 'My plan is to stay in the pool, have my massage at half eleven and then just sit in the jacuzzi all afternoon with my book.'

Ben watched as she eyed the Sixth Formers nervously. 'You have nothing to worry about. No one is looking at you.'

He was right. Looking around she could see girls lying on the gloriously comfortable stone loungers chatting quietly, others making their way into the steam rooms and Harley declaring he was off for his mud wrap.

'What are you so worried about?'

She looked down at her cleavage. 'I'm just so self conscious, it's hardly appropriate a teacher in a bikini.'

'Oh don't be daft! Look at Diane!'

They bounced gently to the edge of the water and peeped over the side of the pool. 'Exactly, she looks great!' Diane was sitting on a cushioned wicker chair wearing a very plain black swimming costume.

'Watch this.' Ben bobbed up and gave a shout, 'Miss Pity, I think I just heard them call you for your first treatment.'

Diane scowled and leaned forward to check the huge silent clock partially hidden by fake green hanging vines. 'It's not till ten,' she huffed, returning to her trashy gossip magazine.

Ben bobbed up again. 'Yes definitely, they called you.'

'Oh for goodness sake,' spat Diane, standing up and marching out of the room, revealing two large wobbling buttock cheeks, separated by a tiny unfortunate piece of black string.

'Bloody hell!' said Kat in disbelief.

'I thought you didn't swear!'

'I don't!' laughed Kat, slowly sinking back under the gloriously calming water.

Diane hadn't minded the false alarm, clearly Ben's way of having another look at her perfect behind, and now with wonder girl being a dirty lesbo she knew it would only be a matter of time for *Perfect Puller* to make his move; a few more struts up and down the pool and he would be begging for it. 'Must be your mistake,' she purred as she edged her way down the steps and into the pool, buttock first. Ben had nowhere to look.

Diane glanced at Kat, devastated that she looked so sensational. 'Miss Spicer.'

Kat smiled warmly as she bobbed gently up and down. 'Hi Diane, how are you?'

She pointed at Freya sitting in the bubbling jacuzzi and sneered, 'Your special friend is all on her own over there. Why don't you go and join her?'

Ben grabbed Kat's hand under the water. 'Yeah, come on I fancy those massage jets!' He bounced quickly down the pool, getting as far away from the costume devouring buttock cheeks as he could.

Freya smiled when they entered the jacuzzi, not just because Kat looked incredible - although that was the main reason - or because Mr Puller was being mischievous about Miss Pity's choice of swimwear, but because she felt lonely; she had not spoken to Bea for over a week. She had been debating the situation as the giggling pair entered the bubbly circle and her thoughts immediately shifted paths. The three of them talked about all sorts of things as if they were old friends and laughed loudly at the experience brought by each new bubble cycle and altered degree of jet pressure. Mr Puller was being incredibly rude, much to their amusement, and Kat was being Kat - funny, warm and interested. This gave her the confidence to assume she understood; she understood that Bea had initiated it.

Ben closed his eyes and rested his head against the smooth marble rim of the jacuzzi, exhausted from the giggles. Kat was clearly embarrassed by his suggestive comments and had turned the setting down to *gentle flow,* which he had to admit was actually very relaxing indeed. He was completely immersed in the healing properties of the soft mineral massage jets and spoke quietly, 'So did you girls get to meet up last weekend?'

Kat had been pulling the soft, sweet smelling, bubbles through her fingers as he spoke and his words made her freeze and look up. She glanced at Freya. 'No...' Ben looked like he was almost asleep. She returned her gaze to the bubbles and spoke quietly, '...unfortunately we didn't.'

Freya read the message in her eyes; maybe Kat was finally ready. She felt the strong beat of anticipation in her heart and moved her hand along the smooth curved seat under the water. Her little finger found Kat's.

Kat didn't move.

Freya felt her heart racing as she climbed Kat's hand further, gently running her fingers up towards her wrist.

Kat thought she had been mistaken at first, but this deliberate tender touch was no mistake. Every second seemed like a lifetime and she allowed herself to enjoy the butterflies that were coursing through her body, firing sparkling impulses to every sensor in her skin. She allowed herself to get lost in the moment; allowed herself, for those split seconds, to indulge in Freya's touch. Then it hit her with a crushing realisation. 'Sorry you two, it's getting too warm in here for me,' she paused and looked at the clock, '...it's nearly time for my massage anyway.' She stood up to leave.

Ben opened his eyes, aware that he had possibly nodded off, 'Is it a naked one?'

She flicked some warm bubbly water at his chest as she passed, hoping he would feel responsible for her embarrassed red cheeks.

Kat lay on the massage table and let the strong, smooth hands soothe away her worries. Her muscles were relaxing, her tensions were easing and she felt the soft music calling her into a state of deep relaxation that she had not felt in months. She had to acknowledge it; it was the only thing affecting her fantastic time at Coldfield and it needed to be addressed. She re-lived the energised touch. The breakthrough she thought she had achieved at *Gail's* watching Bea kissing Freya had been short lived and it was getting harder to suppress her growing feelings and more difficult to restrain her natural desires; especially on days like today where Freya was simply magnetising. She had been funny and mature, smart and sexy and Kat had once again questioned the boundary. She let her mind wander as the essential oils penetrated her muscles and delivered a feeling of pure calmed bliss.

She had walked from the massage treatment room and past the salt water pool with a new found air of lightness, a far cry from the tense, uptight walk of the morning. She headed into the empty steam room and exhaled; it had been an incredible massage. She sat quietly and the wet heat caused a bead of perspiration to slide slowly down her chest. She closed her eyes and inhaled the hot air. She heard the heavy door click closed; Freya walked in silently and sat down next to her. Her white tie bikini was displaying, once again, the perfect stomach and smooth skin that she remembered and her heart pounded as she felt Freya's hand upon her own, climbing her wrist and her arm; all resolve was gone. She moaned as Freya ran her smooth fingers up her neck and deep into her hair, making her body tilt back and arch with desire. There was an intense burning desire in her green eyes and she kissed Kat passionately, with fire, with a yearning that had been building and building in both of them until this moment; this moment of pure passion where their lips met and their tongues devoured.

Kat couldn't stop.

Freya smoothly straddled her lap with her knees on the bench, legs either side of her pounding stomach. She gently pushed Kat's damp hair back behind her ears and kissed her neck, tenderly, longingly, with her purposeful lips finally reaching Kat's black bikini strap. Freya slid it delicately off her shoulder exposing her wanting breast. She found Kat's mouth again and gently ran her fingers down her glistening chest, slowly inching further and further until she curved to the side and cupped her open breast, kneading her nipple with her thumb.

Kat gasped, this was what she wanted. She could not stop it.

Freya kissed her shoulder and then her chest, with her tongue slowly following her fingers to Kat's nipple. She took it completely in her mouth.

Kat leaned her head against the damp wall and bit her lip, the pleasure was intense.

Freya moved her hand slowly down Kat's stomach, gently sliding lower and lower until she reached the top of her bikini pants.

She played with the rim, teasing the material, moving her fingers around the edge, suddenly pushing down and sliding deep into...

Kat jumped up. 'IDIOT!' she shouted, opening her eyes and reaching for the door. The cool air of the room hit her hard and bit her burning cheeks. Freya was climbing out of the salt pool and walked towards her, 'I don't know how to say this but I just know I have to ... you look incredible Kat.'

'Well don't! And it's Miss Spicer to you!' she snapped, storming off to the changing rooms, cursing her own foolish fantasy.

Freya stood shattered, the pain of hurt and embarrassment too much to handle. She dived back into the water and let out a scream of agony. The cool temperature did nothing to sooth her flaming cheeks and aching heart. She surfaced briefly and lunged again to the bottom, curling into a tight ball, desperately trying to halt the slow rise to the top where the truth was waiting, glaring and obvious; Kat didn't feel it, time to grow up.

Freya opened her eyes and saw Miss Mews's long face rippling on the surface. She exhaled and slowly rose to the top, watching the real world come painfully into focus. She gasped.

'Are you okay?' Fiona Mews asked falsely.

Freya ran her fingers through her soaking hair, staring at the ugly horse face of Miss Mews. She suddenly realised why she looked even worse than normal. The garish orange and yellow scarf had disappeared to reveal a large walnut sized mole on her neck, with three long wet hairs hanging from its centre.

Fiona noted Freya's stare and sneered, 'Lovers tiff was it?'

She began to push off from the side.

'If you ever need to make a complaint just pass it on, I'll be more than happy to let the relevant authorities know.'

'Oh piss off Miss Mews,' Freya did not care, 'and by the way, you seem to have some food stuck to your neck.' She darted through the water to the other side of the pool, jumped out and spotted Mr Puller in the hydro room. She explained her stomach ache, which Ben said he required no further details of, changed quickly and left *Cross Hall* in the comfort of her warm, safe, pale blue Clio; embarrassment and hurt quickly turning to disbelief and anger.

Kat threw on the luxurious white dressing gown and slippers that had been handed to her on arrival, and relishing neither made her way to the award winning *seventh heaven* restaurant. She felt strangely

KIKI ARCHER

attired but gently reassured when greeted by the other towelled diners. She stood at the counter gazing, but not paying attention to the carefully colour coded food, green for good, amber for okay and red for don't you dare. She picked up her black coffee, shuffled across the marble floor and sank into a deluxe cream sofa, almost hidden in the corner of the tranquil room; the strangest restaurant she had ever been in. She felt dreadful. She had lost control. She had opened the lid of her tightly sealed box of emotions, peeped inside and now here they were, out, racing around, no chance of ever being contained. Kat couldn't switch it off. She realised with every inch of her being that she wanted Freya; she was in love with Freya. Her mind, with its perfectly rational arguments, had lost the battle with her heart. She felt it. It was real. The conflict was torture.

Freya pulled into the massive driveway and heard the small stones churn under the wheels as the car stopped abruptly. She had been a complete idiot, an infatuated idoliser, so caught up with the impossibly unattainable Kat, that she had failed to acknowledge the perfect reality within reach; the beauty of Bea. The huge oak door opened before she could reach the magnificent wrought iron door knocker.

Bea stood in silence assessing a very bedraggled Freya, she smelt of chlorine. 'Hi.'

'Can I come in?' The request was timid and apologetic.

'Of course,' she smiled, opening the door and revealing the charming entrance hall with its low ceilings, open beams and worn oriental rugs. 'So I didn't miss much then?'

'What do you mean?' said Freya, suddenly conscious of her appearance.

'Well you should still be relaxing at the glorious *Cross Hall.*' Bea had been many times before and the novelty had worn off. She had opted for a personal study day instead and was one of the few who actually made proper use of it. 'Has something happened?'

Freya didn't know what to say, it had all been so clear in the car on the way over; she needed to see Bea, to tell Bea she was sorry, to feel Bea wanting her, needing her, desiring her - unlike Kat who clearly hated her. 'Is there any chance I can have a shower?'

Freya stood in Bea's pristine Jack and Jill en-suite bathroom, pulling on the most comfortable grey velour bottoms she had ever felt.

118

She had no idea Yves Saint Laurent did tracksuits and absolutely no inclination of their cost. She tied her wet hair in a loose knot and peeped inside the mirrored cabinet fixed to the shiny black and white porcelain tiles and squirted herself with Bea's *Miracle*. She loved the scent - '*Modern. Sophisticated. Light-filled. Serene. The splendour of magnolias, serenely balanced by warm, amber notes.*' She put the box back down. Maybe that was the problem. Both Kat and Bea wore sophisticated, grown up perfumes and her own *Dolly Girl,* that described itself as *carefree and mischievous,* was possibly too childish, reminding Kat of the Chianne Grangers of the world who wore Britney, Kylie, Fergie and Jordan, all brought in bulk from Brownhills market. Freya stopped herself and pictured Kat's face as she had angrily put her back in her place, disgusted by her suggestive compliment and over familiar address; no, snap out of it, focus on reality, this is going to be a Kat free Christmas.

'Didn't you bring your bag?' asked Bea, leaning across the large white bed to her iPod docking station, switching Vivaldi's Four Seasons to Rebecca Ferguson's *Heaven.*

'Yeah, but it's in my car.'

'What the car all of that distance away on my drive?' laughed Bea.

'Sorry. I just wanted to come in and see you and then I couldn't be bothered to go back out, and you do have such lovely clothes!' Freya spoke mischievously hopping onto the white quilted divan. 'I've been an idiot and I'm sorry.' She looked at Bea dressed casually but beautifully and finally accepted the truth. Bea had not been judging or critical of her despicable behaviour following their kiss and she had also not been pushy and analytical about the kiss, which Freya realised would have been very difficult. Bea had just been patient, understanding and kind.

'It's okay, I know how hard all of this must be for you.'

'Oh Bea, I don't deserve you as a friend.' She moved up to the soft head board and into the open arms.

'I'm here for you whenever you need to talk and I'll listen to whatever you have to say. I know what it's like being attracted to a woman for the first time and it's scary.' She squeezed Freya's shoulders.

'I know, and I *am* attracted to you.'

'Are you sure?' she asked quietly.

'Yes,' she whispered, gently placing her lips on Bea's.

CHAPTER SEVENTEEN

The exotic buffet was prepared, the mismatched glasses were laid out and the fridge was jam-packed full of drinks. The apartment lounge rang with laughter. Kat, Lucy, Jess, Gary and Ben chimed their glasses together, surrounded by the handmade Christmas decorations that Jess had pinched from school. They toasted each other in preparation for a memorable night; the first guests due any minute.

'So tell me again,' beamed Lucy, already starting to feel tipsy, 'exactly, second by second how did he do it?'

Jess looked lovely. Her auburn hair was tied up loosely with some soft curls falling to her shoulders. The flattering navy blue polka dot dress from the maternity section of *H&M* fitted perfectly; the eating for two had started early. Jess glowed each time she told the story. 'Well, we stayed in this quaint little B&B in Ullswater, the owner was called Marjory and every morning she would say, *"Morning Gary, morning Jess,"* and you would have to say, *"Morning Marjory,"* before she would offer the choice of cereals.' The funny *Marjory* voice continued, 'Anyway that was all charming and we spent our mornings wrapped up walking around the lakes and our afternoons cuddled up in *Marjory's* lounge under *Marjory's* multi coloured crochet throw, playing with *Marjory's* well worn board games.' She beamed at Gary. 'It was idyllic.'

Gary looked like he was about to offer an anecdote but Jess carried on in her animated fashion, clearly overjoyed to recall every last minute of their perfect Christmas break.

'Then on Christmas day, after *Marjory's* home cooked Christmas dinner, Gary took me up to the Aira Force Waterfall and as we stood on the thin cobbled bridge, water crashing either side of us, my knight in shining armour got down on one knee and proposed, box in hand.' Jess flashed her modest sparkler once again to Lucy who had a tear in her eye. 'It was perfect. I'm so happy and I can't wait for March 29th!' she squealed, shaking Gary's knee.

They wanted a very small ceremony in the local registry office, followed by a meal at the plush *Paris* restaurant in town. Both knew where they would rather be spending their money, but had realised some wedding effort did need to be made.

Ben looked devilishly handsome in his crisp white shirt and black bowtie. 'Well we're all thrilled for you and so will everyone else be.' He cheered and raised his glass of potent mulled wine.

Jess glugged her orange juice and shivered with nervous anticipation. 'They know something's going on, I mean me inviting Uncle Barry for a New Years Eve Party, as if!'

'Oh no is Uncle Barry coming?' shrieked Lucy, pouring her third glass of the expensive stuff. She had gone for the sexy Miss Money Penny look to compliment her very own James Bond.

'Hey that's for the toast,' teased Gary, just thrilled with the way everything was turning out. He had loved Jess for an eternity and always knew he wanted children and teamed with his recent internal promotion he felt he had it all. 'I'm a man on top of the world,' he had declared to Ben when the girls were making their finishing preening touches to carefully thought out New Years Eve outfits.

'Well cheers then!' shouted Lucy rowdily. 'Here's to us all! Here's to you Gary and Jess for a perfect future. Here's to me and you Ben for plenty more Christmas dinners at the local Indian, and here's to you Kat for looking sensational tonight!' Everyone whooped. Kat did look sensational in her favourite little black dress, black kitten heels and chunky black bead glass jewellery; her beautiful blonde hair, blue eyes and smile glowing out in contrast.

'Cheers,' said Kat with meaning, determined to put her internal conflicts aside for the night.

'So come on, how was it?' giggled Jess, a fan of the Spicer Christmas dinner. 'Did your sister do her usual?'

Kat had followed the normal routine and spent Christmas with her huge extended family. 'Yes, Kelly and the wonder kids took over proceedings as always and this year we had a rendition of *Annie* by Ava and *Oliver* by Bobby and then they did a *Little Donkey* duet on the violin and trumpet with Kelly taking centre stage singing the vocals!' Kat laughed remembering, 'No one realised that *Little Donkey* was a show tune!'

'How old are they?' asked Ben intrigued.

'Two and three.' Kat laughed, 'and then we had to sing the wee wee song and clap every time Ava used the potty.'

'Ha, and how does that one go?' said Ben trying to drink around the soggy pieces of orange and lemon that were bobbing up and down in his warm red wine.

'Oh I can't remember but it was in a show tune style with actions.' She laughed and shook her jazz hands.

Gary was perplexed. 'So they can play the violin and trumpet at two and three?' His birth and beyond books hadn't focused on when to introduce musical instruments.

Kat was enjoying the energised atmosphere, thrilled that the apartment was once again filled with all of her very favourite people. 'Well yes, Kelly says they can, just like Kelly said they learnt to walk at nine months and speak at ten!'

'They are gorgeous though aren't they,' said Jess glowing inside.

'Oh they are and I can't wait to see what they get in their GCSE's this summer!' Kat loved Ava and Bobby and tried desperately hard to ignore her sister's constant, but well intentioned boasting. The whole family knew that no one was of any importance now the grandchildren had arrived.

Jess's mind suddenly changed direction. 'Shall we do it at the start, or the middle or the end?'

'I think when everyone has arrived. Let's just get them all together and have a toast to us. *Pregnant and engaged!*' hooted Gary, the happiest he had ever been.

'I'm so devastated about my scan though, I was hoping to produce the pictures and just say *Ta dah!*'

Gary smiled, 'Well it's Christmas and you can understand them delaying it, and anyway it will be something else to look forward to.' Everyone chimed their glasses again and the expectant New Year feeling roused them all.

****

Jess and Gary grasped each other's hands tightly as they waited for the midwife, the joyous feeling of their families fantastic reaction and perfect New Years Eve Party was suddenly lost to this stillness; this silent terror where neither spoke and hardly breathed. Jess's scan was supposed to bring joy to the start of the New Year; their New Year as a new family. They had waited eagerly, watching the screen as the sonographer moved the camera around on the cold gel smeared over Jess's stomach, then looked at each other as they noted her slight cough and frown, slightly appeased by her statement of *'don't worry it often takes a while'* and then freezing in terror as she eventually said those awful words, *'I'm really sorry but I don't seem to be able to locate a heartbeat.'* They held hands motionless, silent, as they waited for the arrival of the midwife who would do an internal scan and be responsible for delivering a blow that would crush them for a lifetime or revive them from this quiet state of dread.

****

Kat went with Jess to the hospital. Gary could not bear the thought of being present while the remainder of his baby was removed, dismissed as if never a reality. The first few days of the New Year were dreadful. Jess had walked back into the apartment looking bewildered, and Lucy began to joke about the scan picture looking like Gary, but stopped when she read their faces. The feeling that quickly engulfed the eager, excited lounge was one of complete devastation. It was a feeling that put everything else in its righteous place. Jess and Gary were lost; but neither could find the other, and no amount of reassurance or comfort had any form of impact on their absolute despair.

Jess had entered the lounge in silence and sat on the edge of the leather sofa. 'He just didn't form properly.' She had been wide eyed, staring through the air.

Kat had been close to tears. 'Oh Jess I'm so sorry. What can we do?'

'Nothing.' Gary was empty of emotion.

There was silence in the lounge and the only movement was the slight shift of the shiny Christmas decorations as they blew gently with the rising radiator heat. Kat spotted a stray glass behind the television, missed from the New Years Eve clean up.

Ben squeezed Lucy's hand. She was trying not to cry.

'He's still here, inside me, no heartbeat, just all alone.'

'Oh Jess,' Kat had dashed to the sofa, sank to her knees and held her as tightly as she could. Jess stared straight ahead as a tear fell from Kat's cheek.

****

The waiting room was full of people but empty of warmth. Old posters were falling from the yellow paint chipped walls and the plastic chairs were cold and uncomfortable. No one in the room was talking, but there was the occasional murmur of hushed whispers. Kat walked out of the cold room and went to the lavish reception desk for the second time.

'Yes?'

She tried to stay calm. 'I am not being funny, but my friend is in that room, sitting quietly waiting for the worst experience of her life and still no one is explaining to her why things are running over an hour late.'

The trumped up receptionist stared at the powerful lady who had her black wool collar pulled up against her elegant neck. 'As I said last time, these things happen.'

'Do you know how long it will be?' asked Kat, trying her best to be patient.

'No sorry, she will just have to wait like everybody else.' She swivelled back to her computer, loving the power the job gave her over everybody, no matter how stunningly blonde and beautiful they were.

Kat got two more cheap coffees from the battered machine and sat next to Jess, drawing her chair as close as possible, trying to reassure her that she wasn't alone.

Jess's dark lined eyes betrayed the torment of the past few days. 'At least you won't have to go through anything like this,' she said, staring at a wonky poster about cervical cancer, lacking the emotion and drive to whisper.

Kat realised it wasn't the time to discuss her natural womanly desire to have children, something that had not automatically disappeared when she realised she was gay. 'I guess not,' she whispered.

'It's for the best isn't it.' Jess spoke loudly. 'I mean I never wanted children and I'm too young to get married. It's been a blessing in disguise.' She was monotone and had yet to cry.

'Oh Jess, don't say that,' she hushed, realising it wasn't her friend talking, but a lost and empty soul.

'Jessica Williams.'

Kat tapped Jess's knee.

'Jessica Williams?' the voice was sharper.

'Come on this is us,' she whispered.

Jess didn't move.

'Jessica Williams, D and C!'

Jess burst into tears.

****

Ben and Gary sat quietly in the apartment lounge looking at the large red hands on the oversized black clock. 'She'll be in now.'

'I can take you to meet her if you want?' suggested Ben, still failing to understand Gary's behaviour.

Gary had completely lost it after their scan. The thought that there would be anything wrong with the baby had never crossed his mind. He was just so excited to see the picture and make out the head and spine and legs. He knew from the copious amounts of research that he had done that it would be impossible to tell the sex of the baby until five months, but he was still so energised and eager to just see it, to hear it; and when it was not there he just fell apart. Gary eventually spoke with his eyes wide and his face emotionless, 'No, she will be okay, she's got Kat.'

'But Kat isn't you mate.'

'No it's fine. She doesn't need me.'

'Mate of course she does! She's going to be your wife in a couple of months!'

Gary came to life and spat out his words, 'Ha! As if that's going to happen!'

'Why wouldn't it?'

'Because we were only getting married for the baby, for the baby that's probably in some bin right as we speak.' He broke down. 'I just can't handle it. Look at me, I'm a mess, I can't handle it.'

Ben shook his head and tried again. 'What about her mate? Think about her.'

'She didn't want kids in the first place. She's probably pleased.'

Ben was firm. 'That's not fair and you know it.'

Gary held his head in his hands. It had been a horrific few days, completely unexpected. They had both been so excited, so overcome with the sheer joy of planning for the arrival of their perfect little baby that the notion of this nightmare had not even once entered their minds, why would it? And everything since those awful words, words that neither would ever forget, had been tainted by the irrational thought that possibly the other partner was silently pleased.

'I'm sorry. What am I saying? I don't know what I'm thinking. I don't know what I'm saying. I'm a mess Ben. What am I meant to do?'

'You are meant to get down to that hospital and meet her and tell her you love her and tell her it's not her fault and tell her you want to marry her.'

'I should, shouldn't I.'

'So let's go!' urged Ben, already on the way to the door, reaching for their coats.

****

Kat was fuming with the nurse but contained herself as she put her arm under Jess and helped her stand. She looked up and realised it was going to be a long walk down the corridor to the *minor treatment room*. What an utterly ridiculous name for a room of this type she thought, suddenly feeling a gentle tap on the shoulder.

'I'll take it from here,' said Gary, taking Jess's hand.

****

Ben and Kat decided to stop for coffee on the way back to the apartment, both needed to feel some space. It had been an awful end to the Christmas holidays. The New Years Eve party had been a huge success and all members of both families were genuinely pleased with Jess and Gary's great news. They realised that marriage and kids were on the cards for them eventually and in the excitable New Years atmosphere had all viewed the hurried plans as wonderful and thrilling.

Kat grabbed a table and watched as Ben ordered at the busy counter, desperately trying to ask for two normal coffees, clearly flabbergasted by the confusion and series of question that it involved. He was a good man she realised, and Lucy was incredibly lucky to have won his heart. Their Christmas of cavorting and curries in the empty apartment had sounded like heaven.

Ben slipped into the seat opposite her and added two sugars to his tall Americano. 'How are you, Kat?'

'Me? I'm fine, why?'

He watched her carefully. 'Just because something awful happens to someone else, it does not mean the issues in your own life should take any less importance.'

She didn't need this, especially not now. 'I haven't got any issues, and yes it does, it puts everything into perspective.'

Ben was still trying to connect. 'I like you Kat and I care about you.'

'Thank you, but I'm fine.'

He paused for a moment and went to sip his coffee, quickly changing his mind at the heat. 'Look, I've wanted to say this for a while, but I haven't known how.'

'Say what?' The day had been dreadful and she had wanted to stop for a nice quiet coffee and reflect on the magnitude of these heart breaking events.

'You know what I'm going to say.'

'What?' She was snapping.

'I know.'

'What do you know?'

'I might play the fool sometimes but I know when things are going on. I've seen it.'

'Seen what?' Kat took a large gulp of coffee and burnt her mouth, angry at him for thinking this was the time to discuss personal matters.

'You and Freya.'

Kat's heart pounded, she felt panicked and annoyed. 'Look, I don't know what you think you know, or what Lucy has told you, but there's nothing going on. And anyway nothing like that is of importance on a day like today.'

Ben needed to get through to her. He respected Kat and wanted to guide her in the right direction. She was not the first and would not be the last to embark on a pupil-teacher affair. 'Like I said, care about others, but pay attention to your own life and your own issues as well.'

'Look Ben, I feel uncomfortable talking about this.' All she had wanted was to come here to her favourite coffee shop, enjoy the rich deep aromas that seemed to lure her in every time she passed, and reflect on the past few life changing days and her impending return to school. Her head was so full of everything that she just wanted to talk about nothing.

'I asked Lucy and she denied it, but you know us teachers, we can tell a mile off when the truth is being deliberately lost!' Ben tried to chuckle.

She had started to redden. 'Look there's nothing going on.'

'I can see that, but something has done hasn't it?' Ben was seeing a side of her for the first time, a side that was scared and nervous, falsely cold and emotionless.

'Look this is of absolutely no relevance, but I met her once before I started at Coldfield.'

'Were you together?'

'Ben this is none of your business ... but yes, we kissed, and that was it. End of story.' She was frantically blowing her coffee, nervous and embarrassed by his searching stare.

'But it's not the end of the story though is it? She is clearly in love with you, and you can pour your scolding coffee over me if I'm wrong, but I think you feel the same.'

Kat shook her head. 'I can't have this conversation with you. There's nothing to talk about. My career means the world to me and I will not jeopardise it for anything, not even a silly conversation about infatuations.'

'Is that what you think it is, an infatuation on her part and nothing on yours?'

'Yes,' she snapped.

'Okay, I must have got it wrong then...' he reached across the table for her hands, '...the way you chat like you've known each other a lifetime, the way you look at each other when the other isn't watching, the way you smile when you're together, the way you talk about each other. Kat it's obvious.'

The statement filled her with absolute dread. The last thing she wanted and needed was the wrong kind of attention. 'Don't say that.'

'It's obvious to me I mean.'

'Please just forget about it and please I don't want to talk about it again. There's nothing to say. Regardless of what you think, I'm her teacher and that's it, the end of the conversation.'

'But Kat...'

'I mean it, that's it. Please don't ever bring this up with me again.'

He sipped his coffee. Lucy had told him about Kat's ability to shut down and close off completely. He needed a different approach. 'Cuckoo Kirsty married her old teacher.'

'Who?' said Kat, starting to get really irritated.

'Kirsty Spalding, the Head.'

'Good for her,' she said, sipping her finally sippable coffee.

****

Freya and Bea gently held hands in the pale blue *Clio* that was parked untidily on the huge pebble driveway. Leona Lewis was singing softly in the background.

'I can't believe we're back tomorrow, the time has gone so quickly. I've had such a fantastic Christmas Freya. Thank you.' Bea kissed her hand and watched her scan the numerous large cottage windows.

'Someone might see!'

Bea stroked each of her delicate fingers in turn. 'Freya, they all know.'

She felt a burst of panic. She could not deny that this Christmas had been her best by far, but she was not ready to shout it from the rooftops. 'What? Your brothers know as well?'

'Yes, why? What? Is that a problem?'

Freya released her hand. 'I just don't know if I'm ready for all of this.' She messed with the keys in the ignition.

'All of what? Look, what you do is up to you, but for me ... well I'm happy.' She took Freya's hand again, '...and I'm excited. I'm dating a wonderful, pretty, intelligent, slightly naughty woman and I don't care who knows.'

'Oh my god, Bea, you can't say that!' She was nervously shocked. 'You can't say we are dating!' Freya had enjoyed every moment of the Christmas break, which she had to admit did include numerous dates with Bea - cinema, ice skating, bowling, movie nights, each following the same theme - a vague interest in the alleged activity followed quickly by a search for a quiet corner to engage in their new found favourite activity of choice, heavy petting.

'Well what are we doing?' purred Bea, running her finger up Freya's arm, climbing her shoulder and finding her neck.

She leaned back in her seat and moaned with anguish and desire, 'Bea you can't keep doing this to me!'

She laughed, 'You know you love it, girlfriend!'

'I'm not your girlfriend.'

'What are we then? Friends who kiss and cuddle and soon...' she stroked Freya's red cheek '...when the time is right, make love.'

Freya sat open mouthed, 'OH MY GOD! I need to open the window, this is too much!' She smiled as she fumbled with the handle, Bea was intoxicating.

'Because you know it's going to happen soon. It's been harder and harder to stop ourselves.' Her brown eyes were glistening as she teased.

'Look, I'm being serious now, I'm not ready for people to know. My parents?! As if! Can you imagine?!' She quickly did up the window, Christmas this year had been far too cold. She looked at Bea's eyes, naughtily teasing her own, reminding her of a panther ready to pounce, her full lips glistening, ready for the first bite.

'Come here.' She pulled Freya in and kissed her passionately. This time she didn't bother to look around, instead she closed her eyes, fully absorbed in the power of the embrace.

They were interrupted by a quiet tap on the window. Cal Belshaw was lightly hopping up and down in his expensive silk dressing gown and slippers, making a winding sign with his hand. 'Girls you can always do this inside.' He grinned, thrilled with Bea's recent news.

'Yes thank you Dad, we know!'

He popped his head inside the window, 'I don't mind you kissing in front of me, and nor does your mother.'

'Okay thank you Dad!'

'Come on in then, it's freezing out here!'

Bea tugged Freya's hand. 'Come on, just for ten minutes.'

She rolled her eyes, 'Okay ... but I'm not kissing in front of them!'

Bea pulled a reticent Freya through the large beamed entrance hall into the warm lounge where the open fire was crackling. Silvia Belshaw was adding another heavy log to the glowing embers. Freya had met Silvia a number of times over the Christmas break but was still shocked each time she saw her. Everything was Bea, the deep brown eyes, the flawless skin, the full lips, but with white hair and alabaster skin; she seemed to have a poise and dignity that added grandeur to the simplest of tasks.

'Just throw it in Silvia!'

'Thank you Cal, but it needs to be just so.' She looked at the girls as she effortlessly rose from the inglenook fireplace to her feet, smiling with mother's pride at her daughters beautiful partner. 'Please sit down ladies.'

'Thanks Mum, but we thought we'd just have ten minutes in my room before Freya headed home.'

'No, no, I insist!' commanded Silvia with warmth. The lights were dim and Freya thought she looked almost regal taking her throne in the tall upright armchair alongside the woodpile.

They sat on the large teal sofa next to the fire. The flames had reignited around the new log. Cal sat opposite them in the matching teal fabric seat. Freya felt like she was on interview.

'So girls,' said Cal, leaning forwards and opening his hands, 'what's the plan?'

'Well I was going to head home in a minute. I have lessons first thing in the morning.' Freya nodded, waiting for agreement from Bea.

Bea sighed, 'He wasn't meaning that. Dad, please don't.'

'He's only asking what needs to be asked, darling,' said Silvia steadily.

'Freya, I'm so sorry. I'm used to my parents discussing and debating every detail of my life, but that's not what we came in for. So, no offence, but I think Freya is heading off now.' She glared at her parents.

'No, it's okay. What did you mean?' asked Freya, open to advice she knew she would not find anywhere else. She had never once talked about anything of real importance with her parents. There was no chat about the birds and the bees and she had to completely fend for herself when it came to female issues, too embarrassed to ask when *the drawer* was empty, ending up in the early years using folded tissue paper as a last resort.

'Well,' said Cal, approving of the gloriously pretty, mature girl more every minute, 'I mean what is the plan? Are you going to be open at school? If so when are you going to tell your parents? Which should come first? Will you hold hands in school? Kiss like the rest of them in the common room? When will you take the next step? Assuming you have not done so already. Are you ready for the next step? Do you need some space here alone? Shall we meet your parents?'

'Dad!' yelled Bea, 'we are just fine thank you! Please Dad, she is not used to this obsessing.'

Freya was not sure which was worse, parents like this or her own deliberately naive and illusive pair. 'Wow, I hadn't thought of all that.' This was too much.

Silvia oozed concern, 'Oh you must darling, you must. Be in control of every situation and anticipate its outcome, this way your choices will be confident and thought out, not rash and irresponsible.'

'Mum please. We are just dating.'

That word again, thought Freya, it sounded so strange. Freya is dating Bea. It sounded so wrong.

'So it's secret dating again then Beatrice?' said Silvia, raising her eyebrows but forming no wrinkles.

'If that's what Freya wants, then yes.'

'Thank you,' said Freya quietly, not knowing where to look. 'I just don't know what I'm feeling yet.' She thought of Kat.

'Well surely you feel something for our daughter?' Cal spoke with quiet pressure, delving deep without appearing to dig.

'Of course I do.'

'Okay, so if I can give you one piece of advice?'

'Yep,' said Freya bracing herself.

'Just always be honest about your feelings. If everyone did that then the world would be a much simpler place.'

'If you feel it, then it's real,' concluded Silvia, hands held together pointed under her chin.

Bea knew when enough was enough and ushered a disoriented Freya out of the cosy dim lounge and into the glare of the outside security lights, there were faint specks of snow in the air. They hurried to the car and she crouched at the door. 'I'm so sorry about that.'

'It's okay. I guess they're right. I'm just not ready to be labelled as a lesbian though!'

'It is just a word.'

'Well I don't want it thanks.'

'Why not? Is it such an awful thing?' Bea was starting to take offence.

Freya was confused, this was all so overwhelming. 'For me yes! No, I don't mean that, look I don't know what I mean,' She sighed and looked at Bea. 'I know you're gorgeous though,' she spoke slowly, 'and I know I think you're hot, and I know you're an amazing kisser,' she moved her lips to Bea's ear, 'and I know I can't control myself around you.'

'Me too,' said Bea, moving her mouth quickly round to Freya's. Their kiss was hot and throbbing as the specks of cold snow melted on their burning skin.

CHAPTER EIGHTEEN

Kat returned to school emotionally drained, exhausted from the full on family Christmas, sapped of supportive energy, mind full of conflicting thoughts and unacceptable realisations. The atmosphere in the staffroom had been one of sluggish recognition, Christmas was over, the kids were back, and the term till summer was long. Kat avoided the pull of moaning staff and tried to look enthused, gearing herself up for a second great term, but then Leery Old Lester flicked his new reindeer thong pouch her way and she groaned in despair. An array of new mugs, free from brown circles, had appeared on the wooden staffroom hooks. Kat added her *I Love You Miss* mug to the tree.

'From Freya I presume,' sneered Fiona Mews, with a new paisley neck scarf tied in place.

Kat spoke pleasantly, 'Davey Jakes actually.'

'Davey Jakes?! He hates teachers!'

'Not our fantastic Miss Spicer,' said Ben, grabbing Kat's waist and kissing her on the cheek. 'Good morning Miss Spicer, looking sensational as always.'

'If you like lesbian chic that is,' sniggered Fiona, blowing hot air from her huge nostrils. Kat realised she actually sounded like a horse as well as looking like one.

Ben studied Kat in her tight grey, gently chequered, pencil skirt and fitted black shirt. She had large pale blue beads that matched her dazzling eyes and she looked incredible, so smart and sophisticated yet so stylish and modern. He shook his head in disbelief, how could Fiona be so cruel? 'Says you Miss *exits to the sides*!' He was posing with arms out.

'Not got a haircut over Christmas then Mr Puller?' sniffed Fiona, adamant to get the last laugh.

'No, I see you didn't get your mane cut off either?'

Fiona turned to stalk off and her long black plait whipped his chest as she spun. She peered slowly over her shoulder and flared her nostrils, 'A lesbian pupil-teacher relationship. The governors won't be pleased.' She tutted and trotted off towards her brown woven chair.

Ben walked quickly behind her and grabbed her arm.

'You're hurting me,' she snarled.

'What the fuck is your problem Fiona?' he hissed. 'Leave Kat alone or the governors will hear about your homophobic bullying.' He paused to check he wasn't drawing attention and of the few staff members left in the room most were head down reaching into one of the shiny chocolate tins that littered the tables; the bearded supply guy was asleep; '... you total and utter waste of space.'

'Trouble in paradise?' Dave Lester shouted over to Fiona and Ben. He was considerably deaf from the jungle of hairs and build up of wax in his ears and the muffled show from the kitchenette looked like a lovers tiff.

'Not if she's got any sense,' snapped Diane Pity, having returned from the ladies. She'd caught the comment and glimpsed the scene; there was no way her best fake friend was getting those cheap stylised nails into her hunk of a man.

'Thanks Ben, but there was no need,' said Kat walking along the long freshly painted corridor.

Ben reached up and smeared the pale blue paint with his finger. 'You'd think they'd have done this earlier, the smell is atrocious, and look at this damp bit.' It was always the same with school maintenance jobs, left until the most inconvenient time, or done in the most inconvenient manner.

Kat had apologised to him about her sharpness in the coffee shop - it had been a dreadful day for everybody - but she was still adamant that she did not want to talk about it. 'I mean it Ben. I can fight my own battles.'

'Yes but you shouldn't have to.' He hoped he would gradually wear her down. 'What does she know anyway?'

'Oh nothing, just putting two and two together and making four.'

'It does,' he laughed. 'Is Lucy rubbing off on you?'

'Ha, I don't know where my head is! Is it still only Monday?'

'It's only five to nine,' he chuckled as he swerved into his form room to a cheer of *Happy New Years* from his delighted pupils.

Kat climbed the stairs swiftly, slowing at the top where the hulk of Chianne Granger was leaning a giggling Chantelle Mann over the rails. 'Excuse me ladies, but can we move on to our form rooms.' The smell of cheap perfume was worse than the new B Block corridor.

Chianne sucked her teeth and Kat was sure she heard a faint whistle caused by the buck. She placed both hands on her wide hips and thrust out her non-existent chest. 'Only because it's you, Miss,' breathed Chianne, now smiling, presumably sexily.

Kat's face didn't crack. 'And can you take that pink hoody off as well Chianne, you know it's not school uniform.'

'You wanna see the merchandise don't cha Miss?' she purred winking.

Kat barked, 'Stop talking right now and move it!'

'Alright we're going,' bellowed Chianne in her usual deep voice. 'Mann, get the bags.' Chantelle scooped up the handbags and scurried after the thumping beast.

Most of Kat's tutor group were yet to have their birthdays and the innocence of these eleven year olds was warming. They chatted nicely about their Christmas's and the gifts they had received, genuine excitement still evident in their voices and smiles. Numerous new watches were proudly on display as were the clean coats hanging carefully on the back of their chairs and comic Christmas socks were exposed with the deliberate crossing of knees. Kat sat at her wooden desk and watched, they were a delight and she was really proud of them. 'Come on, who's got a funny story from Christmas?'

Hands flew up, most of them hadn't got funny stories, they simply wanted to share their Christmas with their favourite, genuinely interested, form tutor.

By lunchtime it felt like she had not been away. Kat was back in the swing of things, allowing her classes to have a quick chat about Christmas and New Year before diving straight back into the syllabus; coursework was now the focus in most upper school lessons. Following a chatty lunch with Janet Louza, Kat made her way to the dining hall and her difficult duty position, pleased that Janet did actually seem to have a life after all. Hannah Phag was also meant to patrol the area near the food hatch but Kat couldn't see her and actually couldn't remember ever having seen her on a single duty.

'Hello again ladies, could you please return your trays and make your way to afternoon lessons.' Kat decided to start off politely.

'Wow you have missed me ain't ya' Miss!' spluttered Chianne with a mouthful of cold chips. She pierced her blue *Calypso* with a straw and the crinkled see-through plastic crackled under her large mitts.

'Now please,' Kat spoke firmly.

Chantelle whispered with trepidation, 'Come on Chianne, it's Mr Puller next and he's got those tight trousers on.'

'Oi, I decide when we vacate vicinities!'

'When we what?' Chantelle knew she always got it wrong.

'No you don't, I do, now go!' said Kat pointing at the door.

'Yeah yeah,' muttered Chianne, yanking herself free from the table. 'Mann, get the chips.' Chantelle hastily scooped up the remaining thick cut chips, some splattered with gravy, and cradled them like lost treasure behind a puffing Chianne who had tried to walk sexily to the door; teasing that strict Spicer woman who she thought clearly wanted a slice of the action.

Kat braced herself as she entered her classroom, it was the first time she had seen Freya in nearly three weeks and she did not know what to expect. All she knew was that she felt awful and had to apologise for her outburst at *Cross Hall*. It had been completely uncalled for and out of proportion in response to Freya's pleasant, if somewhat over familiar, compliment. What she had not expected was their late arrival and Bea's smirking apology. Kat had warned her Sixth Formers on their very first meeting to, *'arrive on time or don't arrive at all,'* and in general they did. Today however, the excuse, *'we just lost track of time,'* was unacceptable, and throughout the lesson Kat questioned the intent of Bea's sly wink.

Generally all ten in the A-Level class were performing fantastically. Janet Louza had been thrilled with the exceptional end of term exam scores and the group's coursework progress, which had far outstripped anything Miss Pendleton had achieved. She had requested that Kat lead a Department Inset on her successful *coursework completion strategy*. Kat didn't really have one, most of her students tended to do the work to the best of their ability and hand it in when requested. Big Tom, however, was an exception. Kat sat and watched him gazing out of the window, mesmerised by noisy gulls fighting for ample lunchtime scraps on the littered tennis courts. Today in his new red checked Christmas shirt, smart black trousers and ginger beard he could have been little Jason Sparrow's dad. Jason was sitting tucked in tightly to the desk, feet barely skimming the floor, beavering away textbook in hand, occasionally putting it down to wipe his newly pimpled forehead and push up his wire rimmed round glasses. They were an odd couple, but the best of friends. Kat turned her attention to the table in the

t you mean after our kiss? I know you saw me. I watched
of the club.'

I was going to say I'm pleased for you. Bea is a really
at paused. 'Does she know?'

w what?' Freya was going to make her say it, address the
that had been bubbling under the surface between them
ng.

w about your embarrassing night out with your cousin,
istakenly let a boring old history teacher pounce on you! I
that first lesson must have been awful for you.'

thing has been awful. I only wish you weren't my boring
eacher.' Freya held Kat's eyes.

I am unfortunately.' She looked down at her large
in full of coloured paper and sharpenings from her earlier
ng lesson. 'But I hope I'm not too boring?!'

thing can happen can it?' whispered Freya, softly transfixed
eyes.

shook her head gently. 'No.'

y sat silently.

you feel it though?' she whispered, her heart tender,
wanting to bloom.

closed her eyes. 'I am your teacher; that is what we have.'

ay,' said Freya. She was not going to beg. 'Bea doesn't know
never know, and yes I like her, but she is not you, Kat.'

did not correct her, instead she took her hand. 'If you ever
you know where I am.'

ank you,' she whispered, aching with the affectionate touch.

lay sulkily across the Sixth Form chairs. Everyone had gone
deliberately ignored the sound of the common room door
d lay still with her hands behind her head, until she saw
ing over her. Freya looked flushed. 'You've taken your time.'
rry. Thanks for waiting.'

ell what did she want that so was important that your
ouldn't hear?'

ea, we spoke about that! Please don't call me your girlfriend.'
hat's right isn't it? I'm nothing to you!'

eya had never seen her behave so childishly. She was pouting
g her hair but actually managing to look incredibly sexy. 'I've

corner. Freya and Bea were once again choosing to sit together and if Bea's suggestive excuse was anything to go by she suspected they had become more than reunited friends during the two week break. She cursed herself and watched as they worked quietly. Freya sat with her left elbow on the desk supporting her forehead in her hand, waves of rich chestnut brown hair pushed through her fingers. She wrote quickly, pausing every so often in thought, twisting her pen around the long tassels hanging from her delicate blue and gold scarf. Freya looked up and caught Kat's stare, she smiled and Kat felt her heart quicken.

As the bell rang she gave the final loud and clear coursework deadline date and quietly added a request for Tom and Freya to stay behind. As the class filed out Freya loitered at the back and Tom stayed seated; his beard disguising his red cheeks.

Kat pulled a plastic blue seat into her desk. 'Tom, could you come and sit up here for a minute please?'

'Err Miss, any chance you can come here please?' his low voice mumbled.

'You're a cheeky beggar Mr Wood! No I can't. Get yourself and your thin coursework folder up here now.' Her banter was friendly. 'Freya I'll be with you in a minute.' She noticed Bea still seated in the corner.

Tom lifted his school bag onto his lap, took a long time to stand and shuffled his way to the front, towards the incredibly hot Miss Spicer.

'Okay, take a seat, put your bag down and let's look at what you've got.'

Tom spluttered, his large fleshy ears had turned pink, 'Err my bag's new Miss and I need to keep hold of it.' He was looking at the floor, the outline of her perfect tits bulging against her tight black shirt was too much to handle. He stared at the ground and spotted her elegant ankle and his eyes were drawn slowly up her smooth supple legs, towards the rim of her tight skirt where her crossed legs met. He looked at the board and kept his bag in place.

Kat frowned. 'Okay, whatever. I'd like to arrange some one on one tutor sessions with you after school on a Wednesday, just until we get you up to date with your coursework.'

Tom felt his bag shift, 'Okay.'

'Right, if you don't have any questions then I'd like to start this week. Three Thirty in here if that's okay with you?'

'Yes fine.' His deep mumbling voice was almost inaudible.

'Hey Tom, listen ...'

He couldn't look at her; her incredible blue eyes would be too penetrating and her sexy mouth would be too inviting.

'...I'm really pleased with what you've done so far, there just isn't enough of it.'

'Okay,' he said, trying not to sniff too much of her subtle, yet highly arousing perfume, imagining her stood naked, spraying it on her graceful neck after her sexy as hell morning shower.

'Right, okay. Glad we're on the same page then.'

'Um hm,' he managed, lifting his bulk out of the tiny plastic chair, catching a glimpse of her wonderful cleavage and making a mental note to wear his jockstrap on Wednesday afternoon.

'Okay,' said a slightly bemused Kat as she watched him shuffle out of the room, bent awkwardly over his precious new bag. 'Freya, could I have a word please.'

Freya and Bea made their way to the front. 'Sorry Miss, it was my fault we were late,' said Bea, confidently taking a seat on the front table.

'No it's not about that Bea, just please make sure it doesn't happen again. I could do with a quick word with Freya.' Kat paused and Bea didn't move. 'Bea?'

'Look Miss, you need to know something. Me and Freya don't have any secrets if you know what I mean?' She winked again.

'That might be so, but I would like a word with Freya in private please.'

Freya remained quiet.

Bea raised her perfectly arched eyebrows. 'Meet me in the common room.' She paused on her way out of the door and looked back, moving her long dark hair sexily over her shoulder. 'Maybe you could stay at mine tonight?' she added inappropriately.

Kat listened as Bea's black knee length Yves Saint Laurent boots clipped down the corridor. She got up and closed the door. Freya looked deeply embarrassed.

She breathed in and began. 'I just wanted to apologise for the way I reacted at *Cross Hall*. It has been playing on my mind all over Christmas and I just needed to say sorry.' She carefully recited the speech. 'It was unjustified and uncalled for. I'm so sorry Freya, you didn't deserve that and I hope we can put it behind us and move forward normally.' She stopped and looked up. 'I want the absolute best for you in these lessons and I don't want anything to cloud the

issues. You're online for an A and I breathed and smiled with relief.

Freya had been worried that s tardiness, but this nervous apology had relaxed, took a seat next to the wo beautiful face with its striking features but she resisted the temptation to stare. anything.' She looked for a sign.

Kat didn't know what to say. 'O understand I didn't mean to snap, I just time in that steam room.'

'It is lovely though isn't it Miss.'

Kat met Freya's daring green eye call me Miss.'

Freya felt her heart tingle, not c deliberating over their altercation, but sh their history. She felt buoyed. 'It was pret to be fair it's not like you had much on!' s

'You're getting as cheeky as Big 1 have cleared the air.

'Is that what you and Miss Louza c

Kat smiled, relieved that the ba everyone calls him!'

'Do you know what everyone sparkled.

'Oh I dread to think.'

'Well they call you ... no I think I' highly inappropriate and I don't fancy anot downs!'

'Oh Freya don't! I'm sorry.' She warmth and positive energy that Freya alwa

'It's fine. Look I'm sorry about E sometimes.'

'I'm assuming you two have made up

'What do you mean?' She knew ex needed time to plan what to say. She had or such an open conversation and did not want

Kat gently prompted her, 'Well you Christmas and ...'

'Wha
you walk ou
'...an
bright girl.' I
'Kno
unsaid issue
for far too l
'Kno
where you r
am so sorry
'No
old history
'We
classroom
poster maki
'No
on her blue
She
The
'Ca
desperately
Ka
'O
and she wi
Ka
need to tal
'Tl

Be
home. She
opening a
Freya pee
'S
W
girlfriend
'B
'T
Fr
and flicki

never seen you angry before,' she teased, grabbing her waist, on a high from her previous encounter. 'I think I quite like it.'

Bea wriggled free. 'I'm being serious, what did she want?'

'Who?'

'Who do you think? Your favourite teacher. The gorgeously smart *Madame Spicer*?' She wrinkled her nose.

'Oh nothing, just something about coursework. What does it matter anyway?'

'I'm sure you have a thing for her,' said Bea, carefully watching Freya's reaction.

'Oh give over!'

'Prove it. Prove I mean something to you and kiss me here.'

Freya looked around the empty common room. 'Don't be stupid. I don't have to prove anything.'

'Well do it because you want to then.' Bea's eyes widened seductively as she slowly licked her bottom lip and twirled a long piece of silky dark hair in her fingers.

'You are insatiable Miss Belshaw.'

'You want to call me Miss now do you? I can play teacher if you want. Now come here bad girl!'

Freya laughed and pulled Bea close, bending her backwards as she kissed her with fire.

Chianne thought her thighs were going to explode. Her hefty legs couldn't take much more crouching and her thickset arm was aching from holding the phone against the glass window. There wouldn't be any audio, but who needed audio when there was action like this!

Freya pulled away. 'That good enough for you?!'

'For now,' said Bea, trying to hide her smile.

'What the bloody hell is that?' puzzled Freya, turning to pick up her bag, her eyes drawn to the wobbling black mound that seemed to be hovering at the bottom of the common room window. 'It's fucking Chianne Grangers quiff!' she yelled as she ran to the door.

Chianne quickly slid her phone together and shoved it into her sequined handbag. She stumbled heavily out of the alley, only meant for Sixth Form use, and towards the car park. She didn't get far.

'Oi Granger. What the fuck were you just doing?' shouted Freya.

'English detention, I owed it from last term.' She was wheezing.

'I mean with your fucking phone you pervert!'

'I don't think it's me who is the perverted one round here do you?' she sneered, still gasping for breath.

Bea had joined them outside. It was cold and already starting to get dark. 'You were filming us? You freak!'

'Don't think I'll be the freak round here when I do my upload, lezza's!'

'You fucking dare,' screamed Freya, absolutely fuming.

'What's it worth bitches?' Her swagger had finally returned now the oxygen had completed its long journey around the vast area of mass.

'Get a life Chianne,' huffed Bea, turning to collect her bag.

'Bea?!' shouted Freya, 'she has us on camera!'

Chianne delved into her tiny sparkling school bag and wiggled her phone, smacking her fat lips together around her big bucked teeth, 'Kissy kissy!'

'So?' Bea shrugged it off.

'So she'll put it on her stupid site!' Freya was angrily upset.

'Let her babe.' She turned to Chianne. *Idiot.'*

'Chianne, I'm begging you. Please delete it now. Please.' Freya moved closer.

'What's it worth?' sucked Chianne.

'Please, I'll do anything.'

'Oh grow up Freya,' scowled Bea, heading back into the common room.

Chianne parted her lips. 'Kiss me.'

'What?' said Freya, shaking her head in disbelief.

'As if, you dirty little lezza! Give me fifty quid and I'll delete it.'

'Delete it now?' She had a chance.

'When you give me the fifty quid.' Chianne flicked her solid quiff towards the shop. 'Spar has got a cash point.'

'Wait a minute.' Freya signalled through the window for Bea to hurry up.

'What?' she snapped as she walked back towards the pair stood in the darkening car park.

Chianne loved the winter months with detentions that were only half an hour because of the dark early evenings. In the summer, however, she often had to hang around for an hour and a half.

'Have you got fifty pounds in your bank?' she pleaded.

'Why?'

'She will delete it now if we go over to the Spar and get it out.' Freya was desperate.

'Look at you, it's pathetic.'

'Please. I haven't got that much in my account.'

'Freya, I'm not giving Chianne Granger fifty pounds. I don't care who sees that video.'

'Yes well I do! Please I am begging you!'

'What are you so ashamed of?'

Chianne was getting bored with their bickering, but fifty quid could buy masses of 20/20 and her footage of a very plucky Chantelle Mann secretly sticking a sanitary pad to Miss Phag's green felt skirt had doubled her hits over Christmas. She could wait a while for this upload. 'I'll give you till tomorrow,' she growled, clomping off towards the empty bus stop.

Freya burst into tears. 'How could you? She will show everyone.'

'You have to face up to it sooner or later, you were kissing the face off me! You enjoyed kissing the face off me!' Bea lowered her voice, 'I want you to keep kissing the face off me.' Putting her arms around Freya she whispered, 'What is it you're so afraid of?'

Freya shrugged her off. 'I'm just not ready for people to know.'

'Are you ashamed?'

'Yes I guess I am. Sorry to disappoint you!'

'Fine I'll give her the money tomorrow.'

'Would you?' she urged, lifting her puffy eyes to meet Bea's.

'If that's what you really want.'

'I do, I'm just not ready.'

Bea crossed her arms. 'Okay, so you and I can also wait until you're ready.'

'What do you mean?' she looked at Bea's distant face.

'I'm not going to be your secret Freya.'

'Fine,' she agreed, her only thought to eradicate the damning footage.

'Fine,' said Bea coldly. 'I'll see you at school tomorrow. I'll go and get the cash out now.'

Freya watched as Bea strutted off with her well formed bottom shifting sexily from left to right in her tight black Armani jeans. She was doing it realised Freya; her and Chianne were crossing the road to the Spar. She made her way quickly to her pale blue Clio, got inside and cried. How could she be so stupid? Kissing in the common room, what an idiot! She sat in her cold dark car and shivered, the thought of people seeing the video terrified her. What was she was so afraid of? Freya closed her eyes and shook her head. What is the problem? Why is this so hard? She contemplated Bea's situation. Most people knew about her sexual preference and were generally fine, but then Bea was quite new to the school and it always seemed easier to accept a difference in someone you didn't really know. But what about her and her friends, the ones she had grown up with, what on earth would they think? What would they say? What would Tom think? What would her parents think? A feeling of complete dread coursed through her anxious body. Telling her parents! As if! But what if they saw the video? No, they could hardly work a computer. But what if someone texted them the video? No, no-one knew their numbers. But what if they saw it on the news? Freya shook herself free and leaned her head against the wet steamed up window. Miss Phag was hitching up her infamous green felt skirt, pulling her wispy brown hair free from its bun, throwing the little of it she had over her shoulder and pulling on a black skull and crossbones helmet. Miss Phag straddled the small red scooter, put a sandaled foot on the flame etched exhaust, and sped out of the car park, swerving dangerously into the rush hour traffic. Freya laughed to herself, shook her head and exhaled heavily. Get a grip. She tried to logically work out exactly what was giving her this anxious feeling of panic, this sickening feeling of dread. It was the unnerving loss of control, she didn't have it, Chianne did.

She grabbed her phone and texted Bea. *Just seen u 2 get on bus. Have u given her the money? Did u delete it?*

Her phone beeped almost instantly. *Yes.*

Freya tapped her mouth with the phone, then text again. *Did u delete it?*

Yes

No I mean u. Did u actually delete it? Did u see it deleting?

Yes

U pressed the delete button?

Yes

R U sure?

Sort it out would you! Yes! Oh and thanx for the money!!!

Thank u I will pay u back. Can I come round?

No.

Please, I'm sorry. Please.

No. Sort urself out, work out what u want then let me know.
Fine.

The immediate fog had lifted slightly and she sighed, not yet ready to leave the cold dark car park where she felt safe, hidden and alone. She turned on her music. Trisha Yearwood's *Inside Out* was playing. Kat had mentioned it to a nosy Harley as her favourite all time album and Freya had immediately ordered it on next day delivery from *Amazon*, wanting to hear it, to judge it and to feel it the way Kat had. She sat listening to the words of *Harmless Heart* and cried. *You can run, you can hide, love will still come to find you. You can turn it away, keep romancing the pain.* Tears of grief were trickling down her cold numb cheeks.

'Isn't that Freya? Come on Kat lets grab a lift.'

Kat linked Ben's arm and dragged him towards the school gate. 'No it's only ten minutes walk!'

'Oh come on, it's freezing and it's getting dark!' he pulled free and ran to the lonely blue car.

Kat carried on walking and buried her hands into her deep pockets. She hugged her belted black trench coat into her cold body. The earlier chemistry had been excruciating; an invisible magnetic force pulling her heart towards Freya's, drawing their eyes, electrifying the air and intensifying their senses. Freya had been captivating; her initial endearing apprehension was quickly followed by her charismatic boldness, and her genuine open sincerity had enchanted Kat further and made the close eyed denial of her feelings almost impossible. No, she did not want to revisit it.

Kat heard the rub of Ben's bomber jacket coming up behind her. 'Oh bless her Kat, something's wrong. She was playing some awfully depressing music and had tears streaming down her face.'

'Was Bea there?'

Ben frowned. 'No. Why?'

She had stopped walking. 'Did you ask for a lift?'

'No, I just knocked on the window, saw the tears, heard the awful warbling music and asked if she was okay.'

Kat's heart was aching. 'Was she?' The pull back to the car park was almost too much to bear.

'She said she was fine. She even tried to joke that it was because she missed my lessons! Do you know anything?' Ben's stare was intense.

'No.'

They turned and watched the pale blue Clio drive towards the gate. Freya hadn't got her lights on.

Freya looked in her rear view mirror at Kat racing towards the car waving her arms; her heart started to pound.

'Lights,' puffed Kat as she caught up to the open window.

'Thanks,' said Freya, flicking the switch and edging into the busy road.

****

Lucy was tucked under Ben's strong arm, completely fulfilled with another intoxicating work out. He knew exactly which buttons to press and how to press them. Their Christmas had been the best Lucy had ever experienced and she wanted desperately to keep this gorgeous, compassionate, intelligent hunk of a man interested. Every other relationship had ended in her heartbreak, dumped by phone, by text, by scribbled note, all assuming she wouldn't be too bothered; laid back Lucy, the novelty had probably worn off for her too they all thought.

This time would be different she vowed, gently tiptoeing her fingers down Ben's firm stomach to his even firmer manhood; this time he would fall for her mind as well as her body. 'Did you know the word "penis" is taken from the Latin word for "tail"?'

'Yes,' moaned Ben, finding it difficult to concentrate.

She whispered changing her grip. 'Okay, did you know the average erect penis measures between five point one and five point nine inches?'

'Um hm.'

'And that the Russian mystic Rasputin was rumoured to have an incredibly large penis?' She gently bit his earlobe and tightened her fingers.

'Yeah,' groaned Ben.

'What about the fact that it's extremely rare for an African American to have a penis smaller than five inches?' she moved tighter, increasing the pace.

'Yes!' cried Ben.

'You read that book in my Auntie's loo didn't you!' laughed Lucy, mission accomplished.

He didn't answer, his face was buried in the pillow and his temple veins were visibly bulging.

She was one heck of a woman, thought Ben as he finally emerged from the hot feather pillow, exactly what he needed in his life at this moment in time. Easygoing, funny, great in bed and committed. He looked at her strong features then watched the vulnerability in her gentle brown eyes. She always moved her gaze when he stared, as if scared of what he might discover. 'I love you Lucy.'

Her heart soared, it had worked! 'Oh Ben. Thank you!' She dived on top of him and pinned his arms above his head. She teased his neck with her teeth and whispered, 'I hope it stays that way.' The books had said that when love was declared you had to accept it graciously, enjoy its importance and then independently, at a later time, declare your returning feelings. 'I'm meant to wait to say it. But I can't. I love you too!' She arched her back and lifted her bottom. 'Now come here big boy, this girl needs a spanking!'

Kat sat on the comfy black sofa and reached in her blue school folder for the list of names and numbers. She couldn't concentrate. Jess and Gary were avoiding the racket and taking their time bringing back the Chinese, a start of term treat. She sat phone in hand debating what to do. Duty of care, she thought, finally convincing herself.

Hello. Mr Puller said you seemed upset in the car park. Concerned. Just wanted to check you got home ok. Hope you don't mind got your number from the Cross Hall list. K.

Freya put down her pen and reached across the dining room table; she needed a break from her impossibly complex Biology coursework anyway. Her heart skipped a beat and she darted out from the table and up to her bedroom, away from the watchful eye of her parents who always seemed to sit and read in the adjoining lounge whenever she was working or using the family computer. Freya lay on her stomach and put her head in her cold pink cotton pillow, rippling with excitement. Play it cool Freya, she urged.

Thanks for caring, it means a lot. Am fine, just had a run in with Chianne from Y11 but all sorted now. x

Kat smiled to herself; were there any other Chianne's in the school? She felt relieved at the fast response and put her phone down on the leather sofa, only to pick it up a minute later.

Anything I can help with? K

No, but thank you. Are you ok? x

Yes thank you. Glad we cleared the air. K

Me too, Freya paused nervous of the buttons she knew her fingers were about to press. *I know you feel it x*

Kat cursed herself and quickly deleted her message folder. The front door flew open and a buffeted Jess and Gary ladled with warm white bags shuffled into the apartment, amazed that the noisy tantric workout had not yet finished.

The evening turned out to be a late one for a school night with the five of them sat chatting and gauging themselves on crispy beef and chicken balls, each smiling privately and feeling a warm personal glow deep inside. Kat would have attributed hers to the great news from Jess and Gary regarding their new wedding date - March 29th two years time - a long engagement, but an engagement all the same, with the desire to marry and raise a family and *'live the dream'* as Gary had so lovingly declared; things were on the up. But Jess had noticed Kat's glow before their news and was determined to repay her very best friend's constant kindness with a listening ear, an ear that had been absent for the past two horrific weeks.

CHAPTER NINETEEN

Intentionally, or unintentionally, Kat had spoken with her eyes, tenderly and lovingly, gently conveying to Freya a message that her tongue would not let her speak; and it was glaringly obvious they both felt it. The words were not important. The pauses, gazes, and drawn out breaths were what mattered. Freya understood, and the memory of their emotional conversation in the classroom helped her cope with the fast deteriorating week. Bea was sitting separately in lessons again, Jodi was away in Ibiza and Chantelle Mann was sniggering at her each time they passed in the corridor. She had returned the money to Bea and doubled checked once more that the video had been deleted, to which Bea replied, 'It's gone, just like us.' She was annoyed by Bea's petulance but understood her motive and realised that with her every denial, Bea was getting a slap in the face; a personal condemnation.

So tonight, as Freya looked across Tom Wood's pumping, flashing living room, complete with disco ball, mixing decks and *Limoges* wall plates, she decided to make amends. Bea looked incredible. Naturally sexy. Every outfit hanging perfectly, just like it had on the mannequin and tonight's dark grey tribal print dress with floaty chiffon was no exception. It accentuated her womanly curves and looked absolutely divine. It was Tom's 18th and most of the Sixth Form were crammed into his two bedroom semi. Freya watched as Bea chatted to Poppy Jones, reminding her of a glitzy celebrity visiting an orphanage and talking to the shabby malnourished child. Bea's personality was fascinating and alluring and Freya envied her ability to express her feelings with passion and fervour, but worried about her recent volatility. She stepped over a shiny blue eighteenth balloon and made her way towards the blanket covered three piece suite. 'Hi, can I join you?'

'If you must,' sniffed Bea, deliberately angling her body in the other direction.

Poppy shuffled along the sofa dragging half of the woolly blanket with her. 'I thought you two were friends?' She sipped her drink and decided to be brave. 'In fact if the rumours are to be believed you two are more than just good friends!' The homemade punch seemed to have quite a kick and Poppy felt unusually confident. She saw Bea's glaring face and quickly tried to back track, 'Not that I believe the rumours!' She didn't want to ruin her new friendship with the schools resident supermodel.

'Oh shut up Charity Shop Pop!' snapped Bea. 'No one wanted you here anyway.'

Poppy could not believe that someone had actually called it her to her face. She had know for the past six years that it was her nickname but in all that time no one had ever been cruel enough to shout it right at her, at such a short distance as well. She was close to tears. 'Tom invited me,' she whispered.

Bea bit back, 'It's his eighteenth! He invited the whole Sixth Form! Look, whatever Poppy. Can we have some space?'

Poppy slid off the sofa and crept out of the pumping house. No one noticed her absence, but then again no one had really noticed her presence either.

'That was so mean!' Freya was incredibly tempted to chase after Poppy, to comfort her, and knew deep down it was the right thing to do, but Bea's pull was just too strong.

'I've been stuck with her for the past half hour and she has been going on about her incredibly interesting Biology Coursework and the fascinating way that molecules alter when they're hot and cold or something like that!' Bea's frown relaxed and her face suddenly transformed. 'I'll find her in a bit and apologise. It's just that I feel lost. I feel lost without you.' She looked down at the blue balloons scattered around the floor. 'I love you Freya.'

The pumping bass coming from the black oversized speakers seemed to fade and the multi coloured lights blazing out from the rotating ball seemed to slow. Freya felt disoriented. No one had heard. In fact most people were out in the garden huddled under the large rusty patio heaters, or standing in the kitchen adding their stash of booze to the table, or upstairs going into the rooms that said *Definite No Entry*. But she had heard. 'Oh Bea, can we talk now then? All I've wanted to do this week was talk but you have been so cold towards me.'

'I just don't know what to do. I don't know how to make you love me.'

She frowned. 'You can't make someone love you.'

'So you don't?'

'I didn't say that. I just think we need to talk, and talk properly, and then maybe kiss and make up?' Freya's eyes twinkled and she dropped her head to meet Bea's downcast eyes. 'Please?'

'Will it have to be illicit? Will we have to go into the toilet and do it?' She was still playing moody.

Freya moved closer and pleaded quietly, 'I just need time.'

'But I want you now,' she whispered reaching for her hand.

Tom bounded into the room with his blue pointy party hat lost on top of his huge head, his clean shaven face grinned from ear to ear. *'It's my party and I'll dance if I want to, dance if I want to, you would dance too if it happened to you!* Come on Freya, dance with me!' He went to grab her arm and haul her off the sofa but stopped when he noticed their closeness. 'Oh no. Please no. Freya I thought they were joking?' He pleaded, 'You are not like *that* are you?'

'Like what?' she smiled, stepping up and away from Bea and all that she entailed. 'Come on, let's dance birthday boy.'

As Tom twirled her round the living room, Freya saw the empty sofa.

He grinned. 'Come on let's have a chat. Follow me.'

Tom and Freya had been reserves for the last two years ever since the first house party took place. All of the girls would have a list - only known by them and their closest friends - of the boys they wanted to kiss. Number one would be their ideal, the one they really wanted, but knew they had little chance of enticing. Number two would be a possibility, as long as someone else didn't get in there first. Number three would be a probability, someone you knew liked you and you knew would be interested; they weren't great but they would do. And then if all else failed you had your reserve. The one that by ten o'clock, if no one else had bitten the bait, you knew you could turn to for a good old snog. Freya looked at her watch, it was only eight thirty.

Tom held her by the hand and guided her up his stairs, stepping over two kissing couples who had clearly hit the jackpot and bagged their number ones. 'This is my room.'

Tom could pass for twenty five but still had a Thomas the Tank Engine duvet cover and road print rug on his floor. 'It's nice,' she said lying.

He made his way over to the single bed and tapped Thomas's funnel. 'Sit down.'

She followed his instructions.

'Please tell me you're not a lesbian.' He looked worried. 'Only I heard some people talking about you and Bea making out in the common room or something like that. It could have been the car.' He had heard the rumours but instantly dismissed them, he knew Freya too well and knew her more intimately than he knew any other girl, there was no way he could have turned her gay - what would his mates say?

She shook her head in disgust. 'As if!' Freya realised in that moment, with that simple denial, she was not ready for the truth.

'Okay then, Phew! I was worried she'd got her teeth into you. I mean she's foxy as hell, but you're not gay are you, so she has no chance.'

She messed with her hair and turned to Tom, her wide eyed bewildered act coming all too easily. 'I know. Just because we are friends I guess people are making stuff up. I'm not bothered. People can think what they like.'

Tom grinned. 'Come here then.' He moved heavily towards her and pulled her close, kissing her roughly and moving his large hands clumsily up her top.

She was crying inside.

'Here, touch me here.' He grabbed her reticent hand and shoved it on top of his bulky jeans.

Freya burst into tears. 'I can't.'

CHAPTER TWENTY

Freya couldn't handle it anymore, she had drawn so much attention racing from Big Tom's party that the rumours had escalated and she felt suffocated, terrified. She needed to talk and Kat was coming towards her, marching her way down the chaotic pale blue corridor, asserting herself in a fashion that was simply awe inspiring. She was confident and firm, never turning a blind eye for the ease of a swift journey, but stopping and correcting and insisting and caring, Freya found it breathtaking. Kat could spot a loose shirt a mile off and chewing gum in the mouth with x-ray vision. As they finally met in the middle of the corridor Freya laughed, 'Am I up to standard?!'

Kat smiled, eying her white polo shirt and perfectly faded skinny blue wash jeans. 'Definitely.'

Freya grinned, pleased with the hint of mischief in her tone. 'Have you got a minute?'

'Of course, but I have my Year Elevens next and if I'm late there's bound to be at least one incident to file!' It was the one lesson of the week that she had a slight apprehension about.

'I was wondering if I could come and see you later for a chat? You know our lesson is cancelled right? It's that stupid confidence building day and I've already had to make a ten foot tower out of cotton buds and I've transferred water from one bucket into another without using my hands and anyway...' Freya realised she was rambling '...I have that judo session this afternoon instead of our lesson.'

'I know, any Sixth Form staff that had lessons today have been put on supervision, and I've got...' Kat pulled the piece of crumpled paper, recently retrieved from her jammed pigeon hole, from under her arm, '...Judo.' They smiled. Their secret smile, thought Freya.

Kat noticed the bleach blonde hair first and the huge cleavage second.

'Well I'll see you there...' Freya paused, '...but I was wondering if maybe we could ... maybe go somewhere later after school and have a proper talk. It's really important.' The noise in the corridor was deafening and Freya hadn't heard Miss Pity's stilettos coming to a standstill directly behind her.

'I don't think that will be possible sorry Freya. Let's talk about it in the lesson on Thursday.'

'I can't,' she said confused, 'this is personal and I really need your advice.' She reached for Kat's arm. 'You told me I could come and talk to you whenever.'

Kat stepped backwards. 'Yes you can, but like I said, we'll discuss it on Thursday.'

Freya suddenly realised how Bea must have felt. 'You know what, don't worry about it.' She stalked off leaving Kat and Diane silently eyeing each other like fighting cats, oblivious to the carnage surrounding them in the B Block corridor.

The gym smelt fusty as Kat walked barefoot over the squeaking floorboards. She sat in front of the wooden wall bars on a knobbled bench at the back of the hall, relieving Leery Old Lester - who looked like he had been enjoying proceedings far too much - from his cover. She lifted the first of many exercise books out of her yellow plastic box, tapped her red pen on the bench and glanced up. Kat recognised most of the students trussed up in heavy cotton judo whites and was shocked at how vicious the current move seemed to be. There were about twelve Sixth Formers attempting the basic hip throw, pretending they were being attacked from behind and grabbing their assailant roughly by the arms, flicking their left hip out, pulling the attacker over their right hip and hurling them onto the ground. The bald headed instructor whose tattoo's covered most of his neck kept shouting: 'Maintain your grip, maintain your grip,' but the students didn't and bodies were slamming onto the blue dog eared school gym mats left right and centre. Kat winced and returned to David Haverley's drawing of Tintern Abbey, A+ Merit.

'Right, you're going to have to take over. Here is your *jodogi*, just put it on over your trousers and shirt.' The barking continued, 'Good you're shoeless, you just need to take your necklace off and tie this belt around your middle.'

Kat looked up at the scary bald instructor. 'Excuse me?'

He pointed at Poppy Jones sitting in the corner. 'That one has had enough. Doesn't quite cut the mustard as far as I'm concerned.' He stuck his thick thumb over his right shoulder, 'That pretty one needs a partner and you're it.'

Kat picked up her red pen. 'I'm just here to supervise. I have books to mark. Can't you do it?'

He looked down at the book resting on her knee. 'Looks more like pictures to me love. No, can't pair up male and female, you're up. That sweaty old geezer got involved, show a bit of spirit love!'

'I bet he did,' she muttered, calling Poppy over. There was no persuading her, and Poppy left to join the Library's embroidery session instead.

The instructor glared at Kat. She had no choice so stepped into the massive judo whites.

'Right we've got ourselves a new volunteer, because some people can't stand the pace!' The loud scary instructor shouted in Poppy's direction, possibly not aware that this session was meant to improve confidence and teamwork skills. A couple of the group cheered as Kat took a nervous little bow. She lifted her blonde hair in one sweeping movement onto the top of her head, and wrapped her bobble in place - she always kept a spare one handy for book marking. Kat twisted the band and pulled her silky hair in a tight knot, displaying by consequence her long and elegant neck in all its splendour.

'If you just stand here love,' he almost lifted Kat into position in the centre of the blue mats. 'Right, we're going to look at some mat techniques now. You've got them down,' he threw Kat over his right shoulder and lowered her onto the mat, she still thudded. 'So what do you do with them now?'

'Maybe let go?' she choked.

'No, you do the Makura-Kesa-Gatame, or as it's also known the Pillow Scarf Hold.'

He proceeded to spin to the ground sliding his bent right leg under her right shoulder, locking her head with his right arm and keeping her fixed by holding onto his own knee. Their heads were millimetres apart and he smelt of garlic.

'Can you move?'

Kat shook her head.

'No didn't think so. Right watch it again.'

In one swift action he had lifted Kat from the floor, thrown her over his wide shoulder, clattered her onto the thin blue mat and pinned her into submission. The couple of efforts Kat could see from her squashed position on the ground weren't exactly matching the one just demonstrated, but she could hear whooping and giggling and wails of help from the group who were actually having a fantastic afternoon.

'Right, I've just done it to you, now you do it to her.' He signalled to Freya and shouted at the noisy group. 'Keep practicing, I'll want a demonstration from everybody in ten minutes.' The bald instructor ushered Kat and Freya to the blue mat near the door. 'Right, your turn.'

Kat held her breath and stood in front of Freya.

'Grab her lapels'

She reached for Freya's lapels and gently lowered her right shoulder, nudging her over the top and sliding her pathetically onto the ground.

'Get a grip woman! Show me the hold!'

Kat adjusted her stance and knelt down. She slid her knee under Freya's shoulder and locked her head lightly.

'Bloody hell woman, you'd be dead by now! My goldfish could have done a better job! Get up!' He turned to Freya. 'Right you, pretty eyes, your turn.'

Freya looked at Kat and smiled sweetly before jabbing her hip fiercely and hurling her over her right shoulder and onto the map. She dived into position, pinned Kat down and locked her head tightly.

'That's my girl! Now show Miss Prissy Pants here how it's done!' He turned to the hall. 'Group demonstrations in ten! Bloody hell! Better make that fifteen looking at the piss poor state of you lot!' He marched off shouting insults at the grappling pairs he passed.

They looked at each other and laughed. 'Is he for real?' Kat was rubbing her neck.

'Sorry, I didn't mean to hurt you. Well, maybe I did a little bit!' The last thing Freya wanted to do was appear childish, but their conversation in the corridor had really got to her.

'Right madam,' giggled Kat, 'no more Mrs nice guy!'

Kat did the move again, more powerfully this time, but still one of the few in the hall who actually kept hold of lapels and lowered their partners to the floor instead of letting go and watching them thud. She moved into the hold and immobilised Freya's head. 'Is this better?' she whispered, literally centimetres away from her mouth.

'Yes,' Freya was staring up, remembering the image of Kat's beautiful face moving into hers for their very first kiss, 'but you forgot to hold your leg!' She spun onto her stomach, threw her legs around, rolled Kat onto her back, keeping her hands under Kat's shoulders, and pushed her head onto Kat's chest. They filled the length of the mat, Kat on her back with toes at one end and Freya on her stomach with toes at the other.

The instructor could not even see Kat's head. It was hidden under Freya's body. 'Well you are the gold star pupil aren't you, pretty eyes! Can you remember what it's called?'

Freya lifted her ear from Kat's warm soft chest. 'The Kami Shiho Gatame.' She returned her head and listened to Kat's heart racing.

'Well remembered! You see long legs, if you're not firm in your holds your attacker will soon have the upper hand!'

Kat couldn't see anything. She was face up in Freya's breasts. The pair giggled and laughed as loudly as the other couples with each move picked up perfectly by Freya and poorly by Kat who was quickly thrown into submission and another excruciatingly close contact position. Kat felt the tension and tried her hardest to ignore the agonizing feeling of Freya's perfect body pressing against her own, forcefully changing her position and moving their heads unbearably close. Their cheeks brushed and Kat remembered Freya's incredibly soft skin and the way her rich brown hair smelt deep and intoxicating. There was only about an inch and a half between them in height and their weight must have been incredibly similar, but it was clear to both that Freya was the strongest of the pair. Kat had joked that she hadn't been trying, that it wouldn't be fair to use her full force on someone younger than herself; but as Freya lay on top of Kat pinning her arms above her head into another submission that Kat could hardly pronounce, let alone master, they both knew the truth. Freya was the one in control, she took the lead, she dominated. Kat couldn't help but imagine what she would be like in bed.

Freya saw it. She saw the look in Kat's eyes. For the first time it wasn't a look of empathy or compassion, or a look of love. It was a look of desire. There was a heat in her eyes, a craving. A look of need and want that drove Freya to adjust her thigh and press it firmly between Kat's legs.

Kat closed her eyes and gasped. 'We can't do this,' she whispered into Freya's ear.

'No, not here we can't,' she replied.

Their eyes locked in a state of longing, oblivious to the grappling, thudding and shrieking all around them. Kat's heart was pounding. She couldn't stop it, she wanted Freya more in that moment than she had ever wanted anyone before. The long drill of the bell snapped her back into the room and she dropped her eyes to the mat. She studied the jagged tear in its corner and squeezed the soft multicoloured foam that was peeping through its ripped blue coating. This has to stop. This cannot happen. This simply cannot happen. She lifted her gaze and stared once again into Freya's expectant green eyes. The pain was unbearable.

'Now can we talk?' reasoned Freya.

Kat walked home alone, the cold sharp wind having no effect on her raised temperature. She watched as the red number nine skidded to an abrupt halt at the overcrowded bus stop and was sure Chianne Granger looked over and winked. Kat debated and debated her decision and kept coming to the same conclusion - she had no alternative - they couldn't meet in school for the obvious reasons, they couldn't meet in a cafe for the obvious reasons, they couldn't meet in a park because it was so cold and dark, and they couldn't talk in a car. Freya would be at her apartment in two hours. *Holy Mother of Shit*, she thought, what have I done?

Jess always got home first, able to switch off and unplug at exactly 3.15pm; one of the perks of being the school secretary and not a fully fledged member of staff held behind for meeting after meeting after meeting. She pitied poor Ben and Kat, Year meeting one day, Department meeting another, Faculty meeting every second week, House meeting every term, the list went on. Tonight Kat was coming home early and Jess was excited. Kat was always there for her and Lucy, always thoughtful and caring and interested like any good friend should be, but she did it with a real love and a real concern. She had been her rock over the past few weeks and now it was time for some Karma. The door gently opened and Kat slid her heavy bag onto the wooden floor, she quietly unfastened the belt on her long black trench coat and hung it carefully on the spare hook. She pushed off her black heeled shoes, sighed and removed her soft leather gloves. Kat stood still and slowly rubbed her neck with her warm palm. I have to cancel she ruled.

'You're taking you're time. Come on!' squeaked Jess.

'Oh hi, how are you?' She paused. 'It's Monday, you always stay at Gary's on a Monday.'

'I know, but I've told him he'll have to fend for himself tonight. This, lady, is for you!' Jess lifted her hand to the table where an assortment of beauty products sitting in perfect order. 'We can start with our face and work our way down to our feet.' She pointed at Lucy's ancient, slightly crusty foot spa. 'I have the cucumber mask that you like and I'll do your nails with that new clear polish I was telling you about.' Jess took Kat's hands. 'You're my very best friend Katherine and I wanted to say thank you for everything.' Tears started to form in her eyes. 'I don't know what I'd have done without you.'

'Oh Jess you shouldn't have. I don't need this. You're the one who needs the pampering not me.'

Jess did an excited little jump. 'Well let's enjoy it together then! Go and get your pyjama's on and I'll open a bottle.'

'It's only quarter past four!'

'Oh come on, we deserve it! Go on, move it.' She pushed Kat towards her bedroom. 'I thought we could order a pizza later as well.' She always liked to involve food in proceedings.

Kat stopped and climbed onto the tall breakfast stool. She sank her head in her hands. 'I've messed up. I can't believe it, I've been such an idiot.'

Jess clambered up the neighbouring red leather stool and looked at her anxious friend. 'What's happened?'

'Where do I start?' She was staring at the smooth white ceiling. 'I just don't know what to do. I've got myself into a situation that I shouldn't have and I can't see a way out.'

Jess sat quietly, not moving, just listening, she knew the floodgates were about to open. Kat, against her best efforts, could only keep things bottled up for a certain amount of time, and Jess could see she had reached that limit.

'Okay, so here it is, in all its glory.' Kat smiled and took a deep breath. 'Freya and I seem to have managed to develop feelings for one another. Feelings that neither of us can control. Feelings that I am sure neither of us want. Feelings that are - well for me - so real and so true and so raw and so excruciatingly painful that I found myself seriously considering giving up my whole teaching career to pin her against the wall bars in the school gym and kiss her. Just kiss her. I wanted to kiss her. I nearly kissed her! What on earth was I thinking!?' Kat bowed her head to the glittering black granite worktop. 'I've lost the plot. I've seriously lost the plot Jess.'

Jess sat quietly and watched the turmoil in her friend's eyes.

'I mean, I just need to stop it. I know I have to stop it. I have tried to switch it off, I promise you I have, but I can't. She is so incredibly smart. She was so attentive today and quick to learn, and so eager to master the skills. She is just so full of life Jess. You know, one of those people who energise every single situation, well that's Freya!' Kat could not stop herself, Freya was just so easy to talk about. 'And she is funny and thoughtful and it's as if we have been friends for years. You would love her, I mean really love her. She's the person I've always wanted, but never found.' She sighed and slowed her voice, 'But I know it can't happen. I'm her teacher and I have a duty of care and it can't happen. It's not going to happen and I'm going to stop it.' Kat looked up and bit her bottom lip. 'She's coming here in about an hour.'

'Okay,' said Jess with more calm than she actually felt, 'well I'll put my deep cleansing mudpack away then!'

Kat smiled. 'Oh sweet Jesus, help me!'

Jess was nervously excited. Kat was clearly head over heels for the brown haired beauty that had spent the evening all those months ago mesmerised by her, and now, by some twist of fate their destinies had collided. Jess believed in everything - Karma, Tarots, Palms, Forces of Nature - and this was obviously one of those unavoidable pulls that would happen one way or another. It was meant to be and Jess was excited. Everyone knew someone who had had an affair with a teacher, and everyone who was anyone had wished for an affair with their teacher. But Kat was so proper, so headstrong, so dedicated to her profession that Jess knew what was coming.

She banged her fist against the black granite worktop. 'I'm going to tell her that she's mistaken and that I don't feel it and that I have someone else.'

'But Kat you can't lie! You don't lie!'

'I have to lie, what other alternative do I have?'

'Just tell her to wait for a few months until she's finished school. When is it May? That's when we all signed off. Just tell her you love her and that you want her to wait for you.'

Kat remained firm. 'I can't do that! Anyway who said anything about love? Look I'm not going to lead her on, or make her false promises, or cross the boundary that should not be crossed. I'm her teacher and that is my role and my priority. Period'

'Oh Kat listen to yourself! You're not Mother Theresa for Christ's sake! Just drop a few hints then.'

'And what would that lead to? For the first time ever I have found someone that I can't control myself around. I just want to be with her, to hold her. I want to kiss her.' The thought made her ache with desire. 'I can't tell her because then what do we do? Act normally until the summer? Stop at holding hands? It would just escalate and it would lead to me breaching my code of conduct and that is something I will not do.' She clapped her hands. 'No I have to stop it. I have to stop it now, and then I don't know. If all of your theories are correct then we'll be together when the time's right and when it's meant to be. But that time is not now.'

'Okay so you break her heart, she goes running off to someone else and what are you left with?'

'My career, which means the absolute world to me.'

'More than Freya?'

'Yes.'

Jess knew Kat inside out and realised that no amount of persuasion would change her mind. She understood her predicament and empathised as best she could; but for pity's sake could she not just live a little!?

Kat made her way to the open tiled shower and turned the setting down two notches. She looked up at the large chrome head spraying with force, closed her eyes, stepped forward and urged the cold water to drain her of feelings; to wash away her impurity and make her see sense. She rehearsed the scenario and prepared the speech, but what she hadn't accounted for was Freya's incredible appearance. Kat imagined that she would arrive as she had left her, hair thrown on top of her head, casual sports clothes and trainers in tow. But when she opened the door and saw Freya standing there, she lost her breath. Freya shone with natural magnetising beauty. Her rich brown hair was cascading delicately around her shoulders and her sharp green eyes were twinkling with nervous anticipation. She smiled and her pretty face with its glowing cheekbones lit up with happiness. Her chic white shirt with oversized cuffs was pulled tightly into her navy blue skinny jeans and the long green beads that matched her sparkling eyes hung loosely from her neck.

Lucy was not due home for another two hours and Jess had taken residence in her bedroom, just as nervous as Kat was, hoping for a twist of fate that would see the tragic lovers ending up naked on the lounge floor. She held her breath and listened. Freya had arrived. The door had shut. The voices were muffled. Jess crawled closer to the door and put her ear to the crack. Laughter - good. The leather sofa had just creaked, they must be seated. Sit next to her Kat, don't sit on the pouffe. The leather pouffe squeaked. Stop talking Kat. Stop talking. Let her speak. Let her tell you how she feels. Jess could hear Kat's muffled voice talking quickly, not pausing for breath, saying what she planned to say before her heart tried to change her mind. It took every inch of Jess's willpower to stop herself from throwing open the door, jumping into the room and shouting, 'She loves you! Kat loves you!'

Kat adjusted herself on the black leather pouffe. 'So I wanted you to come round because you said you needed to talk to me and obviously like I said earlier Miss Pity was standing right behind you and I am sure her and Miss Mews are trying to formulate a ridiculous case for some sort of pupil teacher affair that we are meant to be having, so like I said that's why I was a bit sharp in the corridor and why I didn't want to meet anywhere else. Anyway you have dropped me and Mr Puller off here before, so of course you can come and speak to me whenever you need to.' Kat clapped her hands. 'So here we are. What can I help with?' She ran her fingers through her blonde hair and looked up for the first time.

Freya tried to catch her eyes. 'Is that why I'm here?'

'You said you needed my advice on something and I'm more than happy to help.' She paused. 'Look, we both know we have developed a friendship and I value that friendship and I will do what I can to advise you. I can't promise I am qualified though!'

'Okay, well I do need your help, I need your advice on lots of things actually. But do you think maybe we should talk about today first?'

Kat carried on unabashed. She had it all planned out. This was the sensible thing. 'Which part?'

'Maybe the part where we nearly kissed?'

She felt the tops of her ears redden and looked at the carpet. 'What do you mean?'

Freya shook her head and twisted the small green beads that were looped around her wrist. 'Okay. Fine. I'm not stupid and I'm also not prepared to make a fool out of myself so let's just ignore it. Miss Mews and Miss Pity don't have a case. Nothing's going on.'

'I know.'

'Fine. Seriously don't worry about it, it's not important. I guess we don't have anything to talk about then.' Freya spoke calmly but got up to leave.

Kat's heart began to ache so she stood quickly and reached for her hand. 'Please sit down. Please Freya. There's clearly something on your mind. Please, I'll listen. No one can deny we have a good friendship and I value that friendship and I want to help if I can.'

They sat down on the soft sofa together and both felt relief.

Freya didn't want to play games, but she did need advice. 'Bea told me she loves me.' She did not say it to hurt or cause jealousy but that was the effect it had.

Kat felt winded, knocked off guard as if she had lost everything with her one quick denial. It was not what she had been expecting. 'Are you together?' She knew she was poor at reading emotions, but how wrong could she have been?

'In a way I guess yes, we are. Well we were.' Freya could see the effect it was having.

'And how do you feel? Do you love her?' She was cursing herself for believing this magnificent charismatic girl had fallen for stupid old her. She probably wanted to discuss the part today where her pathetic lesbian teacher groaned with desire as she accidentally put her leg in the wrong place. You idiot Kat.

'I don't know how I feel. I'm scared of what I am. I can't face up to what I am. I guess I'm ashamed of what I am.'

'What are you?'

Freya laughed. 'See I can't even say it. I can't even use that word. I like ladies, alright?'

'You're a lesbian.'

Freya laughed and threw a red bobbly cushion across the sofa. 'Don't!'

'What?' exclaimed Kat, she had been serious.

The ice had been broken and both started to smile. 'Can we just be cool?'

Kat giggled. 'Say it. Say "I'm a lesbian."'

Freya grinned and her green eyes twinkled with delight. 'I know you said you were bad at advice, but please, what is this - lesbians anonymous? Shall I stand up and say it?'

'Yes!' laughed Kat.

She stood, flattened her shirt, pushed her wavy brown hair behind her ears and began. 'Hello, my name is Freya Patty Elton and I'm a lesbian.'

Kat threw her head back with laughter. 'Patty? Where did that come from?'

'My birth certificate!' She jumped onto the sofa and slapped Kat's knee. 'You are meant to be helping!'

Raised voices. Giggles. Laughter. Bouncing on the sofa. Jess's knees were starting to ache. Come on Kat. You can do it.

Kat leaned into Freya and looked at her with sincerity. 'There, that wasn't that hard.'

'Oh but it was! I'm just so worried about what people will think of me.'

'Who?' Kat was trying to read her eyes, they looked scared - not of the situation they now found themselves in - but of something else.

'Everyone.'

She realised that this was not about her, it was about Freya. Freya's issues had to be solved before theirs could be addressed. 'But who in particular? Think about who is making you worried.'

'I guess it's my parents mostly.'

'So the person who worries you the most is the person you tell first.'

'You see those words there fill me with the worst dread I could ever possibly imagine experiencing. I can't do that. I can't tell them.'

'Why not?'

'Because it would crush them. They would be devastated. They would be furious.'

'You are their daughter and they will love you regardless. Yes they may be a bit shocked at first, but then they will get over it and you will start to feel comfortable being who you truly are; and then you and Bea can go public.' Kat smiled. 'The bottom line is, if you're sure you are gay, then you will have to tell them eventually, so why not get it done and then you can start living your life properly. Your life, not theirs.'

Freya was so thankful that she had Kat. She also knew that they would not address their personal issue tonight but did not mind, this suddenly seemed of a far greater importance. 'But what do I say?'

'You say "I'm gay."'

'Oh and then they smile and ask me what I want for tea?! Look, I know my parents and I know how they will react.'

'I must have got you wrong Miss Elton. I thought you had balls?!'

'No, my parents will think I *want* balls! I can see how it will go, "Okay Freya so do you want a sex change now as well?" I just can't believe it will be that easy.'

'I didn't say it would be easy, but it will be right. This is the truth Freya, this is you and they have to live with it. It's not like you have changed. You are still the same daughter they loved yesterday, but today they will know something else about who you are as a person.'

'What do you mean today? There is no way I am telling them today.'

'Why not?'

'Because it's not the right time.'

'Trust me, from experience, there will never be a right time. You will wait and wait and put it off until you get found out in the worst possible way and then you'll have lost all control.' Kat smiled, '...and something I've learnt about you today, Miss Elton, is that you like to be in control!'

'I didn't see you complaining, Miss Spicer!' The sparks were back, but this time Kat decided to judge them for what they were - harmless flirting.

Freya broke the gaze. 'Okay, so what about when she says I've destroyed her one hope of becoming a grandmother?'

Kat was shocked. 'Do you believe that? Do you believe you won't have children? Because I know that I will.' She spoke with a genuine passion that touched Freya's heart.

'I don't know, I guess I just assumed-'

'Well don't! There are hundreds of thousands of lesbian parents across the world, and every single study, no matter who commissioned it, has shown that children raised by lesbian parents are of equal, if not improved social development.' Kat was off. 'They have fewer behavioural problems, they have higher levels of self confidence, and they have a greater awareness and compassion for social injustice.' She paused. 'They are not accidental children. They often have mums who are slightly older, financially prepared for their arrival, who ensure there are good male role models in their child's life. They anticipate potential issues arising in school and therefore take a greater interest in their children's education.' Kat finally slowed down. 'You can still have children Freya.'

'How do you do it?' She was in awe. 'How do you know so much about everything?'

'I don't. I just make sure I know what's important, and I know it's important for you to be open and honest with your parents.'

'What if they hate me?'

'Do they love you now?'

'Yes.'

'Okay so they will love you tomorrow as well.'

'Why do you keep saying tomorrow? I'm not telling them tonight. No way!'

'Just do it and deal with the consequences. If they react badly then it's a stain on their character that they will have to live with.'

Freya laughed. 'That's a bit harsh!'

'Not really. If you substitute the word gay for any other group of minority or discrimination then you realise how awful homophobia is.'

She loved the way Kat taught. 'What do you mean?'

'Do it now. "Black people should not be allowed to get married," or "Asian people should not be allowed to raise children," or "Disabled people should not be allowed to teach." Homophobia is a disgrace and if your parents respond badly to your inbuilt sexuality then it's a real shame for them.'

'You are so inspiring.'

'No, I think I just like to get on my high horse every once in a while! Listen, just do it. Do it tonight. You've got nothing to lose but everything to gain. You can live the life you want to live and be the person you want to be. This is who you are and I like who you are. Your friends will still like who you are and I hope your parents will learn to love who you are.'

'And then what?'

'And then you get on with your life.'

Freya's green eyes twinkled. 'Will you help me with that?'

Kat smiled. 'I have a feeling we will be friends for a very long time.'

The silver *Corsa* emblazoned with orange writing and permanent L plates sat quietly in the middle of the empty side street. Bea had stalled again.

'Right, while we're here, we might as well attempt the three point turn.' The edgy instructor sighed and spoke slowly. 'Remember it does not technically have to be three points, take as long as you need, but please watch the curbs.' He had come to dread the twice weekly lessons with Beatrice Belshaw. Yes she was sexy as hell and every older man's dream, but she drove like a granny with cataracts. It was painful.

Bea wasn't listening. She was staring at Freya's blue Clio.

'Restart the engine please.'

Bay two. Looks like those apartments back onto Coldfield Park. Nice views.

'Beatrice? Turn the key?'

Freya must be visiting some relative. No, I know, it will be her mum visiting a friend.

'Thank you. Why have you put your high beams on? Turn them off.'

Which is the lever!?

'Bea, you're high beams. That poor woman. Turn them off!'

Opps that's the water. 'Sorry!' She looked up.

Lucy was striding towards the apartments shielding her face from the fierce headlights.

Where do I know that woman from? Oh here it is.

Lucy lowered her hand, winced and mouthed *thanks*, her eyes still blind from the glare.

Miss Spicer's housemate; you can't forget that nose.

'Clutch Bea?'

Where is she going?

'Whenever you're ready.'

No way. No way! Bea watched as Lucy entered the modern apartment building next to Freya's car.

'Oh for heaven's sake Bea we haven't got all day!'

Bea turned in one point, mounted the curb, churned up the soft grass verge and bumped back onto the street. 'I've had enough now thanks. I'm driving home.' She bounced towards the main road with her hazards accidentally flashing.

Lucy keyed in the code and entered the warm communal lobby. *We've all been there*, she thought blinking and trying to correct her sight. She looked up and wailed! Freya was closing the apartment door and making her way down the hall, and even though Lucy had only actually seen her on one occasion, she felt like she knew her inside out. Kat was forever going on about her, granted it was mostly in the context of her lessons, but Freya did seem to receive a lot of airtime in their apartment. Kat would describe her outfits, her hairstyles, her views on some deathly boring bit of history, neither Lucy nor Jess had ever heard of. She would re tell Freya's funny anecdotes or quick witted responses. She knew her, Lucy knew Freya.

'Oh My God! I'm so pleased to see you! How are you?' Lucy was wiggling her fingers with excitement like a grandma looking at their long lost grandchild for the first time in years. 'You look incredible by the way, I love that shirt! What are you doing here?' She buzzed her own head with her index finger. 'Durrr! You've seen Kat haven't you? I am thrilled! Come here!' She threw her arms tightly around Freya.

Freya could hardly breathe. 'Hello. I remember you from the club. Beyonce wasn't it?'

Lucy put her ring finger to her face and stuck out her bottom. 'Uh oh oh, uh oh oh oh oh!'

Freya felt buffeted, she could hardly remember the woman. 'That was it.'

'Come here!' Lucy dragged her to the brown tub chairs squashed between the tall, slightly dusty, plastic Dragon Trees. 'We've got so much to talk about! Sorry if I look a bit rough - I've just led two hours of pelvic floor! Whatever anyone says, it works, and I'm burning if you know what I mean! Listen to me jabbering on, what's new!?'

Freya sucked on her bottom lip and paused.

'Lucy! Kat must have mentioned me!'

'Lucy, sorry. Harley loves his leg warmers.' That was all she knew.

'Oh good I have plenty more where they came from. Do you want some? Oh no of course you don't, look at you! Kat said you had an amazing dress sense and she wasn't wrong. I said you looked twenty five!'

Freya held tightly to the thick padded arm rests. 'Did you?'

'Yes, when the mountain blew as they say! I said you looked at least twenty five.' She paused, rolled her eyes and put on her best ghetto impression, 'Look at you girlfriend! You ain't no schoolgirl!'

Freya laughed, was that meant to be Welsh? 'So Kat talks about me?'

'When doesn't she!' Lucy was getting carried away, just thrilled at the sight of Kat's *dangerous liaison* sitting in all her beauty in their communal lobby. 'Look, you can always count on me to cut to the chase.' She pulled her chair in as close as was possible. 'Our Katherine is absolutely ... oh shit hang on.' She reached up in the dark and slammed the lobby light. 'She is absolutely crazy for you. Don't tell her I've said this, but this will probably save months of to-ing and fro-ing, she fancies the pants off you Freya. She wants you with a passion that I haven't seen in her for such a long time.' Another strange voice. 'She wants to strum your fiddle and play a sweet tune!'

Freya couldn't help but laugh. 'Has she said this?'

'Well not in so many words, but it's obvious. She is a delicate one our Kat. I know she doesn't seem it what with her power dressing and teacher voice and all that, but she is. She's been hurt before and it has changed her. She has no self confidence.'

'I can't believe that.'

'No I mean with women, with relationships. She really finds it hard to believe people like her. Nice people I mean.'

'Well she's made it quite clear that we're not even allowed to broach the subject.'

Lucy wrinkled her nose. 'What does that mean?'

Freya liked Lucy more and more as the crazy conversation continued. 'She does not want to talk about it.'

'So you really haven't got it on in her store cupboard then? That one needs to get a grip. Look at you! Someone like you does not ... hang on ...' she slammed the button, 'you only get one minutes worth of light. Have you seen these plants? Bloody cheapskates. We have to pay a fee for this area!'

'I like the apartment.'

'Please tell me she took you in her room?' Lucy wiggled her firm bottom in the brown tub chair.

'No, I just needed some advice and she didn't want to talk anywhere else, so we sat in your lounge.'

Lucy fanned her face and blew up her fringe. 'She can't control herself that's why! Look, Kat just needs a bit of gentle persuading. She says you're the smartest student she's ever taught. It's plain as night is day that you're beautiful and I know Kat, and I know you, and you two belong together.'

Freya was wondering if they had met on another occasion, one that she had since forgotten. 'To be honest I don't think she's going to go there.'

'Oh My God! I've just realised that I've been rabbiting on and I've not once asked you if you actually like her! You are Freya Elton aren't you?'

'Yes.'

'Oh Phew, imagine that! Listen, I'm not one to pry or offer my opinions, but is it going to happen? Because if it isn't then I think you should just switch subjects, do Latin or something just as boring instead.'

She laughed. Lucy was as crazy as her dreadful Beyonce dancing. 'No, it's not going to happen. She won't let it happen and I respect that. She's an amazing teacher and I like her so much. I don't want to jeopardise her career. It does mean a lot though hearing what you've said.' She was however not sure how much of it she actually believed.

'Bloody hell, you are a match made in heaven! Fine, both of you play the martyr but remember that old saying - opportunity is a bird that never perches.' She slammed the light.

Freya had been moving her thumb, drawing patterns in the brown brushed fabric. 'Okay thanks, I will.'

'Oh come here loves young dream.' Lucy lifted her out of the seat and squashed her with a full bodied hug. 'It's been lovely talking to you again. Please come and visit us soon, or just visit me, I think you're great!'

Freya laughed. 'Wish me luck.'

'Why?'

'I'm about to go and tell my parents.'

'About you and Kat?!'

'No, about me.'

'Oh you'll be fine. Live and let live as they say.'

'Bye Lucy.' The cold air felt good. What a whirlwind of a woman!

Jess finally plucked up the courage to crawl quietly out of her dark room. She had hoped they would be snogging in the hallway, but as she gently padded on all fours towards the dimly lit lounge she realised Kat was lying on the sofa alone. She was about to pull herself up when the apartment door slammed open and Lucy came racing in shrieking with excitement. She clattered over a four legged Jess and dived hands first across the polished wooden floor, finally coming to a halt against the hot chrome radiator. Jess looked like a dead ant on her back with arms and legs up in the air. Kat sat up. She was glowing. Both could see it and both knew why. Jess had caught the gist of proceedings and Lucy knew all she needed to know - Freya was hot and Kat needed to claim her. They ordered the pizza, much to Jess's delight, and debriefed until every single word, look, gesture and feeling had been analysed and evaluated; but Kat remained adamant. It was not allowed to happen.

CHAPTER TWENTY ONE

Freya did not want to go in. Her confidence and enthusiasm had slowly ebbed the closer she had got to home; the home where her mother and father would be sat reading, patiently pretending not to await her arrival. The floral curtains had already twitched. She gently turned off the ignition, plunging the car into a silent darkness. She shuddered and stayed belted, looking at the house; exactly like her parents - normal. Nothing quaint and quirky like Bea's charming extended cottage, or trendy and modern like Kat's stylish apartment, or even snug and personal like Jodi's one room flat. Just normal. Tar flecked orange bricks, four white *pvc* windows, one red door and seasonal pot plants. Exactly the same as the six other houses curving around the neat cul-de-sac. The floral curtains twitched again. Freya felt a cold sweat course over her body. She could not move. She knew it was coming. She knew she was going to say it. She stayed seated. The red front door opened and Patrick Elton's head peeped out. He stuck his thumb in the air. '*Okay?*' he mouthed, smiling at his daughter.

Freya's heart was racing and her hands were shaking. She fumbled for the clasp at the side of her chair and the swish of the seatbelt made her jump. Her dad hopped across the damp block paving in dry slippers and gently opened her door. 'Come on, it's cold out here. Your mum has put the kettle on.'

Freya looked up and stared. He was always so pleased to see her, always so proud. She started to well up as she made the five metre journey from the car to the house. It was the longest and most excruciating distance she had ever walked. They entered the warm lounge and she felt numb. It would have been so easy to dive on the cream sofa and relax in the familiar comfort of her home, just ignoring her issues and following routine. It wasn't a perfect home, but it was a home where she felt safe and loved. A home where she belonged. It had its own distinctive smell which usually filled her with warmth as she stepped through the door, but this time she had failed to notice it. The lounge, with its swirly gold decor, had hardly changed in eighteen years and the sight of her father sat in *his place* on the cream corduroy sofa filled her with pain.

'Come and sit down Frey.' He patted her seat. 'How was your confidence day?' He was always so interested and always involved.

She walked into the adjoining dining room and reached for the padded leather computer chair, twisted it round and pushed it into the lounge.

Her dad shuffled to the edge of his seat. 'Are you okay?' He stood up and looked at his beautiful daughter now sitting seriously on the high backed chair, she was tapping and twisting her phone on her knee and not giving him eye contact.

Freya could hardly breathe and wondered if she would be able to speak. He was coming over. 'Please just sit down Dad.'

'Sue, hurry up.' He tried to throw his voice around the corner into the old fashioned MFI kitchen. 'Sue, something's happening.' He raised his voice. Was this it he thought? The moment he had been working to avoid ever since he held his beautiful baby daughter in his arms all those years ago. He could not contain himself. 'You're pregnant.'

'Don't be silly, of course I'm not. Will you please just sit down?'

'Oh phew.' He laughed nervously. 'Sorry Freya, but you know me, I'm a worrier!'

She sat in the black upright swivel chair and placed two feet on the floor, putting her phone in her pocket and holding her hands tightly between her legs. She waited.

Sue Elton came bustling into the lounge with the drinks. Normal routine.

Freya shivered inside.

'Here we go. Do you want yours now or shall I leave it on the tray?' Sue Elton always spoke as if she was addressing a five year old child, no matter her audience.

Freya ignored the question.

'Okay, I'll just pop it here.' She saw the look of nerves in her husband's eyes, stopped flapping and sat down. They perched together at the edge of their corduroy cushions, looked at their pale daughter, and waited.

Freya could hear the wooden cuckoo clock ticking gently as she studied her parents' Christmas slippers. It was the same gift requested every year and they managed to find genuine excitement in the new colour, style or material. She bit the inside of her lip and looked up. They were sat open eyed, eyebrows raised, urging her to talk.

'Freya?'

She looked at the three cups of tea, all steaming, all in their favourite personal mugs. Tonight it was a box of *Viennese Whirls* that had been added to the worn flowered tray. She held her breath, she could stop it now. She could make something up.

'Is everything okay?'

She tried to take a deep breath but only managed a short shallow one. 'No,' she whispered. It had started. There was no going back now.

Patrick sat bolt upright. 'What is it?' He noticed the slow tear creeping down her cheek and spoke softly. 'You know you can talk to us about anything.'

Her eyes were sharp. 'Can I?'

'Of course you can.' Her dad pushed himself from the sofa and knelt at her feet. He gently lifted his hand to hers. 'What is it, Frey?'

She shook him away, angry at her tears. 'Don't.'

He looked up at her angelic face and whispered, 'Have you had an abortion?'

'Of course not!' she snapped, wondering how her dad could have possibly said that so calmly.

'Well Sue, she's not pregnant either so we're okay there!' He tried to joke but no one else was laughing. He lightly tapped her knee. 'Shall I try and guess?'

Freya pushed herself backwards on the four small wheels, away from his kindness, and away from his love, physically preparing herself for the emotional chasm she was about to create. 'No, don't be silly Dad.' A tear slid down her pale cheek and she wiped it away. It had all be so clear and matter of fact. It was going to be apologetic but explainable. What she had not expected were her tears.

Patrick rubbed his thinning brown hair and tried to make sense of the situation. 'Are you in trouble?'

Sue Elton had still not spoken.

'No.'

He gave Freya her space and rejoined Sue on the family sofa. Both sat motionless, just waiting.

She breathed in deeply and held her breath. The seconds seemed to crawl and she closed her eyes. 'I just need to tell you-' her green eyes flashed open, more piercing than ever. She looked directly at them. 'I need to tell you that I'm...' she swallowed, '...gay.' She did not want to see their reaction and bent her head to stare at the black rhino skin material peeping through her legs. There was silence. She could not look up.

Still silence.

Freya breathed deeply and lifted her head to the brown flecked carpet, tapping her teeth between closed lips.

Silence.

She wiped away a tear. 'Please someone say something.'

What could they say? They were both cursing themselves. This was the one thing they had not accounted for. Scenarios had been discussed and silent strategies had been in place, most of which had been incredibly successful. How do we stop Freya smoking? Meddling with drugs? Wearing too much make up? Getting in with the wrong crowd? Having sex? Getting pregnant? How do we ensure she does well at school? Wants to learn? Goes to university? Settles close to home? But not this! The thought of needing a strategy to stop her from becoming a lesbian was just incomprehensible. Look at her. She was beautiful. Why would it even cross their minds? If only it had; maybe then they could have avoided this ridiculous scenario.

'Oh don't be so silly Freya. Of course you're not.' Her Mother spoke with scorn and reached for her mug of tea.

Patrick felt a deep pain for the daughter he thought he knew. 'Sue, don't.'

'What Patrick?'

He turned to his glaring wife and spoke quietly. 'If we would have discussed this, then I'm sure we would have decided to let Freya feel like she can experiment with her feelings,' he lowered his voice even further, 'and then we would have nudged her in the right direction.'

'That's what I'm doing.' Sue Elton looked up and stared at her daughter. 'You, young lady, are not gay.' The words were cross.

Freya stared at the pair of them sitting awkwardly on the edge of the cream sofa. They looked like they had just had a massive row. The tension between them was obvious, both blaming the other for missing *sexuality* off the '*to watch for*' list. 'I'm sorry Mum but I am.'

Sue slammed her mug back on the floral tray and tea splashed onto the glass coffee table. 'Freya you are not.' She shifted her body even further forward on the cream cushion so her daughter could feel her full force. 'I don't know what on earth has gone on. Some ridiculous experimentation ... encouraged by Jodi no doubt.' She turned to her husband. 'We should have watched that. Why did you not watch that?' She was furious with him, but turned calmly towards the black chair. 'Freya, *you* are not gay.' She spoke with her hands. 'You are my daughter and I know you and you, my darling, are not gay.' She nodded in confirmation and reached for her mug, now dripping wet.

Freya's transition was one she remembered from her early teenage years. The belittling would begin and her anger would build. She had gradually learnt to control it and actually pity her mother for her righteous piety, but now it was back. The only way to express herself was to lash out. 'I'm gay mother!' she shouted.

'No you're not!'

'Sue.' Patrick had spent many an afternoon playing referee, then eventual peacemaker, and could see the signs a mile off. This would blow up and Freya would act out in the worst possible way just to spite them. What would be the worst possible way now? He panicked, exams were round the corner. 'Let her explain Sue. Don't talk. Just listen.'

Freya was shaking. How dare she? 'I'm going to stay calm, but I am only going to say this once. I do not have to explain anything. All I'm doing is letting you know that I am gay.'

'Letting us know?!'

Patrick scowled. 'Sue, stop it.'

Freya was breathing deeply and trying her best to contain it. 'Yes. Letting you know. I am your daughter and your daughter is gay.'

Her mother shook her head and looked down her nose. 'Listen to yourself! Who on earth do you think you are?'

'Right that's it!' screamed Freya, standing up and shouting at the pair of them, 'Just get lost!' It was all she could think of. She grabbed her keys from the wooden dish in the hall and ran out of the house, slamming the red front door as she went. Her dad just managed to bang the back window of the pale blue *Clio* as it swerved into the road. Freya parked up two streets away, hidden behind a large white van. She was angry, but she was not stupid. She needed to calm down. She laughed with nervous adrenaline - *that went well,* but her smile quickly turned at the corners and her hot tears turned to pounding sobs. She leaned her head against the headrest and looked at the fuzzy grey ceiling, feeling lost and alone, quickly turning to lock her doors - it was almost ten. Freya turned on the music and thought of Kat. Slowly but surely each deep breath seemed to deliver a surprising sense of calm. She remembered Kat's inspiring wisdom and careful guidance and felt a quiet sense of relief; then a feeling of actual achievement. She had done it. It was out there. Kat had been right. The thought of other people now knowing seemed irrelevant. She was in control and they would have to like it or lump it. Freya pulled her warm phone out of her tight pocket. *They know x* she text.

Kat had replied quickly, reassured that Freya was indeed the person she had judged her to be. *Proud of you. K*

Freya knew her temperamental behaviour had improved a lot over the past few years but she still had it in her - the desire to make them pay, to teach them a lesson. Yes her dad had not been too bad, but he could have defended her, he could have hugged her, he could have told her mum to just shut the fuck up.

Have just come out to parents. Didn't go well. Any chance I can stay the night? P.S Sorry x

Bea reached across to her oak bedside table and felt for her phone.

Please do x

****

'Oh darling, come in.' Cal and Silva Belshaw wrapped their silky arms around Freya. 'Family cuddle.' They squeezed hard and the cool material of their expensive Chinese print dressing gowns felt calming. Freya peeped through their locked shoulders; strange but nice she mused.

'Well done Freya,' said Cal.

Silvia nodded in unison and Freya could not help but stare at her white hair looking as magnificent as ever.

'We are so incredibly proud of you, now go and make our daughter happy.' They sang together and stretched out their hands signalling to the curved oak stairs.

Intense, thought Freya, and definitely rehearsed.

'Oh and by the way,' Cal winked, 'we have decided to stay in the granny flat tonight ... give you girls some space.'

The distance between their bedroom and Bea's was further than the distance from Freya's house to her neighbours, and the thought that they would need to stay outside in the converted stables next to the garage was worrying. What on earth did they think was going to happen? She felt embarrassed. 'There is no need, really.'

Silvia raised an eyebrow. 'You haven't seen upstairs yet!' She took her husband's hand and they skipped off together with their arms around each other's waists.

Freya watched as Cal pinched Silvia's bottom, and smiled at her subsequent playful squeal. The noise of their childish giggles disappeared as soon as the huge front door was closed. She heard the lounge fire crackle as she crept slowly up the ancient oak staircase. The imperfect floorboards creaked as she passed down the long wide corridor with its gorgeous oak panelling separating room from room which looked more splendid than usual in the soft low lights. Freya reached the large wooden door at the end of the landing. She knocked gently on a dark swirling knot and waited. She paused and clicked the iron latch down with her thumb. The door creaked open and she saw inside.

Delicate pink and yellow rose petals matching Bea's bold flower print wallpaper had been scattered across the white quilted divan. The wrought iron light fittings were glowing softly with the candle shaped bulbs turned to the lowest settings, and Katie Melua was playing quietly in the background. Bea walked towards her. She looked heavenly. Her white tuxedo boyfriend shirt hung just below her bottom and her warm white socks made her the perfect image of a *La Senza* model. She slowly moved her long dark hair over her head and looked at Freya with deep, penetrating brown eyes.

Her inbuilt sexiness made Freya smile. 'I haven't got my pyjamas sorry.'

Bea maintained her stare. 'You look stunning. Where have you been?'

'Coming out to my parents. I thought I would dress up for the occasion.'

'Did it help?'

Bea's eyes pinned Freya to the spot. She was so intense, but so sexy. 'No.'

They stared in silence and Freya broke first. 'Look I'm so sorry.' She took Bea's hand and sat on the edge of the white bed. 'I have been a complete idiot, I just-'

'I don't care. You have told them and now you chose to come here.' She smiled. 'That's all that matters to me.'

'Thank you.' She did not want to explain so picked up a delicate pink petal and inhaled deeply. 'Is this for me?'

Bea raised her eyebrows in exactly the same manner as her mother had just done. 'No, it's for Miss Spicer.' She watched Freya's eyes dart at her sarcastic comment so softened her tone. 'Of course it's for you. You have my heart Freya and I want yours.'

'Oh Bea.' She drew her into a close cuddle and giggled nervously. 'Do you want to hear about Saint Sue and her wonderful reaction?'

Bea reached up to Freya's lips. 'I want you first.'

Freya had been thrown by the strange comment and tried to behave as Bea would have expected, but as she looked at her full lips and intense stare she realised she did not have to try very hard. Bea was so enticing and so arousing that she leaned forward and met the full lips with her own.

Bea pulled back suddenly. 'Can I ask you one thing?'

Freya tried to concentrate.

'Do you love me?'

She looked at the large white bed and picked up another pink petal, piercing it with her curving nails. 'You can't ask me that.'

'I just did.'

She flicked the damp petal away and took Bea's hands. 'I have just experienced one of the worst moments of my life. I just destroyed the pride my parents had in me and I have finally committed to how I want to live my life.' She bent her head and met the brown eyes. 'I did that for you.'

'Really?' Bea stared intently.

She glanced at the squashed petal on the deep pile carpet. 'Yes.'

'Are you sure there is no one else?'

'No of course not, now come here.' She pushed Bea onto her back and straddled her hips, kissing her hard and silencing her questioning tongue.

The music stopped and Bea rolled onto her side to switch albums. With one click it was done and she rolled back towards Freya, eager to resume their highly charged connection, but Freya was now on her back studying the old black beams that ran across the low ceiling. 'How old is this house?'

'This bit is about four hundred years, maybe more. Why?'

'Do you know the history of it?' She was genuinely interested.

'No. Now come here.' She tugged at her waist and Freya's shirt fell loose from her tight jeans. Bea slowly eased her fingers into the gap and touched the warm, soft skin.

Freya quivered, her sides were usually so ticklish but this she could bear.

'Do you want to go and get ready for bed?' She signalled to the wicker chair where the new toothbrush, soft pink towel and black silk pyjamas were neatly folded.

'Am I staying in here?' She suddenly felt anxious.

'Only stay if it's me you want.' Bea rolled onto her side and waited. After what seemed like an age she felt the bed creak and listened to the sound of slow footsteps heading across the room. She peeped back over her shoulder to see Freya closing the bathroom door. She waited until the lock clicked shut and then listened once again. The buzz was so quiet that she nearly missed it. Bea crept quickly off the bed towards the bag. It was Freya's favourite multi pocket satchel, the one she flung across her body and wore with effortless style. *Which is the bloody pocket?* Bea squeezed the brown leather and its contents, coughing as she unzipped the small pocket at the top. Seven missed calls, two new voice messages all from her parents, and one text.

She clicked on the text, *Did it go well? Call if you want to talk. I really enjoyed tonight. K*

Bea pressed the delete button and scanned Freya's inbox. She could hear the shower running. She quickly clicked on her outbox and was about to return the phone when she saw the message folder named *Kat*.

Freya wiped the steamed mirror and looked at herself. *What are you doing?* She ignored her question and studied the vast array of creams and lotions on the black marble surface. She reached for the attractive container, *Sensai Premier. The Cream*, scooped a large dollop into her hands and rubbed generously onto her naked body. She used Bea's cotton fresh deodorant and cleaned her teeth with the new yellow toothbrush. She looked at herself in the mirror. *What are you doing?* She pulled a face back, arched her eyebrows and raised her shoulders. She stepped into the black silk shorts and pulled the short sleeved buttoned shirt over her head. Bea was not Kat, but Kat was not here, and here was too hard to stop.

'I think I heard your phone buzzing,' said Bea as Freya crept out of the steamy bathroom.

'Thanks. I really should let them know I'm okay. Give me a minute.' She reached for her satchel and sat on the end of the bed. Bea was under the covers. Seven missed calls and two new voice messages. She did not want to listen to them.

Sorry I have disappointed you. I can't help what I am. Staying at Bea's x

She switched her phone off. 'Room for a little one?' Freya smiled and her green eyes glistened.

Bea threw back the white covers and Freya crawled slowly up the bed, licking her lips and trying to look sexy. Her left wrist gave way and she fell face first into the duvet. 'Ha! Look at me the pro!' came the muffled giggle.

Bea smiled softly. 'Come here.' She pulled her under her warm arm and kissed her forehead gently. 'I'm going to win,' she whispered.

'Win what?' she questioned, lifting her head to Bea's.

'Your heart.' She rolled onto Freya's toned body and pinned her hands above her head, staring intently. 'I want you.' She kissed with a passion and a heat that stopped Freya from properly registering her next intermittent words. 'And ... I always ... get ... what I ... want.'

****

Mr and Mrs Elton sat talking, for once, in bed. They did not want to draw attention to their private family issue by calling friends and relatives, and the idea of following Freya in the Volvo just induced visions of a high speed chase and horrific accident, a scenario slightly worse than the one they were currently discussing. So now with the arrival of the text they could relax slightly and really get stuck into solving the issue. Both blamed the other for failing to spot the danger of Freya's close connection with her homosexual cousin, clearly Patrick's fault for having a sister who produced a lesbian child. Both agreed that it was a combination of A-Level stress, lack of recent attention from boys and simple desire to act out - those days obviously not yet behind them. Freya was not really one to follow the fashion but after a quick search of *"lesbian"* on the internet they both realised that girls kissing girls seemed to be all the rage - maybe Freya's attempt to get in with the popular crowd? The list of feasible reasons for her ridiculous statement grew and they took comfort that none fingered them as responsible. So the word *phase* was latched upon and they sat with pen and paper, brains in gear. A plan to be formulated.

'What is the priority?' Sue smoothed her long white nightgown.

'A-Level's,' said Patrick without hesitation.

'Agreed.' A-Levels was written on the pad and underlined three times. She put the pad down and tapped the biro. 'Did you ever imagine we would be sitting here having this conversation?' She did not give time for a reply. 'I mean Freya? Our Freya? She's been a handful at times but this! It just beggars belief.' She shook her head. 'Where did we go wrong?'

Patrick looked at his wife in her high necked frilly shroud, he loved her but she could be so cold at times; this was the most pillow talk they had experienced in years. 'What if she is?'

The reply was sharp and scolding, 'Don't you dare,' she scowled. 'Don't you dare entertain this idea.'

'But...'

'Don't you think we would have known if she was?'

Patrick had fast learnt that an easy life was a quiet life and this involved him keeping quiet for the most part. 'Sorry.' He took her frosty hand. 'Okay, plan of action. We ignore it.'

Sue was frowning.

'We ignore it, we don't rile her, we don't mention it, we just act like normal.'

'Until?' She released his grip.

'Until she has finished her last exam, then we sit down and talk properly.' He smiled hoping his reasoning had won her over.

'I think you mean we tell her properly. We tell her how ridiculous this whole thing is. My only daughter is not gay. My only daughter will get married and my only daughter will have children.'

The thought of playing devil's advocate crossed his mind. 'Fine,' he chose against it.

'But if she thinks she is bringing a tattooed, short haired, leather clad bulldog into our house then she is sorely mistaken.'

'We ignore it.' He leaned over and tapped her pad. 'For now.'

CHAPTER TWENTY TWO

Kat could not wait to see Freya and find out how the news had been digested, and if Freya's lack of reply to the text message was anything to go by then it was probably a positive reaction with the whole family sitting round discussing the future et cetera. As Kat entered the quiet B Block corridor, a smile of remembrance washed across her face, the vision of Freya stood up declaring her lesbianism was one she would find hard to forget. She realised they could easily have been mistaken for lifelong friends the way the conversation had flowed and the giggles had followed. She felt good. Work was good, home was good and the future was looking promisingly bright. The same might be said of Hannah Phag she thought, passing the quiet classroom. Heads were down and pens were scribbling. Miss Phag had even started to alternate her green felt skirt with a grey trouser suit, admittedly the material was flannel but it was a change and so was her new highlighted hairstyle - slightly bowl-esque but a style all the same. Kat looked up and saw them. Bea and Freya were strolling down the pale blue corridor towards her. They looked great, both with their long brown hair bouncing away and their smiles of conversation glowing on their attractive faces. Bea noticed her first. The look was one that Kat could not quite place, was it hostility or possibly pride? Bea was a hard person to judge and admittedly Kat had got her wrong in the past, but now as Bea grabbed Freya's hand and smiled falsely she reassessed her judgement.

Freya felt the heat of Bea's hand and panicked. She looked at her intense brown eyes, fierce with pride, and decided to go with it. Freya breathed in, lifted her head high and looked straight ahead. Kat was there. Their eyes met and she felt a pain so wounding that she tried to flick Bea away, but her clasp was too tight. Freya felt sick. Kat held her gaze and smiled gently as they passed without a word.

Kat was stung. Whether it was the sight of them together or the look of apology in Freya's eyes that evoked her hurt she did not know. What she did know was that she had been a fool - again. To make matters worse a smug Diane Pity was clipping her way up the corridor. Today it was a skin tight black and white stripy dress with pink heels and a pink arm bracelet, where on earth did she think she was going, thought Kat?

Diane stopped in front of her and stood on tip toes to peer over her shoulder. 'At least she has the age right now.'

'Pardon?' sighed Kat.

Diane nodded her head, 'Freya Elton. I said at least she has the age right now. Shame about the sex.'

Kat realised she was worth nothing and stepped to the side in an attempt to walk forward.

'Cat got your tongue?' sneered Diane.

She started to walk. *Breathe. Breathe.*

Freya pushed open the metal B Block doors and stepped out onto the icy concrete. She was fuming. Bea must have seen Kat and taken her hand deliberately, marking her territory or possibly claiming her trophy. Freya tried to release the ever tightening grip but Bea quickened their pace. 'You're hurting me,' she said, finally breaking free.

'Yes well you're hurting me too.' Bea stopped walking and glared at Freya, her dark brown eyes were popping out like daggers. 'It's all or nothing.' She took a sharp breath and tried to compose herself. 'Let's just face this head on. Let's just get it out of the way.' She took another deep breath and reached for Freya's waist, drawing her close and softening her voice. 'Everyone could know by the end of the day and we will be old news by the end of the week.'

Freya was annoyed and confused, but Bea was so powerful and intoxicating and the experience of the previous night had been so completely incredible that she struggled to reason. 'I just don't want to rub it in anyone's face, that's all.'

'Who?' Bea let go of her hold. 'Look you either want this or you don't.'

Freya looked at the highly passionate, highly charged temptress stood inches away and impulsively kissed her cheek. 'I like you a lot Bea.'

'Ai Ai!' jeered Chianne on her way to the cool down zone. What a pair of weirdo's, she thought, especially that tanned, pouty one; first paying her twenty pounds to film them kissing and then fifty pounds to delete it.

CHAPTER TWENTY THREE

Kat's term ended up uneventful and frustrating. She did not have the same issue as other staff, chasing students for unfinished coursework, or cramming in extra lessons in a vain attempt to finish the syllabus. Everything ran smoothly. Her examination classes met their deadlines and even Big Tom handed in a final essay of good length and quality. Kat had enjoyed their private tutoring sessions and was bowled over by a letter of thanks from his parents attached with a very expensive bottle of bubbly. They cared about their son and their son cared about Miss Spicer, enough to work harder for her than any other teacher in the school. His proposition of a date to celebrate their final session was met with a kind smile and polite decline. Diane Pity and Fiona Mews had cut back on their catty remarks and poisonous eyes - possibly because there was very little for them to see; Freya had been distant and very hard to get hold of. Bea would shunt her out of the lessons, take her off site at lunchtimes and hang around outside the classroom when Kat requested a private word. These rare personal moments were tension filled and hard to judge and Kat refused to trust her instinct that swore the feelings were still mutual. If they were, then why had Freya failed to respond to her occasional text message? Kat's routine would be the same, a romantic DVD surrounded by her loved up housemates, a bottle of wine and a burning desire to reach for her phone. She managed to stop herself for the most part, but a couple of messages had been sent. *How are you? Here if you need to talk? K.* She even once suggested a meeting, much to her embarrassment when no reply was received. *Hello have booked a court with Lucy at 10am on Sat. Do you fancy a knock about? K.* Kat tried to blame Freya's distance on the upcoming exams. She was a conscientious student and would most likely be spending these final few weeks revising and preparing for the highly important A-Level's. She cursed herself for even daring to send the messages. It was probably this hassling that explained Freya's reluctance to stay and chat at the end of her lessons and the reason she had not popped up for any private lunchtime gossips. Kat was confused. The very least she thought they had was a friendship.

Kat was being honest when Lucy and Jess had quizzed her on Freya's apparent relationship with Bea; it did not bother her. Kat would much rather Freya experimented with Bea and determined that women were indeed what she enjoyed. At least Freya would know for sure, at least she could test her feelings and grow in her own confidence. Somehow Kat had convinced herself that it would be a short lived affair, but now as Ben and Lucy sat in the apartment lounge discussing, once again, the school's popular lesbian power couple, she decided it was time to acknowledge Freya's choice and move on.

Jess saw the look of hurt in her eyes and realised that Kat was indeed bothered so tried again to sell her the idea of a speed dating night. 'Don't be ridiculous Katherine! You'll get so many matches!'

'If we go, what will you do?' Kat spoke with her back to the black sofa, shaking her head.

'I'll stand at the bar.' Jess was thrilled that the idea was finally being entertained.

'What and look over at me the single saddo moving from table to table in a vain attempt to get someone to like me.' She stuck out her bottom lip.

'As if Kat! Look at you,' shouted Lucy. 'I didn't like that Freya from the moment I saw her.' She was moving her head in a jerky fashion. 'Who does she think she is, flaunting herself with that Eva Mendes look-alike?'

Kat fidgeted on the wooden floor, still uncomfortable discussing her feelings openly in front of Ben - who, much to her dismay, had now replaced her and taken permanent residence next to Lucy of the left side of the sofa. 'She is a student in a relationship with another student.' She nodded in conclusion, 'That is the way it should be.'

'And it looks like a pretty red hot relationship if you ask me!' Ben fanned his face.

'We didn't,' scowled Lucy. 'We'll come as well won't we.' She nudged his wide chest.

Kat reddened and flung her head, once again, back onto the leather sofa. 'My embarrassment does not need an audience thank you all the same.'

'You'll get loads of ticks! ' Jess had taken her time to explain the process of three minute meetings followed by scores and possible matches displayed privately on the internet. Kat had nothing to lose, decided Jess. She had been so down recently that a boost to her confidence was definitely the best medicine. 'I'll sign you up now.' She reached for her pink laptop, anxious to commit. 'Here we go, *Gail's* on Thursday. The twenty to thirty category starts at eight.' She typed quickly. 'Done.'

Everybody giggled apart from Kat who closed her eyes and shook her head in utter disbelief.

Kat was still shaking her head as she caught Jess's eye from her lonely table complete with red tablecloth, red plastic rose and blank score sheet. She was a sitter and would hold the position as a variety of eligible women came and went. She sipped on her dry white wine, needing something stronger. Jess was looking over with pride and Kat felt like a child on her first day of school, mother in the window, checking she got a good seat. A net of pink balloons opened from the ceiling as the klaxon made a loud and penetrating sound. Kat watched as the waiting women descended on the tables, banging shiny balloons out of their field of vision. Kat wriggled on her hard blue chair and sat upright. She messed with her hands before deciding to hold them together on the table. She paused - too much like a teacher, and moved them to her knees. She watched as the large figure approached her table. The woman was as black as the night and her gender a mystery to most, a mystery not helped with the deep husky voice that followed. 'Betty Jean,' she thrust out a hand.

Kat stood to greet her and noticed the smell of petrol.

'Mechanic.'

'Hello. I'm Kat.' She smiled warmly, disguising her sudden feeling of complete horror at the frightful situation. What on earth had she been thinking? She would much rather be alone for the rest of her life than be degraded to this dreadfully desperate experience.

Silence.

Betty Jean nodded, 'Nice tits,' and continued her stare.

Kat moved her right arm to her opposite shoulder. 'You too.' She was shocked and could not think of anything else to say.

'Is that meant to be a joke?' Betty Jean looked down at her red checked shirt and flat chest.

Kat raised her shoulders nervously. They were only ten seconds in.

The dark face remained serious. 'I don't want no commitment or nothing. I just want sex.'

Kat coughed.

Betty Jean's face had not cracked. 'But I wear the strap on.'

Kat fumbled for her drink and took a large swig, clocking a worried looking Jess through her shaking wine glass. 'I'm not really into that sorry.' She thought about getting up to leave, but she couldn't, what would people think? That she was too good for them? That was the last thing she was.

'What, strap on's or sex?' Betty Jean looked like she was about to attack.

'The former?' she said apologetically.

'Suit yourself. Thought you looked a bit prudish when I walked over.'

'Sorry,' she offered.

'Oh well I've got fourteen more to go, so no shit on me sweetheart.'

They sat in silence for the remaining two minutes with Betty Jean spending the majority of time scratching her imaginary balls.

The klaxon sounded and Kat started to breathe again. Betty Jean thumped to the next table and left her sweaty seat for Marcy who looked like a Poodle and sounded like a Chiwawa, gushing that they would do nails, lunch and shop, but only after she had checked her schedule as her life was so full to bursting. Kat hardly spoke and her desire to call it a day was almost fulfilled when Jodi Elton plonked herself down in the blue plastic chair.

'Ello ello ello, Miss Spicer! What brings you here?' She grinned.

Kat wanted the ground to open up and swallow her whole. 'The same as you probably.' She was deeply embarrassed.

Jodi teased her blonde Mohican seductively and winked. 'What cruising for punany? I'm not being funny, but last month I got a ninety percent match rate and I've worked through fifty percent already.' She talked with a swagger that didn't match her tiny childlike stature.

'I don't think we've officially met.' It seemed so long ago when Jodi was making her excuses and leaving a bewildered Freya in the arms of her soon to be teacher.

'No, but your staff picture on the Coldfield website is hot and so are the braces you were wearing with those high waist trousers in the activities week photo's. I always check the monthly uploads.' She winked and puffed up her chest, 'You clearly recognised me though. I'm not one to forget am I?'

'I guess not,' said Kat, devastated at the situation and depressed with the incessant chat.

Jodi poked Kat's hands that were clasped together on the table, 'So come on Teach, what are you doing here?'

She returned her hands to her knees. 'Just trying to meet someone nice I guess.' She studied the lime green swirl on the drink stained carpet and wished desperately for the klaxon to sound.

'Well here she is.' Jodi patted her raised chest then paused. 'Actually scratch that. I don't tread on toes, so you and I are a no go. Sorry about that Teach.'

'Not to worry,' she said relieved. She smiled and lifted her hands to touch Jodi's arm noticing the string of tiny star tattoo's moving from her wrist to her forearm; they actually looked quite pretty. 'I'm sure you will get snapped up anyway.'

Jodi calmed down and spoke genuinely. 'You know you really are as nice as she described.'

'Am I?' She knew exactly who Jodi was talking about and so did the pain that suddenly returned to her heart.

Jodi nodded and her blonde Mohican flopped slightly to the right.

Kat could not help herself. 'Is she happy?'

'Do you really want to know?' she questioned, raising her eyebrows and lifting the red heart piercing to a new height.

Kat twisted her glass and sipped her wine slowly. 'Probably not.' She returned the drink to the table and gave her full attention. 'This is about you anyway, so tell me about yourself.'

This was too good an opportunity to miss, so Jodi rattled on nonstop about her prowess as the ultimate lady lover and her desire to one day bed her old French teacher, even though she was now going on fifty.

The noisy klaxon sounded and Kat reached gently for the starred wrist. 'Please don't mention this to Freya. I'm embarrassed enough as it is.'

As Jodi looked into the deep blue eyes and felt the soft fingers on her arm, she understood, for the first time, Freya's dilemma. 'If that's what you want.' Freya's actions suddenly made sense to her.

Kat nodded and reached for her bag, hoping to escape as the familiar table shuffle commenced, but as she went to stand a gentle hand brushed her tense shoulder. 'Please don't tell me you're leaving?'

Kat looked up and saw the pretty woman with rich auburn hair smiling kindly at her. 'No, sorry, I was just -' She sat back down and composed herself. 'Hi, I'm Kat.'

'Rachel. Okay shall I start?'

Kat smiled, she seemed normal, but then what was normal in this completely abnormal situation. She would never be able to look at the *Gail's* 'quiet room' in the same way again. It was usually so trendy and relaxing but now it was garish and cheap with its bunting of hearts stretched from bar to bar and its dreadful *Sunday Morning Love* songs CD on repeat. 'Please do, I'm not very good at all of this.'

'Oh I don't know if I believe that.' Rachel's eyes smiled and Kat began to relax. 'Okay so I'm Rachel. I train horses. I had my heartbroken by a girl a while ago and I'm just starting to get my life back on track.' She smiled and paused for a moment. 'Sorry if that was too much? I just want to meet someone nice,' her eyes scanned the room, 'someone normal.'

Kat laughed. 'Well scratch number one and number two off your list then.' She composed herself. 'Sorry. Okay I'm Kat. I'm a teacher and I also just want to meet someone nice.' They smiled shyly and the conversation flowed quickly and easily, both startled when the klaxon sounded, sure that the time had been shorter this round.

Kat chose to stay and endure the remaining ten candidates and added a tick to number eight and number eleven. The final klaxon sounded with three short bursts and the wedding march boomed out over the club's surround sound speakers. She watched as the women cheered and whooped, deciding that she must indeed be uptight, boring and lifeless. Defeated, she made her way back to Jess at the busy bar and tapped her score sheet with raised eyebrows. She would try and be enthusiastic for Jess's sake. 'Three ticks.'

'Is that all?' Jess grabbed the sheet.

'Hey! I'm proud of that. Three women that I might ... possibly .... maybe ... want to see again?' She had only taken part for Jess whose intentions had been kind, even though the outcome had been dreadful.

'But they have to tick you too and only then do you get a match.' She bit on her lip, worried. 'You might have sold yourself a bit short.'

'Thanks!' She linked her friend's chubby arm. 'Let's go. I'm a bit peckish anyway.'

Jess beamed. 'Yes good idea, we can get take out and then check the scores on my laptop. They promise a result within the hour.'

Kat looked over and saw Rachel pinned between Betty Jean's arms at the bar. 'Sounds great.'

Jess phoned through the order and Kat changed quickly into her soft blue fleecy pyjama bottoms. The apartment was always so warm and cosy that she never had to worry about wrapping up, so pulled on her thin strapped white vest top. She pushed her feet into her fluffy white pompom slippers and made her way into their lounge.

Jess looked over at Kat and considered putting the phone down, she would never look as good as her if she kept up this love affair with the Balti man. A rich voice sounded in her ear asking how she was and what she would like to order this fine evening. Jess snapped back into the real world and listed her lengthy request. She skipped over to the sofa and put her small hand across Kat's bare shoulder, squeezing her perfectly toned arm. 'Moment of truth, Katherine.'

Kat picked up the pink laptop and entered her code. She was nervous, not at the possibility of a date but at the possibility of no dates. Her deep seated fear of rejection once again being proved correct. She closed her eyes and prepared for the worst.

'Two matches!' said Jess trying to sound upbeat. What on earth was wrong with that third person she thought?

She looked at the bright screen and winced. 'Okay, so I got Rachel the horse trainer and Dana the vet.' She scanned the page, 'What happens now?'

'Well you click on their names and you'll get their mobile numbers,' Jess raised her shoulders, 'then you decide if you meet again.'

Kat closed the lid and put the laptop on the floor. 'Great, well thanks for that, it was a real eye opener.' Job done, Jess was happy. No way was she ever going through that again.

'Aren't you going to ring them?' She fished for the computer.

'No. That whole evening just wasn't my style and I can safely say I will never ever do it again.' She paused. 'But thanks.' She realised that Jess was slowly and surely returning to her bubbly old self with the whole dreadful experience of the start of the year seeming to bring her and Gary even closer than before and she did not want to knock her in anyway.

Jess pulled Kat's head onto her chest and held her tightly. 'At least we've got a curry coming,' she giggled.

Kat lay in bed completely at ease, what a wonderful Saturday morning lie in. She stretched and yawned widely. Two more weeks and the Sixth Form and Year Eleven would be on study leave. Relaxing in bed she wondered how Kathy from Cover would fill her eight empty lessons - probably with Year Eight PE, Miss Titley was always off with one sports induced injury or another. Kat reached down for her phone and turned it on. A rare weekend without plans. She contemplated calling Emma who had continued to send a monthly check in message requesting a meet up and spot of fun. She had so far politely declined, but the thought of company seemed appealing and for the first time Kat realised she must be desperately lonely to even entertain the idea. The phone's standard message tone bleeped.

Hello, we got a match. A bit spontaneous but do you fancy meeting up for coffee this afternoon? Costa on the high street at 2pm? Hope so. Rachel. (Number 4!)

Kat felt silly and pulled the warm covers over her face. She touched the phone and it lit up her dark den. *Ok. See you there. Kat. (Table 7!)*

She heard the heavy bag being dragged across the wooden floor and listened for the apartment door to close. Ben was off to play rugby and Lucy would be tucked up in bed, TV on, waiting for her Saturday morning's viewing to commence. Kat jumped out of bed and knocked on the white door.

'Hold on.'

Lucy was pulling a wrinkled black T-shirt on as Kat popped her head in. 'Room for a little one?' She jumped into the ruffled bed and tried to ignore the definite smell of sex.

'How did it go?' asked Lucy, wriggling under the covers and back into her pants.

Kat held out the phone.

'Get you Miss Speed Dater!'

'It was dreadful,' admitted Kat as her eyes were drawn to the jeering television. What on earth did Lucy like about this trash?

'Are you going?'

She paused unable to move her gaze, the DNA results suddenly of upmost importance. 'Um ... yes,' she spoke without looking.

Lucy snuggled into Kat's shoulder, 'Great, we can have a morning of telly and toast and you can tell me all about her.' She too looked at the noisy screen. 'I'll make the first round in the break. Then you can make a cuppa in the next one.'

'Sounds good to me,' said Kat snuggling down, her eyes transfixed by the unfolding drama.

Where had the time gone, thought Kat, as she walked briskly down the high street? The metal table and chairs sitting outside were damp and empty and Kat felt a lovely glow of warmth as she entered the rich smelling coffee shop. She spotted Rachel immediately in a maroon leather booth, smiled and raised a cupped hand to her mouth.

Rachel shook her head and signalled to the large mug already on the table. Kat ordered her normal white coffee using the requested language and stood carefully adding the milk. Her morning had been fantastic, messing around with Lucy, watching and talking absolute drivel, laughing at her latest raunchy escapade with Ben. But it wasn't until this moment as she slowly swirled the milk with her thin wooden stick that she realised she was actually quite nervous. She breathed in and turned around. Rachel got up from the booth and was standing to greet her. Her auburn hair was as lovely as she remembered and her soft brown eyes were still glowing with warmth.

Kat placed the coffee on the dark table and kissed her smooth cheek. 'Nice to see you again.'

'You too,' said Rachel with genuine meaning.

They sat, drank and chatted, mostly about the dating night's mix of contestants, quickly relaxing into one another's company. Kat hoped that the sexual spark missing from their first encounter might ignite, but it didn't. Rachel looked lovely, sounded lovely, and would probably make a lovely friend, but she had friends. What she craved was romance. Rachel returned to the booth with two more coffees and paused for a moment, looking serious. 'I don't want to be one of those people who talk about their ex, but I do want to mention something early on.'

Kat put her new steaming mug back down. 'Okay.' She waited.

Rachel slid gently into the private seat and her fine features suddenly looked anxious. 'I just can't stand games.' She looked at Kat directly. 'My ex really messed with my head and I would rather just hear the truth and get on with things. So if this date doesn't work out then it's honestly no problem, just let me know.'

She smiled. It was refreshing to hear such openness. Everyone had baggage of some sort or another and she would much rather hear it all in full before she fell for the person in question. 'I will,' she paused, nosy from her morning of prying chat shows, 'do you still see her?'

Rachel exhaled heavily and cast her eyes down in despair. 'I try my very best not to! She was so manipulative and so controlling, everything was mind games with her. I won't go into it, but it was not nice.' She nervously twisted her large steaming mug. 'I wasn't the only one though. I know it sounds awful, and you will probably not want a second date,' she looked up, 'but she was younger than me and still at school and it turns out that she was two timing me and messing up some other girl's life as well.'

Kat thought back to the televised real life dramas, the best bit the results or unexpected final guests. 'What happened?'

Rachel shook her head with the memory. 'It was horrible and I won't bore you with it, but the other girl ended up in hospital with a breakdown or something. She was apparently one of the brightest in the school and ended up missing all of her exams.'

'That's dreadful.' Kat sipped her coffee, enjoying the sensational gossip, realising how a morning with Jeremy Kyle could change you.

'I know. Things got messy, the school were aware of the situation and she was forced to leave.' She picked up her coffee and took a small sip, relieved with her own openness. 'I think she went somewhere else. I hear tit bits every now and again'

'Not Coldfield was it?' said Kat laughing, not expecting the next response.

Her eyes widened. 'Yes.'

The school had attracted lots of new Sixth Formers but this was too close for comfort. Kat suddenly felt sick. 'Please tell me her name was not Bea?'

Rachel nodded slowly. 'Do you know her?'

'I teach her.'

Kat raced home anxious and concerned. What should she do? What could she do? Exams were in less than a month and Freya had the world at her feet, any interference may prove disastrous. But in the same respect, no interference may prove even worse. She flapped with her leather shoulder bag and reached for her phone. 'Jess are you home?'

'Yes hun, why? You sound like you're running. Was she that bad?'

'No, no she was fine. She has baggage but she was fine.' Kat puffed as she spoke. 'Get the kettle on, I'll be back in ten. Major advice is needed!'

This sounded promising, thought Jess. Maybe Rachel had been wonderful and Kat, being the person she was, had a dilemma regarding her remaining unrequited feelings for Freya. If only it had been that simple, thought Jess, as the story unfolded. Lucy had gone to join in with Ben's raucous post match beer circle, she had become quite the regular and Ben's team mates envied him with a passion for bagging a fit bird that could actually drink. Gary was on a nine-five and so Jess and Kat had the apartment all to themselves. Kat explained in detail what information she had glistened, admitting that it was hard to dig deeper when Rachel realised she actually taught Bea. She seemed to panic about potential repercussions and stayed tight lipped regarding specific details. It was obvious that Bea still had a hold over her, but Kat had grasped the basic gist. Bea was manipulative and controlling and not to be trusted. When she heard herself retelling the story she realised that it all sounded so familiar, an ex with a grudge. Who didn't think their exes were a screw loose? Kat knew that she did. So as the conversation and advice flowed and Monday morning came, Kat realised she was in an impossible situation. Bea and Freya seemed happy enough working quietly during her penultimate revision lesson. There were no wide eyes or internal screams of help coming from the back corner table, so she carried on as normal but tried to catch Freya's eyes at the end of the lesson as she was heading quickly towards the door.

Bea saw the look, stopped and pulled Freya by the wrist back to the front desk. 'I just thought you'd like to know that we have both been accepted into Edinburgh University.'

Kat looked shocked, the last she had heard was that Freya was applying to Birmingham on the same three year teaching course that she had recently completed. 'Congratulations,' she managed, feeling hurt. She really was so far out of the loop now that it was embarrassing.

Freya remained silent and Bea shifted her weight from one hip to another. 'Oh and another thing, I passed my driving test on Saturday and if Freya's a good girl then I'll add her to my insurance.' She slapped Freya's bottom. 'Do you drive Miss Spicer? Only I often see you walking in the rain. Cars can be ever so expensive these days can't they?' She spoke with false concern.

'I like to walk.' Kat returned her cold stare. Enough was enough. 'I met an old friend of yours on Saturday actually.'

Bea instantly lost her strut and started to mess with the gold zip on her very expensive Gucci bag. 'Good for you,' she mumbled, pretending to be busy.

'Rachel I think she was called.'

Freya looked up from her motionless stance.

'No, I don't know anyone called Rachel. Come on, my car needs a Christening.' She grabbed Freya's hand and pulled her out of the room, ordering her to go ahead and unlock. Bea dashed back into the classroom and leaned over Kat's desk with her brown eyes piercing. 'You'll regret that *Kat*.'

Kat was lost for words and watched as Bea raced out of the classroom in a fury. She sat and waited for too long, debating what to do. Time was wasted. Time that could have altered the course of the next ten minutes.

Freya felt Bea link her arm and pull her close. She had learnt in situations like these that it was best not to ask. Bea was passionate and Freya had loved the passion at first, but had quickly learnt that it came with a definite unpredictability, a temperament of high sensitivity and an erraticism that was previously well hidden. Bea had a short fuse. Freya would let her explain in her own time, and anyway there was bound to be a logical explanation for her lie, just like there had been with the other discrepancies she thought she had noticed. They were good together, she remembered, as they paced arm in arm down the B Block corridor to the usual "Hi's" and "Hello's" from all and sundry. A popular power couple Bea had called them. Popularity was not important to Freya but it felt nice to be accepted and liked. The sharp fresh air of the car park returned her memory to the hurt caused by Kat. Her failure to enquire further about her family's reaction was painful enough but then to change her number without so much as a word was a real blow with each secret message being returned as undeliverable. It did not matter anyway as Kat had clearly moved on, spotted three times, or possibly four, by Bea in close contact with the mystery blonde. Freya knew she could not compete with someone of such glorious sounding beauty and her age as well, Bea guessed around thirty. It had all worked out for the best, nodded Freya, stooping to climb into Bea's sensational red sports car, still desperately trying to shake off the image of Kat's emotion filled eyes.

Kat raced out of her classroom, down the L shaped stairs and through the long B Block corridor. Her heeled shoes were clipping quickly as she picked up speed, desperate to catch the pair. The issue was not rescuing Freya, but reprimanding Bea. How dare she tower over her desk and point her perfectly manicured finger in her teachers face? Who on earth did she think she was? Kat flung open the double doors and saw Freya climbing into the red car, the outline of the L plates was still visible just above the black bumper. Freya did not hear her shout. She shut the door and was surprised when Bea accelerated towards the exit before she had a chance to reach for her seatbelt.

Bea looked in her rear view mirror and then stared ahead. *Come on. Come on.* Little Jason Sparrow was edging out of the junction in his tiny, old style *Mini*. He passed his test over a year ago, but the invisible distance between his seat and the steering wheel and the way his head just about popped over the bonnet, made him look like an incredibly nervous driver.

Kat was catching up. She walked briskly towards the school gates, dodging slow moving students on their way home. The Mini had gone and Bea's red car was waiting noisily at the junction. She was indicating right. Kat was metres away and could see from the sudden wave of movement at the bus stop that the red double decker was approaching. *Great.* She would have time.

Bea looked backwards then forwards. She had to go. The bus would be slowing. *Clutch, gear, accelerate, accelerate, come on, oh hand break -*

This will show them, thought the bus driver speeding up, aiming to pull in at the far end of the stop and allow someone other than that awful Miss Piggy to get on first. *What the -*

Kat reached for the back windscreen with a closed fist and almost lost her balance as the car jerked forwards into the road. Kat heard the piercing screech of huge double tires. She looked up and saw the bus. The noise of the impact tore through her body. The red double decker slammed the passenger side of the car with such force that Kat keeled over. She was crouched with knees bent, covering her mouth with both hands when she heard the screams. There was chaos at the bus stop. Students were running and screeching. Others were frozen in terror. The bus had finally stopped and the red car sat hissing, side on, in front of its dented bumper. Kat ran into the road and stood at the shattered window.

Freya did not feel the thud, but she did feel Kat's eyes calling her, begging her to stay awake. It was too late. Kat's beautiful face was the last thing she saw.

CHAPTER TWENTY FOUR

Kat sat in the empty waiting room watching Mr and Mrs Elton through the clear glass. She saw the tall dark haired doctor walk down the bright white corridor and open the door to the shiny room. The doctor closed the door and Kat watched as he drew his white clipboard into his chest. With a slight shake of his head, Mrs Elton fell to the floor. Silence.

'Kat.'

Kat felt the stroking hand first and her own hot tears second. Jess was once again crouched gently by her bed.

The familiar voice was soothing. 'It's okay. She's okay.'

Kat wiped her wet cheeks and tried to calm her irregular breathing. She sat up and rubbed her face as dark shapes and shadows came into focus.

'You were shouting again.'

She was embarrassed. This was the third time in the last month. 'I'm so sorry.'

'The same one?' Jess asked quietly.

'No, I was in the waiting room this time.' She took a deep breath. 'What's wrong with me?'

Jess had consulted her manual of dreams and was confident with her answer. 'You think you've lost her. Your subconscious is dealing with the realisation that you've lost something precious.' She took Kat's damp hand and squeezed it lovingly. 'But you've not lost her to that crash, you've lost her to Bea.'

Kat knew she was right, but wanted there to be another explanation. 'I think it's because I was there, in the hospital, I met her parents and I felt their terror.'

'But she was fine.'

'I know.' Kat knew her best friend was right, because at that awful moment of impact, all she wanted was Freya. Freya was all that mattered in her life.

Jess climbed into the warm bed and snuggled on her side, resting an elbow under her head. 'What were they like?' It was the middle of the night but she didn't care, Kat clearly needed some company.

Kat quivered as she remembered the way she had escorted an unconscious Freya in the ambulance to St Joseph's and met her parents as they came racing into the hospital reception full of panic. 'The dad was very quiet and the mum just went on and on at him about how she would change everything and just accept her daughter's lifestyle as long as she was okay,' Kat laughed, 'which she was, but then I saw Freya's mum with Bea and there is definitely no love lost between that pair.' She lay silently, wondering what to do. It could not go on like this. 'I'm going to tell her.'

Jess had been waiting for this moment for so long. 'Oh I'm so pleased.' She needed confirmation. 'When?'

'They sign off tomorrow...' Kat looked at her clock, '...today and it's their prom tonight-'

'Your prom, Miss Spicer! You have to go.'

Kat could not bear the thought of it. All teachers of Year Thirteen were expected to attend and share the magical evening with their protégés, but she already had her excuse planned out. 'I don't know, maybe. Anyway when the holidays start I'll try and contact her through the tennis club or something.'

Jess shook her head in disbelief. 'Can you not just talk to her?'

She could still not quite believe it herself. 'I know this sounds ridiculous, but she is never on her own. Bea is like a blood sucking limpet who watches her every move and things have got so much worse since their accident.' It was true and had been so incredibly frustrating for her, but she had managed to give Freya a private smile and word of good luck for the A2 history paper as she waited outside the exam hall for her name to be called; Harley Adams and Beatrice Belshaw had already gone in.

'Lucy's going.'

Kat smiled. 'I know, bless her. Poor Mr Puller is going to break a few hearts tonight.'

'So might you,' giggled Jess, winking in the dim light.

'That, I can tell you right now, is a guaranteed no.'

****

Kat was sitting at her allocated table in the main hall with six empty boxes in front of her. The Year Elevens and Sixth Formers were returning from their study leave, to sign off from school and supposedly return all borrowed books now that exams were over. She watched as Chianne Granger burst through the open fire exit doors wearing a pair of sunglasses that were slightly larger than her micro denim hot pants. The matching denim waistcoat and black fish net tights made Kat think of Madonna in the early eighties, a Madonna dressed as a very fat Miss Piggy. Her empty sequinned clutch bag was going to disappoint her subject teachers, but the knowledge that they would never have to see Chianne Granger again more than made up for their missing books. She was strolling over to Kat, presumably provocatively, with one leg sexily crossing in front of the other. She winked.

'Hello Chianne. How can I help you?' Janet Louza had had the pleasure of taking bottom set GCSE this year and Kat was ever so grateful to have avoided spending any more time with Chianne and her gang than she already had done.

Chianne lifted her tongue to her lip glossed top lip and waited. Okay that would have been long enough for Miss Spicer to absorb her beauty. 'You will be pleased to know that *moi* is taking history A-Level with you next year.' She pushed up her nonexistent chest and winked.

Kat coughed quietly and adjusted herself in the seat. 'So you're hoping for a C then?'

Chianne sucked her buck teeth. 'No problem Miss!' She returned to her purring, 'September 6th, I've got that date in my diary, see you there Spicer.' She tucked her sequinned clutch bag under her arm, Kat could no longer see it, and span around, shaking her booty as she disappeared into the *signing off* room.

Kat smiled privately and watched the excited buzz of the hall. The Year Eleven's were in their own clothes, thrilled to finally display their own style to their teachers, testing the image they would carry on into the Sixth Form. Others were just thrilled that they would never have to set foot inside Coldfield Comp ever again. The Sixth Formers were all wandering around with teary eyes, saying heartfelt thank-you's to their never to be forgotten teachers, thank-you's that would inevitably get more heartfelt and emotional as the day of the prom progressed. Kat heard the rustle of bags and turned around to see Bea and Freya weighed down with plastic carriers full of textbooks. 'Hi girls,' she said nicely, her eyes drawn to the faint scar still visible on the left hand side of Freya's head. She had been so lucky. The window had broken and cut various parts of her body, but all had healed well and she had gained consciousness quickly in the hospital. Forty eight hours later she was home - and back in Bea's arms, thought Kat, bringing herself back to the bustling room. 'Are these all for me?' A stack of books had been plonked on her desk.

Bea hit Kat with one of her dirtiest stares. 'Obviously.'

She just did not understand. What was Freya still doing with her?

Bea took control once again. 'Come on Freya, *she* was the last, so let's go and sign off and start proceedings.' She looked at Kat with thin eyes. 'We are having hands, feet, nails, hair and make-up all done for tonight and we need to fit it in before our pink limo arrives to take us in style.'

'Are you coming?' asked Freya, desperately trying to show her warmth, but Kat was too busy eyeballing Bea.

'Try and stop me.' She maintained her stare.

She turned to Bea. 'Could I have a word with Miss Spicer on her own please.' Freya sounded timid.

Bea span around and stared at her. 'Fine, but you know what will happen.' She marched away from the table towards the signing off room.

Freya was broken inside, but she had no choice. 'Sorry I need to go. Maybe catch up later?'

'Hope so,' whispered Kat, deciding enough was enough. It would have to be tonight. Freya had already gone.

Bea felt Freya's presence once again at her side. There was nothing in this world she could not have if she wanted it. Last on the list were those three little words, Freya had still not said it and it was really starting to anger her. She signed the sheet first and Freya followed suit, both receiving an odd hand shake from the Head, at least they thought it was the Head, they had only seen the woman from afar on a couple of occasions. Bea took Freya's hand and walked back through the hall in full view of Miss Spicer and out of the open fire doors into the glaring summer sunlight. If changing a digit of Kat's number and fabricating stories about her new love interest wasn't enough, then the threat of passing on damming information about her kiss with Freya, private tennis match and personal meeting in Kat's own home, seemed to have worked. Freya rarely breathed her name anymore. It took quite a bit of manipulation to extract the full story, but Bea had succeeded, as she did with all aspects of her life. If you want it, get it, she thought, as she pulled her black Prada sunglasses onto her head and marched Freya to their first appointment.

Diane Pity and Fiona Mews stood up from their seats and craned their necks as they watched Kirsty Spaulding cross the busy hall towards Kat's desk. What a fantastic day they thought - taken off timetable to just sit and collect books, prom tonight and watching the final downfall of the highly irritating Miss Spicer. Fiona trotted to Diane's desk and they stood shoulder to shoulder, revelling in the vision of Kirsty Spaulding directing Kat to her office. They realised that their dossier must have been read and digested and was now about to deliver its fatal blow. How would they have managed without the help of that gorgeous, tanned, but unfortunately gay, Sixth Former?

'So long Spicer,' sang Diane.

Fiona flared her nostrils. 'At least we won't have to see her ugly face tonight.'

Kirsty walked in silence, nodding at the odd student who passed her, absolutely no idea of names. She buzzed open her office door and the rich aroma of coffee was comforting, even though Kat knew this was not going to be a comfortable meeting. The way Diane and Fiona had stood from their empty tables and peered over with such personal pride made her worry.

The office door clicked closed and Kirsty flicked off her shoes, jumped around and grabbed Kat's arms. 'What are you waiting for?' she cheered.

'Pardon?'

'Oh don't start that again! She has just signed off. You're free. Go and claim her!'

Her heart started to quicken. 'Sorry?'

Kirsty lifted what look like a manual from her desk and thrust it into Kat's chest. 'Courtesy of Miss Mews and...' she clicked her fingers, 'the one that dresses like a hooker ... Pity. Can you believe it? Forty two pages! I mean neither of them write that much when planning or marking, but forty two pages - unbelievable.'

She opened the front cover of the blue file. *Grievance filed against Miss K. Spicer - Behaviour unbecoming of a staff member.* There were times and dates, details of supposed trysts, even a list of text messages she had sent. *Bea,* thought Kat. She was fuming, but also deeply embarrassed. 'I am so sorry.'

'Oh get over yourself!' Kirsty was pouring two Malt Whiskeys into large crystal tumblers. She tapped the buzzing screen on her desk. 'I told you before, I know exactly what goes on in this school and your behaviour has been exemplary.'

She needed to be honest. 'I kissed her.'

Kirsty had quickly separated the truth from the lies. 'Before your contract officially started,' she paused taking a huge swig of the expensive potent liquid, 'and anyway, you should have carried on! I would have turned a blind eye. Me and my Trevor were at it all over the place.' She closed her eyes. 'Mr Spaulding. PE. We did it on the trampoline, in the swimming pool, even in the staffroom once. I was only fifteen!'

Kat gulped her Whiskey.

'Now he *was* a good teacher.' She moaned in remembrance. 'Still is mind you, although his cavorting with Year Tens has stopped now.'

'Is that how old you were?' Kat was trying to keep her composure, in this once again incredible situation in this quite incredible Head's Office.

'That's when we first progressed from kissing, if you know what I mean.' She ribbed Kat with her elbow with no response. 'Oh lighten up Miss Spicer.'

She lifted the blue file. 'What does this mean?'

'It is all irrelevant drivel. It means nothing.' Kirsty waited for the smile but it did not arrive. 'It means you go and win her back from that dreadful Beatrice Belshaw. Her parents are an absolute nightmare. I only took her on a managed move because they offered to pay for a new statue in the entrance hall. I was thinking of getting an Angel.'

Kat remained quiet.

Kirsty put down her whiskey and stood still. 'Are you telling me this is all lies?' She tapped the dossier that she was still holding. 'Are you telling me there are no feelings there?'

Kat shrugged her shoulders slightly.

'Well if I find out you've not told the fabulous Freya Elton, then I'll be having a quiet little word in her ear, just like I will with those two awful hussies out there.' Kirsty was slowly but surely creating her own private dossier on the pair of them, which she hoped would eventually put an end to their miserable presence at her fast improving school.

'Please don't,' said Kat feeling quite emotional.

'Come here big girl,' whispered Kirsty, reaching up to hug her tightly. 'You've had a fantastic year and I'm so excited about results day. Your predicted scores could nudge us ahead of John Taylor's for the first time in thirty years.'

'I hope so.'

'See you tonight.' It was an order, and Kirsty watched as the remarkable Miss Spicer left her office, probably in a greater turmoil than before. That one just needs to loosen up a little, she thought, as she threw a tiny mint into her mouth and squeezed her black shoes back on, ready, once again, to meet her people.

CHAPTER TWENTY FIVE

Kat and Lucy perched against the tall red breakfast stools, neither wanting to crease their beautiful dresses. Both aware that a dainty rise from the lounge sofa was a near impossibility. Ben, with his smart black tuxedo, did not have that same issue and admired them from afar. Lucy looked lovely in her new teal, shimmering taffeta, knee length gown. Her shoulders were bare and Ben smiled at the strength clearly visible in her arms, softened slightly by the delicate rose corsage replicating itself like a waterfall down the side of the dress. Kat however, looked sensational. She was a mixture of Grecian charm and evening elegance as the long black chiffon layers of her stunning evening gown split, unveiling a glossy satin fabric underneath. Ben's eyes flicked up to the band of glistening beads wrapped under her chest, accentuating her already incredible figure. Her hair was pulled up in a complex knot fastened with small white flowers and her features looked even more striking than usual. Ben realised he was staring and reached across the black sofa for his phone. He began to dial the number for Coldfield Cabs, twenty past seven should do it; the venue was pretty close. As he reached the final few digits the apartment door crashed open and Jess and Gary galloped in both clutching a small black photograph. Ben put the phone down.

'It looks like I'm destined to marry pregnant,' shouted Jess, a tear of joy in her eye.

Gary was visibly choked. 'How do people fancy a Christmas wedding?'

Jess handed her twelve week scan photos to Kat and Lucy and cried with delight. They had secretly planned to try again, but had no idea it would actually happen so quickly. Ben dashed to the fridge and grabbed the expensive bottle of Moet. No one else had noticed their nervous energy or the delicate way Gary would place his hand on Jess's stomach during their weekly film nights. He had, and he was prepared, just in case. 'Cheers guys. I had a feeling.'

Lucy banged his strong chest with her teal clutch bag. 'You did not!'

He nodded, 'I did.'

'Oh look at my man,' she cooed as Ben passed around the glasses, 'isn't he simply the best.'

Glasses chinked together and a mixture of happiness and pride washed over Kat. Despite her initial false protesting, Jess was desperate to become a mother and a wife and had been since the day she met Gary all of those years ago.

Their impromptu celebration led Kat, Lucy and Ben to miss the start of the Coldfield Prom and avoid the much deliberated style of student arrival. Word in the venue was that Bea and Freya's pink Limo had been somewhat overshadowed by the huge Hummer hired by the PE gang. Big Tom and Little Jason had also made a memorable entrance whizzing down the steep drive of *Tuckrup Hall* on green children's pedal tractors. General consensus in the buzzing grand hall was that top spot went to Poppy Jones who landed on the acre in front of the country house in a small two-seater helicopter. Rumours were rife that her family had won a small fortune on the premium bonds. Kat listened to the excited buzz as she studied the huge seating plan. She looked around at the girls in their beautiful ball gowns and boys in their stylish suits and checked the plan again.

'Sorry. We did not think you would be here,' sneered Diane, looking horrific in an orange and yellow striped micro dress with orange nails, eye shadow and lipstick to compliment, '...and I have no idea who you are?' She looked Lucy up and down and Lucy openly cringed at the way Diane's yellow crimped hair clashed hideously with her garish orange colour scheme.

Ben reached for Lucy's waist with two hands and gently kissed her on the lips. 'This is Lucy Lovett and she is my very delicious, very delightful girlfriend.'

She reddened. An audience had started to form.

He kissed her again. 'In fact, she is the love of my life.'

Lucy looked into his wonderfully caring eyes, oblivious to the cheers of 'Go Sir!' and 'Get in there!' and knew she could die happy. What was that saying? Oh well it doesn't matter now, she thought, kissing him back and finally noticing the whistles.

Diane was fuming. She might have lost that battle for now, but there was one she was adamant she had to win. She spun on her heels and headed to the stage. Where was that microphone?

Kat scanned the large dining room, complete with huge shiny banners and floating helium balloons, the buzz was electric and every proudly dressed person knew the carefully prepared and greatly anticipated evening would be remembered for the rest of their lives. Kirsty Spaulding had given Kat the last bit of confidence she needed to finally do what she had dreamed about doing from the moment she set eyes on Freya at the back of her class all of those months ago. She searched the room once again, her eyes drawn to the huge pink and white balloon arch standing proudly on the stage. *Where was she?* It was now or never. She had been restraining her heart for too long. Soon Freya would understand.

Diane tapped the black microphone noisily and wiggled her bottom on the centre of the stage. 'Hello and welcome to Coldfield Prom two thousand and twelve!'

The crowd in the hall were not particularly responsive. No one liked Miss Pity and all were aware that she had done little to help them in her supposed role of prom co-ordinator.

'Can I get a *yeah*!?'

One quiet *yeah* came back.

She stopped wiggling and stood up straight. 'Sorry I forgot you are all grown adults now!' She laughed on her own. She had been practicing her fairground voice, aiming to sound like one of those women from the waltzers shouting, "*Do you wanna go faster?!*" It was not working. 'Anyway, without further ado, let's start this momentous evening.' She clicked her fingers and Aerosmith's *I don't want to miss a thing* started to play. 'We have decided to announce this year's prom couple at the start of the evening so the lucky pair can bask in their glory all night.' She placed a hand on her hip and did another embarrassing wiggle. She reached sexily into her tight top for the warm brown envelope nestled snugly in her orange laced bra, this bit had been practiced and perfected and she was sure of the wolf whistles of delight to follow. There was silence and a couple of the girls looked away in disgust. Diane realised she was dying on her feet and decided to make it quick. 'Okay, ninety percent of you voted on the school intranet last week and the results are...' She clicked her fingers and the drum roll sounded.

People had started to pay attention to the dreadful Miss Pity as she clicked her fingers again and the drum roll increased in volume. They were actually getting quite excited. Diane clicked her fingers once more and it was deafening. She had requested two free periods from

Kathy from Cover in preparation for tonight's proceedings and was pleased the effects were finally raising anticipation. 'In third place ... Dave and Grace!' The waltzer voice had returned. There was polite clapping, no one really liked Dave and Grace, they had been together since Year Eight and reminded most people of their mums and dads. Diane was shimmying all parts of her body and jigging strangely on the spot lit stage. 'In second place .... Paul and Eve.' The cheering had begun as the runner up's raised their hands and gave a polite nod. Diane stared across the balloon filled hall and spotted Kat stood quietly by the door. 'That means in first place .... the wonderful .... the revolutionary ... the modern ... and perfectly suited Bea and Freya!' She clicked and Aerosmith was raised to full volume. It was the first time Kat had seen her. She looked incredible in a knee length ivory dress, with a black ribbon sash tied daintily round her waist. She glimpsed her black floral corsage as a swarm of people surrounded the pair and pink balloons engulfed the hall from the ceiling.

Bea grabbed Freya's hand and hauled her up onto the stage. Kat watched as she leaned Freya backwards, kissing her with passion. Diane Pity and Fiona Mews were attempting to place gold plastic crowns upon their heads without spoiling the crowd's sensational view. The room had exploded into cheers of congratulations and shouts of approval. Clearly well loved, realised Kat, as she reached for the door.

The warm air was comforting and she lifted her head to the dying evening sun, only one thing for it, she thought, as she reached for her phone. Kat made her way around the corner of the wonderful old brick building and found a small wooden bench where she sat and let the evening glow soothe her spirits as she waited patiently for the taxi. Lucy followed her out and desperately tried to change her mind, but she was adamant. It was time to go.

Kat spent the short journey staring out of the window, looking at nothing and thinking of everything. She tried to analyse her feelings and could not decide whether it was the hurt, or the loss, or the embarrassment, that made her want to disappear and start afresh, somewhere new. Somewhere where nobody knew her. But by the time she entered the empty apartment her personal sorrow had turned to annoyance. Annoyance at herself for feeling grief for something that had never really begun, annoyance that Diane's silly little games had clearly had their desired effect and annoyance that she had walked away, let Diane and Fiona win. Let Bea win.

Kat picked up the scribbled note on the kitchen table. *Staying at Gary's - invited the in-laws round!!!! P.S: This is my 6 months notice - it's been a blast!* It finished with a smiley face and a stick woman with a big baby bump. Kat held the note against her heart and felt like crying. Jess had been so completely devastated by her miscarriage but had quickly realised that a child was exactly what she and Gary wanted, they wanted it more than anything in the world. Lucy had made some comment about not needing what you've got until it's gone and Jess had for once agreed. She replaced the note and quietly made her way to her bedroom, carefully stepping out of her inappropriately expensive dress, and climbing into her soft blue pyjama bottoms. She untied her hair and pulled her favourite tight white vest top over her head, collapsing on the bed and sighing as she dimmed the bedroom lights and reached for the small silver remote. Relax and calm down, she thought, as she clicked it three times and Trisha Yearwood's *Second Chance* started to play. She lifted her hands to her face and felt like crying as she mouthed the words to her favourite song, *'Just close your eyes, reach for the moment before it slips by. Here is your second chance, take it and fly'.* She heard a noise and opened her eyes.

The apartment door clicked closed and hesitant footsteps tapped gently across the wooden lounge floor. There was a long pause and Kat listened again. Her bedroom door slowly creaked open. She climbed off the bed. This was real. This was happening. She heard the music, *'you trust what you feel, you take that first step,'* took the hand and shut the door, pulling Freya close, and kissing her with a wanton passion that was reciprocated by an incredible burning desire.

Lucy's keys dropped to the floor.

Freya pulled back and was about to speak but stopped at the look in Kat's eyes; she understood. They both understood. Freya thrust her lips against Kats and pushed her by the waist towards the edge of the bed. The lighting was romantic and the music was tender but their kisses were raw and intense.

Kat reached the mattress and pulled Freya down on top of her, enjoying the weight pressed against her own lusting body. She rolled her over and straddled her waist, feeling the netting of her skirt against her own bare toes. Kat looked into her sharp green eyes. 'You have no idea how much I want you.'

'Show me,' said Freya, pulling at her neck and dragging her in for another explosive embrace, months of pent up feeling finally bursting out with a force and a power that neither of them could control.

Kat was aching. This was incredible. Freya was incredible, rolling her over and pinning her arms, using her strength to overpower and dominate. Kat returned the energy and kissed her hard forcing them up into a seated position with legs wrapped tightly around each other's waists.

Kat pulled away and looked deep into her green eyes. She maintained her stare as she slowly ran her finger across Freya's bare shoulder and down her smooth back, speaking gently for the first time. 'Is this what you want?'

Freya's heart ached with shame. 'This is all I have ever wanted.' She wanted to explain, to make her understand. 'I had no choice, she said you would get-'

Kat placed her finger on Freya's panicked lips. 'I know.'

Freya held the forgiving gaze and kissed her gently, feeling Kat's soft touch return to her shoulders, to her back, to her zip. She sat with her legs cradled around Kat's waist and felt her zip begin to open. She closed her eyes and put her arms around Kat, drawing her shoulders tight against her own body. The zip opened slowly, every notch sending a shockwave of anticipation through her body. She moved Kat's wavy hair to the side and looked down her back to find the base of her tight white vest top. She reached for the hem and walked it upwards, but their chests were so close that it hardly moved. Kat leaned backwards and Freya felt a rush of adrenaline as she watched her slowly lift up her arms. Freya pulled the white top up and over Kat's head to reveal her perfect breasts and highly aroused nipples. Kat rested backwards on her arms and let Freya stare. She waited and watched as Freya returned her eyes and slowly pulled down the front of her unzipped dress. It was Kat's turn to stare and she realised she had never felt so aroused. She pulled Freya in for a deep penetrating kiss and their hard nipples pressed together sending electric pulses all over their highly sensitive bodies. She leaned backwards, drawing Freya onto her body and rolled her over as she pulled the pretty ivory dress down to her ankles and off over her feet. Kat carefully undid the buckles on the black sparkling kitten heels and dropped the shoes to the floor, turning to look at Freya. She was perfect. Kat crawled up the bed and straddled her wonderfully toned waist, reaching for Freya's hands and lifting them up to her own desperate chest.

Freya felt Kat's nipples, they were so hard and erect and her every touch seemed to cause a moan of desire. Kat looked incredible sat above her, resting on her hands and moving her head back in pleasure. Freya increased her pressure and each groan aroused her further. She wanted to experience Kat's touch. 'Kiss me,' she gasped wantonly.

Kat knew what she meant and leaned forwards taking Freya's pert nipple into her warm mouth. She teased it with her tongue and sucked it hard, drawing it out further as she heard Freya's cries of satisfaction. Their passion was heated as they both pulled at the others last piece of remaining clothing. Kat lay gently on top of her, parting her incredible legs with her own. They gasped simultaneously, both wet with desire, moments away from ecstasy. She took Freya's hands and pinned them out to the sides with her own. They kissed and their contact was so close, so intense, and so complete that they felt like one. Kat slowly moved her body in a smooth rhythm and together they felt the heat. They felt it build and rise and they moaned deeply, cheek to cheek, neither experiencing anything as overwhelming as this before.

Freya said it first. She felt her body take over and her pulses strengthen, tightening until she could control it no more. 'I love you Kat,' she whispered, gasping in ecstasy, throbbing with pleasure.

Kat felt Freya's intense pulse and tried to slow herself, but it was too late. She heard the words as her own desire took over and pushed her over the edge into a moment of pure elation. Kat moaned loudly and gasped for breath. 'I love you too.'

They lay quivering together, neither wanting to move the pressure that still caused a delayed, occasional, throb. Kat finally rolled onto her side and brushed a wave of chestnut brown hair from Freya's damp cheek. She stared into her sparkling green eyes that were alive with life. 'I want you.'

Freya looked back into the deep blue eyes and read their meaning, a meaning that she had seen from the start. 'I know. I have always known,' she looked away; '...it has always been you.'

Kat pulled a soft curl, she did not need details, but this she wanted to know. 'What about next year?'

'How else could I make sure she got as far away from us as possible?'

Kat halted her soothing touch.

'My first choice is still my first choice.'

She smiled and rolled on top of Freya, kissing her playfully. 'University Halls can be ever so expensive ... if you need accommodation we have a spare room going.'

'Well now that I'm here,' grinned Freya, returning the perfect embrace.

The End x

The sequel to 'But She Is My Student' is called

'Instigations'
by Kiki Archer

Out Now!

www.kikiarcher.com

Twitter: @kikiarcherbooks

Facebook: www.facebook.com/kiki.archer